QUIVERFULL

Quiverfull

Inside the Christian Patriarchy Movement

KATHRYN JOYCE

Beacon Press, Boston

Beacon Press
25 Beacon Street
Boston, Massachusetts 02108-2892
www.beacon.org

Beacon Press books
are published under the auspices of
the Unitarian Universalist Association of Congregations.

12 11 10 09   8 7 6 5 4 3 2 1

This book is printed on acid-free paper that meets the uncoated paper
ANSI/NISO specifications for permanence as revised in 1992.

Text design by Tag Savage at Wilsted & Taylor Publishing Services

Author's Note:
The only names to have been changed in this book are those of Joanna Stoors
and Dr. Singer, which I have done at their request. All characters in this book
are individuals. There are no conflated or composite characters.

Library of Congress Cataloging-in-Publication Data
Joyce, Kathryn, 1979–
    Quiverfull : inside the Christian patriarchy movement / Kathryn Joyce.
    p. cm.
    Includes bibliographical references and index.
    ISBN-13: 978-0-8070-1070-9 (hardcover : alk. paper)
    ISBN-10: 0-8070-1070-7 (hardcover : alk. paper)
    1. Women in fundamentalist churches—History. 2. Patriarchy—Religious
aspects—Christianity. I. Title.
    BX7800.F864J69 2009
    277.3'083082—dc22   2008036051

To Michael and Bonnie Joyce

Contents

In the corners of fundamentalist Christendom across the country, an old ideal of Christian womanhood is being revived. It looks like this: the "biblical" woman wears modest, feminine dress and avoids not only sex but also dating before marriage. She doesn't speak in church or try to have authority over men. She doesn't work outside the home, but within it she is its tireless center: homeschooling her children, keeping house, cooking bulk meals, and helping her husband run a home business or ministry. She checks in with her husband as she moves through her day to see if she is fulfilling his priorities for her. When he comes home, she is a submissive wife who bolsters him in his role as spiritual and earthly leader of the family. She understands it's her job to keep him sexually satisfied at all times and that it's her calling as a woman to let those relations result in as many children as God wants to bless her with. She raises families of eight, ten, and twelve children, and she teaches her daughters to do the same. She's not the throwback to the fifties summoned in media-stoked "mommy wars"; she is a return to something far older.

It's hard to estimate how many women are following this standard of "biblical womanhood" that's being taught through the self-named patriarchy movement. But it's a prevalent lifestyle among the booming homeschooling population, which the U.S. Department of Education counts as currently having more than one million school-age children, and which homeschooling advocates say easily has double or triple that number. Patriarchy and what we might call "the submissive lifestyle" also are increasingly advocated through a number of mainstream conservative churches that urge a return to "complementarian" notions of manhood and womanhood modeled on roles of female submission and male headship. Complementarianism is promoted and organized in part through the work of interdenominational groups like the Council on Biblical Manhood and Womanhood, which proselytizes evangelical churches to adopt conservative doctrines on gender. And the theology of submission and headship has garnered the support of the second-largest denomination in the United States, the sixteen-million-member Southern Baptist Convention (SBC), which in 1998 released a statement urging wives to graciously submit to their husbands.

When moves like these come into the news, such as when former presidential candidate Mike Huckabee was revealed to be a signatory to the SBC's submission statement, commentators anxious not to offend stumble to find a suitable gloss for this theological mandate, or they ignore it altogether. Likewise, even when the pronatalist, anticontraception motivations of the antiabortion movement are made clear, as when some U.S. pharmacists began refusing to fill birth control prescriptions for unwed women or for any woman who intended to use the pill as contraception, media reports rarely dig into the theological grounding and real-life implications of their arguments. The implication of the anticontraception position is the "Quiverfull" belief system: that women should accept every child as an unconditional blessing and that family planning is immoral. Media coverage has thus far failed to connect the individual pharmacists, portrayed as conscientious objectors standing alone with their religious beliefs, with the growing ranks of anticontraception activists at their backs. When I first began looking into the phenomenon of pharmacist refusals in 2004, coming to the issue as a secular feminist who writes about religion, I was shocked to hear the explicitly anticontraception message of the pharmacists' advocates and the deeply antifeminist politics of their allies. I was more surprised to realize the detail and complexity of the antifeminist lifestyle these allies proposed for women in its place and how well the movement was already organized.

In a movement guided by religious literalism, theology matters. Or, as proponents of the patriarchy revival like to say, "Ideas have consequences." They're quoting the title of conservative philosopher Richard Weaver's book, which presents an antiegalitarian argument for hierarchical social roles and communitarian norms, where majority morality trumps individual rights. When members of the patriarchy movement quote Weaver, they mean all the particulars of his book: the universal truth of biblical literalism that informs his community sensibility, the prizing of agrarian family independence, and certainly the disdain for egalitarian ideas like feminism. But they also mean a more general point: an all-purpose "I told you so" to a society that has embraced, even to a limited extent, modern notions of women's autonomy, broad definitions of family and love, and a high valuation of individual rights and fulfillment that, as they see it, can threaten the good of a community at large. When the lumbering conventional wisdom of centrist politics gets around to registering the effects of these ideas—sexual revolution ideas, in short—Weaver's fans smile ruefully: they could have told you that feminism would lead to nothing good.

It's a familiar scenario: the Christian right operating in its classic mode of assigning blame for a national calamity—from the twin towers to divorce rates and teenage pregnancy—to opposing worldviews, whether secular, liberal, or feminist. What goes less examined is the competing set of ideas that informs the Christian right. These certainly have consequences as well, and the consequences appear from time to time in the media as rekindled debates on submission or the raising of the principle in domestic violence cases. Like dispatches from a shrouded world, they're prodded rudely and shallowly, then forgotten. The worldview behind them remains fuzzy.

That's a shame, because these ideas about gender hierarchy and women's roles have a yet broader resonance throughout the evangelical church as a whole, where not just the abstinence ideals of chastity and virginity find heavy play through teen projects like purity rings and balls, but the notion of male headship and female submissiveness is a part of the basic theology of the church. Here, in mainstream evangelicalism—churches that fundamentalists consider worldly shells that have lost their Christian "saltiness"—the same language of biblical marriage roles directs the sermons and the pastors' books for sale without acknowledging the fierce denunciations of feminism that fundamentalists know is the heart of their fight.

Take as an example the New Life Church in Colorado Springs, Colorado, the vast megachurch founded by former National Association of Evangelicals president Ted Haggard, an icon of boastful evangelical power, who very publicly fell from grace in 2006 during a scandal involving drug use and a male prostitute. The schadenfreude of liberal critics aside—Haggard had been a sneering opponent of gay rights—Haggard's fall was a particularly heavy blow in Colorado Springs, where he and his wife, Gayle, a stay-at-home mother to five who dropped out of Oral Roberts University "to support a man of God," were long established as the first couple of the Christian community.

The two cowrote a breezy, heavily illustrated marriage guide, *From This Day Forward: Making Your Vows Last a Lifetime,* that, postscandal, seemed to epitomize for many the hypocrisy and unrealistic demands of the Christian right: that a "wife loves her husband with unflinching devotion," seeks to please him, love him, and above all help him, since, as the book warns, men have affairs with coworkers because they "are drawn to the women who help them do their task." Likewise, a husband has household authority in a marriage structured after government chains of command, even if it's suggested he temper his headship with a servant's heart. Disobedience to these roles, write the Haggards, "is the number one reason why marriages are unhappy...If you ignore the structures of your marriage relationship, you are vulnerable to disaster."

Little wonder that when Ted Haggard fell, a fellow megachurch pastor, Mark Driscoll of the Seattle-based Mars Hill Church and a leader in complementarian doctrine, would take the opportunity to chastise Gayle Haggard by insinuation. Writing about Haggard on his blog, Driscoll delivered this pastoral insight: "It is not uncommon to meet pastors' wives who really let themselves go; they sometimes feel that because their husband is a pastor, he is therefore trapped into fidelity, which gives them cause for laziness. A wife who lets herself go and is not sexually available to her husband in the ways that the Song of Songs is so frank about is not responsible for her husband's sin, but she may not be helping him either."

Such veiled blame may be why Ted, in a letter of apology and leave-taking read aloud to New Life Church on November 5, 2006, felt the need to excuse Gayle from any responsibility for his actions, telling the congregation that his affair had nothing to do with their marriage. But for the stunned congregation at New Life, the words of the Haggards' marriage book likely held renewed relevance, as did the example of Gayle, who "at every stage of life," Ted had written, had asked him "what she can do to most help me," and who had led the women of New Life Church in a plethora of women's Bible Studies and cell groups devoted to teaching the notion of submissive biblical wifehood. Gayle's lessons, explained one student of Gayle's Five Aspects of a Woman cell group, taught her about women's distinct roles and men's greater authority for fulfilling God's needs.

While Ted's letter of apology and resignation was read aloud to the congregation, remembers journalist Lauren Sandler, the crowd was silent and stiff. But following that, a letter from Gayle was read, addressed to the women of the congregation. The church reacted with an astoundingly different response, laughing, crying, and giving the absent Gayle a standing ovation. The *Colorado Springs Gazette* reprinted it in full. In the letter, Gayle passed on a distinct message, providing another lesson to the women of the church: this was no rupture in the marriage, but a continuation of her life's role.

Telling the women that she knew their hearts were broken, Gayle said that she still loved Ted with all her heart and was committed to her marriage vows until death. "If I were standing before you today," she wrote, "I would not change one iota of what I have been teaching the women of our church. For those of you who have been concerned that my marriage was so perfect I could not possibly relate to the women who are facing great difficulties, know that this will never again be the case. My test has begun; watch me. I will try to prove myself faithful."

Sitting beside Sandler, a woman who had sat through the entire service with clenched fists gasped. "It was electric," says Sandler. "I think they all felt their own test was just beginning." After years of leading New Life women, Gayle was saying, "Even I can be tested." Amid the weeping prayer groups that gathered in New Life's World Prayer Center to pray for Pastor Ted and the possible resurrection of his good name that James Dobson had hinted at, there wasn't a word of dissent. No one asked, as they had with Hillary Clinton or would with Silda Wall Spitzer, why Gayle didn't just leave him. "Everyone knew," said Sandler, "of course Gayle is going to stand by him, because she's the role model for them all, especially now, for the perfect Christian wife." In a corner of the World Prayer Center a group of women was praying exclusively for Gayle, and they said that just as they'd looked to Gayle when things were going great in her marriage, now they'd really be watching her. "They felt that Ted would come back, and that Gayle would show them how to do this, that Gayle would bring him back."

"I don't know when they stopped watching her," Sandler said a year later, after the ecstasy of pain had faded from Colorado Springs and Ted

Haggard had debased his fallen angel status with a clumsy fundraising letter to his former congregation that smacked of a worse indecency than the scandal.

Gayle, failing to effect the miracle of resurrecting her husband, loyally retreated from public life, illustrating a final lesson to her disciples. As Sandler described, "If one has to fall that low to stand by her man, she will." It should be a lesson to outside observers of the patriarchy and submission doctrines as well that to follow these ideas to their conclusion can mean, in very real ways, to disappear.

PART ONE

·

WIVES

CHAPTER ONE

Massachusetts Hope

"I've watched my wife counsel a lot of young ladies who are considering marriage, and she always asks them the question, 'Are you willing to call your husband "Lord"?' There will be dead silence in the room." At the podium, a handsome and charismatic man in his early forties mimics in mincing tones the single women's response to his wife's evocation of 1 Peter 3:6, which describes Sarah showing submission to her husband Abraham by naming him "lord": "'Are you kidding me? I only have one Lord: Jesus Christ!'" He continues, mincing no more: "We're not talking about Lord as in the Creator, but your earthly head. And one that you have to follow, even when he makes bad judgments. Are you ready to do the most vulnerable thing that a woman ever can do and submit yourself to a man, who you are going to have to follow in his faith, who is incredibly imperfect and is going to make mistakes? Can you do that? Can you call your husband 'Lord'? If the answer is no, you shouldn't get married."

Doug Phillips, the founder of Vision Forum, a prolific publisher of homeschool curricula and one of the most influential proponents of the conservative Christian patriarchy movement now flourishing among homeschoolers, is addressing between three and four hundred people gathered at the massive Digital Federal Credit Union convention center in Worcester, Massachusetts, for the feature address of the Eighteenth Annual MassHOPE Christian Homeschool Convention. His keynote speeches are PowerPoint presentations—The Wise Woman's Guide to Blessing Her Husband's Vision and The Homeschool Vision for Victory. *Vision* and *victory* are key words here, referencing Proverbs 29:18, "Where there is no vision, the people perish." It's a verse interpreted by would-be patriarchs as a warning to cast a bold vision for the future of their families and "the church militant," so that their children and the church at large keep a lofty goal in sight: victory for the Body of Christ in reclaiming the earth as their own. Preparing for this work is the common thread through all of Phillips's media, products, and even toys, which are showcased several times a year in a stunningly produced high-gloss catalogue featuring numerous pictures of his family—he uses his children as models—and the extensive and wholesome-looking Vision Forum clan at home in San Antonio, Texas.

In Massachusetts Phillips's lecture draws the largest crowd of the speeches that day. The main reason most families come to the event, priced at sixty-five dollars per adult, is to shop for homeschooling materials, and here there's an arena floor full of vendors hawking books, CDs, and DVDs for the instruction of both mind and soul. The materials provide counsel for raising pure children who resist worldly temptations, and not just those of drugs and sex; dating and attending college away from home are equally verboten. But, as evidenced by the booths rented by political action groups such as the antifeminist flagship Concerned Women for America, Phillips and other leaders know that this is fertile ground for spreading their ideas, their theology of the family.

Vision Forum's sales table is in a league of its own: it is a multimedia onslaught of Christian revisionist history, highlighting the role of Providence in the settling of Jamestown and New England and the hand of God in general world history. They offer beautifully bound editions of Puritan classics and Victorian-inspired descriptions of family life, following Phillips's belief that homeschoolers should not be borrowing or making Christian copies of "government school" materials but should rather build a thoroughly Jesus-centered education from the ground up. As one of Phillips's fellow travelers, R. C. Sproul, Jr., writes in his homeschooling text, *When You Rise Up,* godly education means that the sovereignty of God is the baseline fact of all further knowledge, so that even elementary addition problems—two plus two equals four—follow not from any internal logic but from seeing the addends as Jesus's twos and His four: an acknowledgment that Jesus invented and rules over math, that He is in fact "the reason for" math.

But Vision Forum's passion—its heart—is in books, tapes, and CDs that stress the necessity of building large family dynasties, generations of families with six, eight, ten or more children to raise a godly seed for

Christ and the salvation of America, and that lay out the guidelines for how men and women should behave. Following the philosophy that all education and play is inherently religious—and that ideological neutrality is therefore impossible—Vision Forum offers well-stocked, sex-segregated children's product lines, the Beautiful Girlhood and Adventurous Boyhood collections. These lines forge gender fidelity through an assortment of Victorian-inspired (yet multiracial) dolls, aprons, and cookware to start training your daughter for successful wifehood now; or conversely, expensive swords and musketeer outfits, camping gear, and Second World War canteens to instill in your boy his sense of nobility and obligation to protect and lead the women in his life. For adults, the gender-training materials are even more explicit. The Biblical Patriarchy collection for husbands includes titles such as *Manliness, Manly Men Write Manly Letters,* and *Poems for Patriarchs*; the Virtuous Womanhood collection for wives includes *Verses of Virtue, The Role of Women,* and *What's a Girl to Do?*

The homeschooling families of Massachusetts that browse through these offerings don't stick as rigidly to the dress codes of their southern and Midwestern brethren—the denim jumpers and "prairie wear" that are such a staple of homeschooling mothers' wardrobes that they've merited their own self-deprecatory parody among homeschooling moms online in the "Prairie Muffin Manifesto" as well as other more pointed jabs. But the family bearing among the crowds of shoppers is still marked: one mother and her group of five daughters arrive in the traditionalists' uniform of long, homemade skirts and uncut hair. Another mother leads a brood of blonde teens in matching, modestly loose cargo crops. A father guides his three eldest sons, all in matching green nylon rain jackets. It's practical for the large families that homeschoolers tend to have, but it's also a mark of the emphasis on autonomous, stand-alone families over modernist ideas of the individual. These families don't want to be beholden to the state; they'd rather follow older notions of kin and clan and the strict role definition for members within the group, justified by an attitude of *us, our family,* against the world.

On stage, and manning the Vision Forum tables, Phillips and his all-male cast of employees wear matching outfits of khaki pants and blue blazers. The employees, many of whom are interns traveling with Phillips as part of their "entrepreneurship" training, have the same tidy, close haircuts, and all hew to the guidelines of brotherly accountability: they

grow visibly uncomfortable when speaking to a single young woman beyond a simple purchase exchange and will pull over another employee for
propriety's sake. In a world where dating is discouraged in favor of the
growing conservative Christian trend of "courtship," anything that could
hint at unauthorized, improper mingling of the sexes is avoided.

With Phillips, the uniforms have another function besides identification of "family" borders. When Phillips is not addressing the crowd
but answering questions privately with members of the audience, one of
his employees stands to the side taking notes, lending the informal conversation—even as seen by viewers across the conference hall—an air of
political authority and importance. This is no accident. Phillips and his
faithful see themselves at the forefront of a cultural battle, and they know
well both the real criticism their positions draw and the invaluable tacti-
cal advantage of appearing under siege by a powerful enemy.

But on stage, Phillips and his identically dressed son, who operates a
Mac-generated slide show, intersperse their radically reactionary message
with a folksy show of their own well-crafted hearth and home, project-
ing for the crowd a series of pictures of the Phillips clan, at eight children
and counting: Joshua, Justice, Liberty, Jubilee, Faith Evangeline, Honor,
Providence, and Virginia Hope. "We call them *Shayneh kepelehs*, which is
Yiddish for our 'pretty little heads,'" Phillips says, hamming up his character as a converted Jew, which some in the homeschool community interpret as Phillips bestowing an extra modicum of "chosenness" on his
mission. The extended Vision Forum "family" appears in the slide show
as well: a cast of more than sixty employees and employee family members, many of whom are children, standing in front of the Alamo, squint-
ing in the Texas sun, a model to be emulated across the country with the
arrival of the Vision Forum catalogue in the mail.

Phillips likes the Alamo—as he likes other masculine images from
the past, such as the Jamestown settlers, the Puritans, and the *Titanic,* for
which he's named a father-son association—for its image of men standing together at a line drawn in the sand. "We go there each year to remind
ourselves that we are in a battle for our families, for our children's hearts
and souls. Men, put this verse up on your doorposts for when you feel
discouraged: Nehemiah 4:14. 'Do not be afraid of them; remember the
Lord who is great and awesome, and fight for your brothers, your sons,
your daughters, your wives, and your houses.' This is an incredible mes-

sage—pick up and fight—and what every man should be saying to his family. We're going to fight."

The notion of a Christian nation declaring itself at war against its secular humanist countrymen is one by now overfamiliar to most Americans. Phillips's father, Howard, played a part in the creation of that national battle. Howard Phillips, a Russian Jew who married an Irish woman and started his family in Boston, where Doug was born, later converted to evangelical Christianity and was a servant to the Republican Party during the Nixon era. Eventually he broke away to form the far-right Constitution Party and has chaired the Conservative Caucus since 1974. At an alternative Jamestown celebration held by Vision Forum in Virginia in 2007, Doug Phillips reminisced on stage with Jonathan Falwell, son of the late Moral Majority founder Jerry, shortly after the elder Falwell's death. He reminded the preacher's son of growing up together, when both were young boys attending meetings with their fathers and men such as Paul Weyrich and Tim LaHaye, other leading lights of the Christian right, then still in its infancy. "I remember there was a day," Phillips pressed, "when my father and some others convened with your father and said, 'Jerry, you need to lead the charge. Let's call it the Moral Majority.'" For decades, the Phillips family has been in the business of waging war against the familiar *bêtes noires* of the Moral Majority and their manifold successors in the ever-expanding universe of religious right activism: reproductive and gay rights, women's liberation and the Equal Rights Amendment, modern definitions of family, and media control.

But in recent years Phillips, as well as many other more mainstream religious right leaders, has taken the battle home. While they have a great deal to say to men, through ministries ranging from the emotional Promise Keepers of the '90s to Phillips's testosterone-driven lessons in manliness and patriarchal home leadership, increasingly they argue that the battle begins, and can only be won, with Christian women. And the way they want women to fight is not to "battle" as most of us might recognize it, not as the world knows it, but as true believers do: by dying to themselves as Jesus died on the cross, by bowing down to the headship of their husbands, by laying aside their own ambitions to further the cause of the Lord and his representatives here on earth—the men God put in authority over them, their fathers first, then the men that they marry.

There are four main verses of Scripture that conservative Christians point to for reference in delineating men's and women's roles: Proverbs 31, which catalogues the attributes of a godly wife and describes virtuous women as valuable "above rubies"; Titus 2:3–5, which instructs, "Likewise, teach the older women to be reverent in the way they live, not to be slanderers or addicted to much wine, but to teach what is good. Then they can train the younger women to love their husbands and children, to be self-controlled and pure, to be busy at home, to be kind, and to be subject to their husbands, so that no one will malign the word of God"; 1 Peter 3:1, which holds out an oft-repeated promise that wives' submissive behavior can be used to win unsaved husbands to the Lord, "Likewise, ye wives, be in subjection to your own husbands; that, if any obey not the word, they also may without the word be won by the conversation of the wives; While they behold your chaste conversation coupled with fear"; and perhaps most potently, Ephesians 5:21, which provides the model for Christian marriage in the relationship of headship between Jesus Christ, the bridegroom of Revelation, and his waiting bride, the Church: "Wives, submit to your husbands as to the Lord. For the husband is the head of the wife as Christ is the head of the church, his body, of which he is the Savior. Now as the church submits to Christ, so also wives should submit to their husbands in everything."

These verses, Phillips tells the crowd, are the "best-kept secret of modern Christian marriages" in a time when the church is modernized and afraid to preach the Bible's truths about men and women. "Ladies," he says, "I need to ask you some questions at this point, and these are tough ones. They're tough because I want to ask you questions that will bring you to determine, are we doing our very best to honor Christ's vision? One: are you ladies ordered by God to teach your husband or to listen to your husband? If you think you have to teach your husband because he's a dummy, we have some work to do here. Even if you're right, that's not the point—do you think of yourself and your life's mission to be your husband's completer? A helpmeet suitable to him? I can tell you right now, if you don't start thinking in those terms, you will never be a wise woman, and you will never bless your husband. You can't fully understand how to bless him unless you know how God created you to bless him. You are a helpmeet. The Bible says that man is not made for the woman but the woman is made for the man. If you have a problem with that, take it up with the Creator, not Phillips. I'm just quoting. Until we get comfortable playing those roles, we'll never be at peace. But if we accept those roles, whew! Half the battle is diminished already just by the fact that we accept God's creation order."

He chastises the women in the audience not to struggle after careers but to accept as their realm the care and management of the household. He encourages them to win the beautiful "adornment of humility"—the characteristic that God promises is a woman's crowning grace, the "meek and quiet spirit which adorns you with magnificence"—through submission to their husbands and to keep their eyes on their assignment from God, no matter how lacking their husbands may be. The women need to realize they aren't the ones to fix their broken husbands, but can only help them by prostrating themselves before the Lord, humbling themselves, and encouraging, serving, praising, and ennobling their men.

Above all, Phillips warns them, they are not to nag. His son changes the slide to a cartoon image of a dripping faucet beside the Bible verse, "A constant dripping on a day of steady rain and a contentious woman are alike." "Are you a dripping faucet?" Phillips asks the women in the crowd. A man who is criticized by his woman, rather than being able to enjoy her submission to him, Phillips warns, is liable to flee. "If you are 'drip, drip, drip,' you are giving a message to a sinful man who would be tempted to respond sinfully. You know his vulnerability to saying, 'Take me outta here now!' To a bar, to the men, wherever, but out of here." Phillips describes the Bible's conception of an "odious" married woman who, like the contentious woman, steps out of her place, a breach in hierarchy that disquiets the earth to a degree that it cannot bear. Likewise, an indiscreet woman, he says, is a bejeweled swine or a rottenness in her husband's bones. God gave us such shocking portraits of bad women for a reason, says Phillips: to warn women away from their natural, sinful inclinations to be unsubmissive, to rebel against God-given authority— something that, Phillips says, husbands read as "I don't love you, I won't follow you."

"In the Bible it talks about a day when you had only pusillanimous, mollycoddled, effeminate men, and women who are taking over the lives of the men." He quotes Isaiah 3:12, "Children are your oppressors and women rule over you." This, he reminds, is God's curse on a sinful nation.

"Ladies, instead of fighting this,"—Phillips's voice fills with a whine of struggle, imitating a woman tugging on a rope—"'Give me my rights!

I'm intelligent!' realize that you're not losing anything. What you're doing is embracing the gift that God gave you. This is what God gave you to be able to change the world. You don't need to be a man; you don't want to be a man. You want to be a woman. And if you say, 'I love this, I love this,' God will change the world before your very eyes."

"We're the reclamation generation," Phillips says, and the whole world is at stake. With diligence in right biblical relations between husbands and wives—the most pivotal issue before the homeschooling community today, and the foundational question that determines how the children will be raised—and a commitment to pass the model down the family line, a reclamation of the family and country, and yes, even Massachusetts, for God is possible. And it starts at home, with wives who "encourage their husbands but never rebuke them. [Who] seek to build the kingdom his way. Would you please bow your heads in prayer with me? Father, in Jesus's name, would you please give us the victory?"

CHAPTER TWO

The Church Comes Home

Conservative Christians may say they have no use for feminism, but increasingly, over the past twenty years, feminism—that is, sworn enmity to it—has become a rallying point for conservative and orthodox believers ranging from evangelicals to Catholics to Mormons to Reformed Protestants to fundamentalists, almost a stronger organizing principle than particular doctrines themselves. Feminism, as they see it, is what started it all. Mary Pride, an early leader in the homeschool movement and publisher of the influential *Practical Homeschooling* magazine, was also author of *The Way Home: Beyond Feminism, Back to Reality,* a book published in 1985 that did much to recreate the homeschooling movement along patriarchal and militantly fertile lines. Pride sees feminism as combining a range of ills from communism to self-worship to witchcraft. The influence of feminists, she writes, can be seen in the "victimization" of women through no-fault divorce laws; in casual sex, which lowers women from protected wives to the level of "unpaid prostitutes"; in vice peddling, such as cigarette and alcohol companies "cashing in" on displaced homemakers whose husbands have left them; and in lower wages for husbands with the abolishment of the gender-weighted "family wage" (paying men more than women on the argument that they were working to support dependents, while women were working for "extra" income). Not to mention what Pride sees as the cause-and-effect slide from socially sanctioned birth control to legalized abortion.

But the most troubling aspect of feminism to Pride, along with a wide-ranging band of fellow believers, whether they call themselves patriarchalists, antifeminists, complementarians (as opposed to egalitarians, feminism's mild evangelical cousins), or proponents of biblical manhood and womanhood, isn't any of its specific sins, but its acceptance by Christians, allowing the philosophy of the enemy to strike at Christ's church.

"Christians have accepted feminists' moderate demands for family planning and careers while rejecting the radical side of feminism—meaning lesbianism and abortion," she writes. "What most do not see is that one demand leads to the other. Feminism is a totally self-consistent system aimed at rejecting God's role for women. Those who adopt any part of its lifestyle can't help picking up its philosophy. And those who pick up its philosophy are buying themselves a one-way ticket to social anarchy." Pride isn't suggesting some easy reversion to the Ozzie and Harriet model of the 1950s, but something more extreme. "Feminism is self-consistent. The Christianity of the fifties wasn't. Feminists had a plan for women. Christians didn't."

But since, and in large part due to, Pride's writing, Christians do have a plan: a "whole-cloth," integrated lifestyle for women. It is not about independence and self-fulfillment but submissive wives following the leadership of patriarch husbands, working at home to educate their children and support their husband through his work, rest, and ministry, and "dying to the self"—a Christ-like self-abnegation and acceptance of God's plan for their role in life as helpmeets to their husbands. This biblical womanhood, encompassing homework, motherhood, and wifehood as they were lived not in the 1950s but in a notion of preindustrial, pre–household appliance times, is what Pride calls a "total lifestyle"—as comprehensive as the pervasive influence of feminism, which has reached every part of women's work lives, biology, and thinking. And this time around, the antifeminists intend to be fiercely diligent—rooting out the worldly, "feministic" ideas and influences in their churches, entertainment, and own thinking and making sure it doesn't come back.

In a way, to that minority of American women who actually do claim the title "feminist"—a rarity bemoaned by both feminists and antifeminists alike, who both see the majority of women living out feminist ideals without recognizing or acknowledging their roots in the women's liberation movement—this heated attention and estimation of feminist power is strangely flattering. Nobody has taken the feminist threat to decency and order this seriously since the 1970s. But it's less amusing to realize that the movement against feminism, including all its unacknowledged aspects, such as the acceptance of women's careers, the expectation of pay equity, a greater degree of sexual freedom and bodily self-determination, more equitable divisions of housework and child-care, and shared decision-making between husbands and wives, is being undertaken on a large scale by a coalition that goes far beyond the home-schooling community with its separatist ethos, yet which has echoed the ideas of men and women as extreme as Doug Phillips and Mary Pride with surprising fidelity.

John Piper and Wayne Grudem, both Reformed Baptist preachers and theologians, are leading members of the Council on Biblical Manhood and Womanhood (CBMW), an organization founded in 1987 with the goal of fighting feminist or egalitarian influences in the evangelical church. Piper and Grudem targeted the modest trend of "Christian feminism," a gentler notion of equality than mainstream feminism that was sparked in part by moderate theologians questioning the long-held assumptions of evangelical churches that women should be barred from positions of church authority or, in some denominations, from speaking in church at all. Christian egalitarians also believe that the church shouldn't discourage women's careers outside the home and that family planning decisions are best left within the family.

But even such tepid endorsements of gender equality were threatening to established patriarchal traditions, and the CBMW was formed as a rebuttal. The Council, which today spreads its message through the sixteen-million-member Southern Baptist Convention, the conservative Presbyterian Church in America, and the evangelical ministry Campus Crusade for Christ, grew out of the publication of the "Danvers Statement," an antiegalitarian document signed by dozens of theologians and pastors whose names have become synonymous within evangelical circles with Christian antifeminist activism. They include Beverly LaHaye, founder of Concerned Women for America and wife of *Left Behind* author Tim LaHaye; Dorothy Patterson, wife of Paige Patterson, one of the architects of the conservative takeover of the Southern Baptist Convention; Mary Kassian, a leading writer and conference speaker on biblical womanhood; CBMW board members Pat Robertson and Paige Patterson; and a number of men pushing the evangelical church toward Reformed theology, more commonly known as Calvinism or Puritanism: John MacArthur, Jr., R. C. Sproul, Sr., D. A. Carson, and dozens of others. Heavyweight contenders in the theological-political realm have also contributed essays and support to the CBMW, such as Albert Mohler, president of the Southern Baptist Theological Seminary, which steers the doctrine of the mammoth denomination. In an essay for CBMW, Mohler called for courageous action in reestablishing traditional gender roles throughout American Christendom. And Piper today disseminates his complementarian theology through his popular "Desiring God" ministry, church "plants" (expanding a network of churches like a franchise from his own Minnesota-based church), and conference series.

The Danvers Statement, which stands as the Council's call to arms, holds that "widespread uncertainty and confusion in our culture regarding the complementary differences between masculinity and femininity," the promotion of feminist egalitarianism, ambivalence toward motherhood and homemaking, calls for female church leadership, and "growing claims of legitimacy" for "illicit" sexual relationships—that is, gay rights—had all jeopardized the authority of Scripture, making theology too confusing for "ordinary people" who depend on the Bible's literalism for direction. Such laity, the Council warned, would be thrown into uncertainty, and perhaps doubt, by an "evolved" standard on gender that seemed to contradict the given Word: if God's revelations on the sexes were up for modernization, why not the rest? And the careless threat to the faith, they argued, was all in the name of the church accommodating the world rather than seeking to shape that world to the standards of the gospel.

The founding purpose of the Council was, in short, to counteract these influences by promoting a biblical view of the relationship between men and women, at home and in the church, through academic and popular publications. They sought to encourage lay people to study Scripture as a literal guide for biblical gender roles and relations and apply these guidelines to their lives, and thereby heal "people and relationships injured by an inadequate grasp of God's will concerning manhood and womanhood; to help both men and women realize their full ministry potential through a true understanding and practice of their God-given roles, and to promote the spread of the gospel among all peoples by fostering a biblical wholeness in relationships that will attract a fractured world."

In other words, the Council on Biblical Manhood and Womanhood sought to make marriages that look like a return to well-ordered harmony an advertisement for the church. In a world grappling with the growing pains of new demands for marital fair play and with the breakups of marriages where partners no longer felt obliged to sacrifice their needs and desires for the sake of an unequal partnership or to stay in unions that had simply been a bad match from the start, the Council hoped the appearance of secure, settled marriages would draw people to the faith. Sensitive to the appeal of feminism to people concerned about domestic violence and the abuse born out of male domination of women, Piper and Grudem lay such abuses of power at the foot of feminism as well, arguing that "wife abuse (and husband abuse) have some deep roots in the failure of parents to teach boys and girls about true masculinity and femininity. The confusion about sexual roles explodes in violent behaviors." In this way, abusive men, passive men, and gay men could be linked together as sinners failing in their roles as men in a culture that has lost its way.

Shortly after the formation of the Council in 1991, Piper and Grudem, along with a number of their fellow Council members, published a guidebook for their mission, *Recovering Biblical Manhood and Womanhood: A Response to Evangelical Feminism,* composed of essays by pastors, theologians, and a handful of women (three out of twenty-two authors were female). In a new preface to the book, reprinted in 2006, they argued that the urgency of leading "Christian women back to a joyous embrace of godly male leadership in the church" was that the core of the issue was biblical authority—the truth of Scripture itself. "If we write off, ignore, or distort the Bible's teachings on gender roles, then we are bound to do so with everything the Bible teaches," they wrote. Acceptance of these teachings amidst a culture that had departed from them, they recognized, depended on acceptance and insistence of the literal truth of the Bible as the divine word of God rather than seeing it as a culturally influenced, time-bound document that represents the patriarchal views of the men and culture which put the words to paper.

As Mary Kassian writes in *The Feminist Mistake: The Radical Impact of Feminism on Church and Culture,* the threat of feminism is a three-stage process that ends with the rejection of God: "Feminism began with a deconstruction of a Judeo-Christian view of womanhood (the right to name self); progressed to the deconstruction of manhood, gender relationships, family/societal structures, and a Judeo-Christian worldview (the right to name the world); and concluded with the concept of a metaphysical pluralism, self-deification, and the rejection of the Judeo-Christian deity (the right to name God)."

In other words, by allowing women to declare for themselves who and what they are, the definition of manhood, the meaning of which complementarians find principally in manhood's differences from womanhood, comes under attack, as do hierarchical relationships within marriage. Eventually, God's word and God Himself become an image considered in the eye of the beholder—whatever we want Him to be—and therefore no basis for hard and fast rules to live by.

Or as Al Mohler writes, "We must choose between two unavoidable options: either the Bible is affirmed as the inerrant and infallible Word of God, and thus presents a comprehensive vision of true humanity in both unity and diversity, or we must claim that the Bible is, to one extent or another, compromised and warped by a patriarchal and male-dominated bias that must be overcome in the name of humanity. For biblical traditionalists, the choice is clear."

Piper, Grudem, and the CBMW wanted to fight this growing amorphousness of gender and duty, so they set about the business of defining what Scripture says man and woman should be. Piper's findings on the inherent truth about men and women come down to this: "At the heart of mature masculinity is a sense of benevolent responsibility to lead, provide for, and protect women in ways appropriate to a man's differing relationships. At the heart of mature femininity is a freeing disposition to affirm, receive, and nurture strength and leadership from worthy men in ways appropriate to a woman's differing relationships." In short, action and reaction. Though Piper has instruction for men and women alike, as Phillips and Pride do, his emphasis is similarly on women's roles, and on the necessity of women accepting their roles first in order to start the process of returning to these biblical ways of relating: "A significant aspect of femininity is how a woman responds to the pattern of initiatives established by mature masculinity....Mature femininity [is] a disposition rather than a set of behaviors...[such as] a disposition to yield to the husband's authority and an inclination to follow his leadership."

These roles play out beyond the marital relationship as well, and Piper gently explains to women that some roles of authority in society at large are too close to masculine-appropriate power for women to fill: "Roles [that] might stretch appropriate expressions of femininity beyond the breaking point," wherein she is too much in control over other men, "are roles that strain the personhood of man and woman too far to be appropriate, productive, and healthy for the overall structure of home and society."

Then, codifying the discomfort male employees may feel under female supervisors, Piper describes a continuum along which women—and those who hire or appoint women to positions of authority—should consider the appropriateness of a woman performing a certain job or task. A woman's suitability for any position of authority should be rated along two scales: how personal the relationship between the man and the woman is, and how authoritative is the type of leadership the woman has over that man. By this scale, a woman city planner, who shepherds male drivers through her traffic patterns, may be acceptable as she is never directing a man face-to-face, but a female boss instructing her subordinate, especially in an unacceptably masculine leadership role such as a principal and her teachers, a college professor and her students, or a police officer and the citizens she may control, all "involve kinds of leadership and expectations of authority and forms of strength as to make it unfitting for a woman to fill the role." (The same standard of distinctions was at the root of a 2008 controversy at a Catholic academy in Kansas, where a female basketball referee was forbidden from calling a high school boys' varsity match, as it would place her in an unbiblical position of authority over men, even men too young to vote.)

Rather, in an Orwellian turn of phrase that can't help but summon the slogans of Margaret Atwood's dystopian feminist classic, *The Handmaid's Tale*—wherein women's freedom *to,* to work, to vote, to drive, to control their bodies and sexual lives, was exchanged for a dubious freedom *from,* from the dangers and sexual threats of independent life in the world—Piper suggests that women discover their true "path of freedom" in God's good design of femininity. "There are sensations of unbounded independence that are not true freedom because they deny truth and are destined for calamity...one [woman] is encumbered by a parachute on her back and the other is free from this burden. Which person is most free?...This false sense of freedom is in fact bondage to calamity which is sure to happen after a fleeting moment of pleasure."

Or, as Mary Pride might say, "You and I don't have a choice between slavery and uncontrolled freedom. We have a choice between slavery to self-indulgent sin or slavery to God." It's in these formations about the conception of and impossibility of freedom that we can glimpse, through the media-muddied filter of popular consciousness, what was once the radical promise of feminism—as the late feminist writer Ellen Willis wrote, "that there really is such a thing as liberation" and that a truly democratic community of equals is possible in something other than thought—and what, ironically, only feminism's sworn enemies seem to accept as an idea with great potential consequences. In a way, feminism's antagonists are the only ones who give its central idea credit for having the radical potential to shake the status quo of several millennia and threaten the heavy history of patriarchal religions that, seen from a secular standpoint, serve to rationalize and uphold those inequalities.

Hence the need for a literal and absolutist trust in the authority of God's word, which Christians must obey, whether or not they understand its fairness in the eyes of the Lord. As Raymond C. Ortlund, Jr., Senior Pastor of Christ Presbyterian Church in Nashville, Tennessee, and author of a book on "spiritual adultery" called *God's Unfaithful Wife*, declares, "Because God is ultimately the one who shapes our lives, I have to conclude that God is not interested in unlimited equality among us."

CHAPTER THREE

The Men Who Would Be Kings

Fifteen miles from Williamsburg, Virginia, on a country road in Charles City County dominated by plantations turned bed-and-breakfasts, four thousand ultraconservative, largely homeschooling Christians gathered in June 2007 to correct a national mistake. After the country had marked the founding of America's first colony with mixed sentiments earlier that spring, they intended to do Jamestown right. The women wore hoop skirts, bustles, bonnets, and mob hats. The men wore tricorns, feathered musketeer hats, or top hats; they carried swords. "Maidens," that is, girls, wore aprons, while "heroes"—boys—donned armor or coonskin caps.

They came to Fort Pocahontas, a plot of land appended to former president John Tyler's family estate on the James River frequently used for Civil War reenactments, to celebrate the founding of the Jamestown colony four hundred years ago. "Jamestown Quadricentennial: A Celebration of Our Providential History"—a weeklong gathering of home-schooling families organized by Vision Forum—was a key example of the Vision Forum drive to create a fully Christ-centered, religious worldview for homeschoolers to draw on. Through speeches, sermons, and guided revisionist history tours through Old Jamestown, the celebration paid homage to a number of favorite themes, including God's providence in settling the nation and the belief the early colonialists were a God-chosen and God-led people with a special holy mission. And it offered an opportunity to dress up in colonial drag: no small draw for a community that eschews many of the other common lubricants of social festivities. Most importantly, though, it was a live demonstration of the ideal society that ministries like Vision Forum have in mind when they exhort their followers to revive the culture: a return to values not even of the Victorian age but of the Puritan societies represented by the Massachusetts Bay Colony and their European brethren who lived under religious law in Calvin's rigidly pious Protestant community in sixteenth-century Geneva.

But the grounds for Vision Forum's quadricentennial were only superficially about celebrating history. The nation held official ceremonies in May but replaced the word "celebration" with "commemoration" after black and Native American members of the planning committee protested that "you can't celebrate an invasion." Veteran activists such as Jesse Jackson and Al Sharpton spoke at the official commemoration, and new exhibits at the Jamestown Settlement museum spoke to the colony's history of "human bondage and the displacement of Virginia Indians." A *New York Times* review of the exhibit noted that Queen Elizabeth's visit to Jamestown would find "not the triumph of British influence, but the triumph of ambiguity, discomfort, and vague multiculturalism."

Phillips and his followers were incensed. Jamestown needed a real celebration, he said. "Who wants to come to a birthday party where you're angry at the parents and you lament the birth?" Or as he wrote in a May op-ed for a right-wing news site, *World Net Daily,* "At what should be a crowning moment of blessing, celebration, and thanksgiving to God, America is being held hostage by savage philosophies reanimated from the grave and marching on Jamestown." "It's down on Western Christendom, up with spirit guides," he was quoted elsewhere on the site.

But at the celebration on the Tyler grounds, Phillips was buoyant, dressed as an old-time town-fair master of ceremonies. He wore the standard Vision Forum outfit of blue blazer and khakis, but topped with a straw porkpie hat. He dashed back and forth from a chair outside the ceremony's big tent, a carnival-sized canopy, and the podium on stage, where he was in charge of introducing speakers and performers: pastors preaching a message about "covenantal history" and Christian leaders who served as guides on Vision Forum's annual New England "Faith and Family" Christian heritage tours in Plymouth. When I caught up with Phillips, following him out of the tent after he introduced a young folk singer named Charlie Zahm, he elaborated on his motivations: "If you go on the national commemoration Web site, you'll find that not the natives, but the settlers were cannibals; that they were terrorists against the environment; that there was a holocaust; that the settlers were guilty of lynchings; that a genocide took place. You need something more than the oral tradition [of indigenous populations] to defend something like that."

Rev. Joe Morecraft III, pastor of the Cummings, Georgia, Chalcedon Presbyterian Church and a speaker at the celebration, summarized the gathering's complaints more succinctly: "Jamestown, for the first time in the history of the nation, is getting bad press."

Some might call it an overdue balancing of the scales, a much-needed nod to the varied experiences of a pluralistic society as well as a recognition of contemporary historical findings that challenged the old stories of the nation's founding. But that wasn't how it played at Fort Pocahontas. Traveling from as far away as Oklahoma and Washington state, thousands gathered to proudly defend the Jamestown settlement not just as the cradle of the republic and American free enterprise but, more importantly, as the "beachhead" of American Christianity: the site of its first church, first baptisms, first (Protestant) conversions, and the first institution of the Decalogue-based common law.

"We don't believe that this is Israel, this is perfection, the 'city on the hill,'" Phillips continued. But they do see it as something, and something tied closely to a somewhat belligerent, somewhat self-conscious assertion of traditional Anglo-Saxon, and particularly Scots-Irish, heritage. On stage, Zahm, who Phillips would like to see named "America's Balladeer," alternated between patriotic standards, traditional British Isles folk songs, and a rousing version of "Dixie" that brought the audience to its feet—a musical potpourri that mirrored Vision Forum's self-conception as an heir to both Southern traditionalism and the Protestant Reformation of sixteenth-century Scotland. (Vision Forum incorporates this into its ministry with group homeschool "Faith and Freedom" tours of Reformation landmarks in Scotland.)

One of the songs performed by Zahm was dedicated to Phillips's father, Howard. It was a mournful, militant rendering of the old Irish rebel song, "Minstrel Boy," a cappella save the whirling baton of Zahm's traditional Irish pan drum accompanying his soaring tenor voice: "The minstrel boy to the war is gone / In the ranks of death you'll find him / His father's sword he has girded on / and his wild harp slung behind him." The song was updated during the American Civil War to include a Revelations-inspired verse, envisioning an eschatological return of the minstrel boy "one day" and the launch of "a world such as Heaven intended." I recognized it as the song Sean Connery dies to in the film adaptation of Rudyard Kipling's story "The Man Who Would Be King," in which two wayward soldiers of the British Empire travel through the Hindu Kush to Afghanistan to become gods. They perish nobly at the hands of the indigenous pagans they were trying to civilize and improve, though in the film, the traditional lyrics are replaced by the Lutheran battle dirge "The Son of God Goes Forth to War."

It is Doug Phillips's favorite movie, and it's a fitting reference for the celebration of Jamestown's spotted history, but Phillips, catching this easy resonance, clarified, "Not that I'm an imperialist." And that's believable; beyond its archaic politics, the draw of the classic film is much like the swelling melody of "Minstrel Boy" in its gallant send-off for soldiers doomed to death. A similar sentiment of tragic nobility permeates Vision Forum's mission: sons of God going forth to war with kingly crowns to gain. It's the moral Phillips looks for in all his retrieved heroes of the faith, acting out Providential, God-ordained roles through history.

"Jamestown laid the foundation for the real spiritual birthplace, which was the Plymouth colony. Jamestown gave us our firsts before that: our first churches, worship services, Thanksgiving, first charter based on the Great Commission. We do believe that God has been involved in our history, that we see His hand at work, active and real, and not just distant and far off and uninvolved. God is not just transcendent from the earth. He's with us every minute, and He's been part of this nation."

And He was also at Jamestown that weekend, honored through hot-air balloon and boat rides, historical tours, reenactments, artillery demonstrations, and the laying of a Scripture-engraved children's monument and time capsule. And certainly He was present in directing the team of adolescent cadets standing guard around the fairground in military dress of vague inspiration. They were young trainees from the Air Land Emergency Resource Team, or ALERT, program—an official-sounding name for what is neither a civil defense nor an emergency response team, but rather a Christian ministry for boys seventeen and older run on military school lines under the umbrella organization of Bill Gothard's Institute in Basic Life Principles.

Gothard's Institute, the source of a deeply influential set of Christian teachings among homeschoolers, is a $63-million per year business that enumerates a series of "nonoptional" spiritual laws calling for strict authoritarian child training, including a fundamentalist condemnation of worldly modern music and toys and an ethos of unswerving obedience to one's proper authorities in all jurisdictions in life. Through the 1970s, Gothard, a fundamentalist youth pastor who graduated from the evangelical Wheaton College, ran a series of youth seminars teaching his "Basic" principles that drew up to twenty thousand attendees per seminar, leaving a Gothard alumni base of an estimated two and a half million former students. In recent years, this influence has made Gothard a bogeyman of the left, but these days his influence is more discreet: through a quasi-secular training program for municipalities and secular institutions called the Character Training Institute, which has spread the ideology of the Basic Life Principles, sans explicit Scripture references, throughout civil society. One curriculum targeted at women prisoners teaches lessons on "Moral Purity," "Proper Submission," and "Yielding Rights."

That ALERT's young soldiers of the faith are shy and stammering teenage boys just on the cusp of becoming young men is no indictment of the movement's success but rather a glimpse of the raw material from which the patriarchy movement shapes its stern, undoubting future leaders. From such children, programs in manliness such as ALERT or Phillips's own internship program mold a staunch regiment of dedicated young men who, over the course of several years, gain the confidence and uniform worldview of patriarchy leaders several decades their seniors.

It's how Phillips was shaped, according to Fredrick Clarkson, a veteran religious-right watcher and author of *Eternal Hostility: The Struggle between Theocracy and Democracy*. "He was homeschooled and raised to be a revolutionary," says Clarkson. In this light, the trust and expectation poured into a unit of blemish-prone seventeen-year-old boys are less laughable. The imperative for Phillips's generation and those younger, Clarkson says, "is to understand your place in history. Because if you don't, you don't know what to do with your life. They are given a vision of themselves as big actors, so that if you act like you have power, maybe then you will."

. . .

In speeches and sermons delivered under a peaked, thirty-five-hundred-person tent, the celebration drove home one point, that Jamestown was settled in order to fulfill the Great Commission, Jesus's mandate that his followers spread his word and make converts of all the nations. Jamestown's founding mission was to evangelize and convert the Native Americans from what Phillips termed the worship of "spirit gods," "devils," and "animism" to that of Jesus Christ. (A post at Phillips's Web site underscored this sentiment with a mock advertisement for the celebration created by a Vision Forum reader, transforming the iconic *Jaws* movie poster to show a submerged, toothed Jamestown ship—the Quadricentennial's logo—menacing a Native American woman paddling a canoe on the surface above. The legend at the top of the mock poster read: "Just when you thought it was safe to re-embrace paganism…")

In their addresses, Phillips, Jonathan Falwell, and a number of their fellow speakers approvingly cited Jamestown's 1606 charter. That document explained the settlers' mission as "propagating of Christian Religion to such People, as yet live in Darkness and miserable Ignorance of the true Knowledge and Worship of God, and may in time bring the Infidels and Savages, living in those parts, to human civility, and to a settled and quiet Government." Phillips claims the colonists were motivated by a sense of religious, and not racial, superiority, thereby perversely casting Jamestown as an early model of "racial unity." He admits that such mission-oriented settlers "did see a tension between their God and the gods of the pagans" and allows that the resolutions to those conflicts may have been "imperfect." But, Phillips said, the settlers brought with them not just the gospel, but also a "dominion vision for establishing a land of freedom."

This begins to get at the heart of Phillips's mission. "Dominion" is a scriptural term taken from the "Genesis command" to be fruitful, multiply, and take dominion of the earth. It's a phrase that's taken on a number of fretful interpretations by liberal critics who study the aims of the "Dominionist" or "Christian Reconstructionist" movements: calls to return to biblical government, with varying degrees of fidelity to Old Testament law and punishments. Phillips sugarcoats this in the context of Jamestown: "We're talking about [settlers] believing with all their heart that part of their mission is to be fruitful and multiply and take dominion of the earth. To come and to claim—dedicate—the land to Christ. So that's exactly what they did. They planted a cross [on Jamestown's beach] and said, 'We are dedicating all work and all we do to Christ.'"

What this means in practice is detailed by the proponents of Christian Reconstructionism, namely, the founder of the movement, R. J. Rushdoony, and his intellectual heirs at the California-based Chalcedon

Foundation, the preeminent think tank of the Reconstructionist movement. Rushdoony is the author of an encyclopedic body of work, including the immense series on Reconstructionist law, *The Institutes of Biblical Law,* published in 1973. He was one of the early advocates, in modern years at least, of recognizing America's providential history and God's hand in guiding the nation. If only men would exercise dominion over the earth, he argued, they could remake the world as a Christian one. His ideas influenced generations of prominent Christian right leaders, ranging in style and theology from Jerry Falwell and televangelist Pat Robertson to the libertarian Reconstructionist writer, and Rushdoony's son-in-law, Gary North. Rushdoony briefly dabbled in "cobelligerent" national political movements with theological rivals—that is, setting aside fierce doctrinal differences to work together against common enemies— in organizations such as *Left Behind* author Tim LaHaye's secretive social conservative networking group, the Council for National Policy, and the pan-evangelical Coalition on Revival with another prominent Christian right theologian, Francis Schaeffer.

Rushdoony is rumored by some to have personally converted Doug Phillips's father, Howard; in any case he was certainly a close friend to the elder crusader. At Rushdoony's eightieth birthday, Phillips introduced him as "the most influential man of the twentieth century" due to his foundational work on Christian homeschooling, his unrelenting push for the institution of biblical law, or theonomy (obeying God through fidelity to orthodox Christian documents), and his singular efforts to "reconstruct" society in law, education, science, religion, and the family along the lines of the Bible.

Reconstructionists following Rushdoony are generally postmillennialists. Distinct from premillennialist Christians who believe that Jesus's return is imminent, postmillennialist believers have generations to work on crafting a godly society that will preface their Savior's return. While postmillennialism is shared by a broad spectrum of Christians far beyond Reconstructionists and represents a range of eschatologies, Reconstructionists believe that their work in creating God's kingdom on earth will be total, a grassroots changing of hearts and minds from within society that will convert all souls before Jesus's return.

Morecraft, a contemporary proponent of Reconstructionism whose Georgia Chalcedon Presbyterian Church is linked to the Chalcedon

Foundation in California, has explained: "We see the ultimate end of the Kingdom of God to return the rule and reign completely to God. And that," he admitted, "would become some kind of theocracy."

But the theocracy envisioned by Reconstructionists is not the familiar dystopia imagined by many progressive critics. It's more a theonomy, meaning that God's law from the Bible is still binding on his followers, but its power is divided into separate spheres of power, with numerous moral laws relegated to the jurisdiction of the family and the church. There's a temptation to look for Rushdoony's influence in the wrong places, aligning his thought with the clumsily crusading Bush administration and the publicity of a Christian political class determined to take power in any way possible. Rather, as Michael McVicar, a scholar at Ohio State University who studies Rushdoony's work, explains, Reconstructionists are probably most influential at the grassroots level, where there has been the birth of a multitude of church "Reform" movements across the nation, in multiple denominations, that have gone on to spur and effect far larger changes, seeking to alter society from within by proselytizing a message of obedience to God's will.

Though the founders of the movement have almost all been Calvinists who see their theology as a faithful extension of the Reformed church of colonial Puritans, they evangelize other conservative and fundamentalist churches outside the Reformed community. In 2006, Rushdoony's adult son and other movement leaders planned a countrywide tour to convert fundamentalist churches to the cause. Today, Morecraft says that leaders of the theology include Baptists, Methodists, Episcopalians, Catholics, and certainly a host of independent fundamentalist and Reformed pastors. But even broader, he says, "Beyond those who would identify themselves as Christian Reconstructionists, our influence goes into many of the leading conservative organizations of the New Right today."

The Reconstructionist movement is marked by a deep libertarian streak, which would inevitably color their version of theocracy. And in any case, McVicar says, many Reconstructionists viewed Bush, at best, as a well-intentioned buffoon. "Their theocracy would be decentralized, no ruling body of clerics." The death penalty that Reconstructionists notoriously advocate for gays, adulterous women, disobedient children, and "witches" would be dealt out under very strict circumstances. "It's modern man's propensity to interpret everything in terms of the state. But that's not what Rushdoony wanted. He wanted to bleed the state to death."

One avenue is through homeschooling, which Rushdoony advocated as a means to fight back against a secular public school system. Homeschoolers are often made of the same thick, antistate cloth, often referring to their Christian brethren who send their children to "government schools" as "Canaanites." The late Rushdoony himself argued that Jesus had delivered the strongest blow to "statism" with his existence, setting the stakes for a long battle between "Christ and state." And moreover, McVicar stresses, Rushdoony's work on biblical law cannot be separated from his advocacy at the libertarian, agrarian-minded Volker Fund, where Rushdoony "churned out memo after memo arguing that what we've got to do is get back to the countryside and start homeschooling our children, living off the land, breeding, and getting back to the basics of American society."

Jamestown and the Puritan colonies, or at least the Vision Forum imagination of them, are ideal representations of what the deconstructed, decentralized state of the Reconstructionist order would look like: a collection of autonomous patriarchal households under the authority of the local church. America before democracy. Not even Calvin's Geneva, an early center of the Reformation in the sixteenth century governed by Reformed theology—described by Scottish reformer John Knox as "the most perfect school of Christ that ever was on the earth since the days of the Apostles"—fit the bill for Rushdoony, who described his work as a correction of Calvin's settlement. Rather, the reconstructed country would be what McVicar calls "a pre-Enlightenment, medieval view of a God-centered world" wherein individual men are unable to reason outside of God's will: a basic transformation of our assumptions about society. (The moniker "medieval" was no slight; it drew the praise of the Chalcedon leadership.) It would be a form of Christian feudalism. There would be no king and no barons but individual Reconstructed men, all church members and land owners, following no legal body or authority but the church and the laws laid out in Deuteronomy and the New Testament.

There's a certain near-dandyism in this image as well that's evoked by the aesthetic focus of many Vision Forum publications and productions, which dedicate significant effort and attention to crafting the correct image of the ideal Christian family. This family is not frumpy and awkward but rather features handsome and muscular fathers decked out in colonial gear and an assortment of carefully selected girls and women who possess the movement's beauty ideal: somewhat fragile, pale, and demure, yet with a regal bearing as royal daughters of the church. Doug Phillips evokes this stately standard when, in a speech to a group of young girls, he describes one of his revisionist Christian heroines, a Hawaiian princess who was so devout, so gifted, and so kind that at her untimely death all of the peacocks in Hawaii cried. Phillips's artistic focus on the details may have been learned from the example of Rushdoony, who was said to carry himself with an air of gentrified nobility, and kept a flock of peacocks himself. Clarkson, who met Rushdoony during the 1996 Republican National Convention in San Diego, when Rushdoony and the Constitution Party were hosting their own far-right convention across town, found the father of Reconstructionism "a terribly, terribly dignified man," well manicured and suited like a 1930s banker, as befit a man with Rushdoony's sense of authority. "He thought of himself as playing a certain role in the history of the world, of humanity, of God's history."

As for lesser lights under Reconstructed rule? "Where men rule as patriarchs, an aristocracy of godly men," McVicar speculates, "everyone else falls by the wayside." For example, there would be a form of Reconstructed slavery, or at least indentured servitude. And women would certainly be secondary citizens, not property owners. The protections against abuse that would swell under such legal inequality are thought to be in the divine guidance that follows fidelity to Scripture. "They assume that, if you get your theology right, and live biblically, bounty will follow. And man's rule, if he's ruling according to God, will always be just."

. . .

Ideology like this sparked some controversy and actual bad press in Virginia. The week of their arrival, Williamsburg's local paper, the *Virginia Gazette,* ran two items on the celebration. The first was a letter from Rev. Peter Bauer, a Baptist pastor and secretary of the Charles City Clergy Conference, which disassociated local churches from the doings of "an out-of-state political organization with its own particular political agenda." "We applaud any attempt to give God glory," wrote Bauer. "But we take a stand against Vision Forum's attempt to tie its own political and social agenda to the Gospel." The paper further ran a separate article labeling Vision Forum a cult, a description that angered the event's organizers and celebrants, who countered that Vision Forum is an Internet-based ministry, not a sect or denomination with enforceable rules.

Geoffrey Botkin, a filmmaker and associate of Vision Forum who often functions as Phillips's right-hand man, dismissed the "cult" label as hateful and as the hallmark of lax and uneasy Christians "who know that they're disobeying God's word" and are therefore hostile to Christians more faithful to the Bible. Botkin said celebrants came to be around like-minded families and to discuss Jamestown "without the constraints of political correctness." They sought to openly profess their admiration for a society in which "it was really impossible to separate religion, economy, and society because within their civil government, all were integrated" and to reclaim Jamestown as part of America's "covenantal history," where God made an agreement with His chosen people. Following such a covenant, Botkin explained, means that when God's people are obedient, they are given protection, but when they are disobedient, they are chastised as a parent would chastise a child. "The Creator is very specific about how He wants [His people] to live, very specific about how they should behave and bring up their children as disciples."

Botkin traced America's disobedience to the mid-1800s, when government began to assume roles that were intended for families alone. Encouraging a return to cellular family independence and limited government is part of Vision Forum's mission, and followers often refer to their community as the Covenant Church and themselves as Covenant families (language that is emblematic of the Reformed Presbyterian churches that Phillips and many of his followers are a part of). And as for the lifestyle of the attendees, Botkin says—the families of eight, ten, and twelve children, or the one with fifteen that he met and photographed—that isn't something that can be transmitted by force or coercion, but only by the good example of orderly families. In this way, he saw the children at the celebration (including his daughters, unmarried women in their early twenties who have written a book endorsing stay-at-home motherhood for women) as part of a leadership generation, one clearly defined as young boys being trained for positions of prominence and young girls being raised, as Botkin's daughters were, to see motherhood as their "high and noble calling."

"I see the leadership of America in this tent," agreed Marshall Foster, founder of a Christian heritage organization, the Mayflower Institute, explaining the connection between abundant progeny and cultural renewal. "Look twenty years down the road and think about it. You raise up a godly seed, and a lot of them, and those people will do what the Scripture says: your children's children shall inherit the land. Not that your children's children will take the land, as has been presented this year [through the nation's official Jamestown commemoration], but they'll lead [the people] to God, to Christ. This isn't just an event or a tent revival. This is the result of twenty years of hard work and discipline in raising godly children and love for our country made manifest right here."

Phillips, in introducing Jonathan Falwell—attending to deliver his late father's intended speech—made a similar point, recalling the meeting between the elders Falwell and Phillips that led to the formation of the Moral Majority. Jonathan Falwell repaid the Father's Day compliment to the Phillips family, thanking Howard Phillips, seated in the front row, and rousing the audience to a standing ovation. "There are many out there who want to change our history," Falwell read from his father's notes. "We as Christians must never let this happen. Thanks to the great work of men starting in the early 1970s, we had Reagan in the White House in the early '80s. We must have the same vision and hope that God is still there and can change our nation."

It's a "changing of the guards," said Paul Jehle, a conservative Christian author whose Christian historical works include a defense of the Puritans involved in the Salem witch trials. Just as the daily ceremony of watch-shifts that had occurred in the Jamestown colony, he said, a new generation was due to rise, taking their places in the long stretch of covenantal history. "Those who have gone before—the Rushdoonys, the Falwells, the Grahams—it's necessary that we watchmen take their place. When you begin to remember, you become qualified to be the new guard at noon."

CHAPTER FOUR

The New Reformation

"In a way, the roots of this story go back to Westminster [Theological Seminary]," Susan Wise Bauer tells me as she navigates through a toll booth while caravanning behind her husband as they drive south from the Jamestown area to the Carolinas for a vacation at the shore. Over the phone, I can hear her children in the backseat. Bauer, the wife of Peter Bauer, the minister who criticized Vision Forum's Jamestown event, is one of the preeminent names in homeschooling, having cowritten a book with her mother—who had herself homeschooled Bauer back in the "dark ages" before it became the conservative religious movement it is today—that became a perennial bestseller among homeschoolers.

Bauer and her husband, minister of an interdenominational church, live in Charles City in southern Virginia on the strip of land where the Jamestown settlers landed and dedicated their colony to God. Vision Forum's Quadricentennial also landed not ten miles from their town, and Rev. Bauer felt compelled to distance area conservative Christians, particularly members of his largely interracial flock, from Vision Forum's message. At the time, in Jamestown, Vision Forum angrily wrote off Bauer's letter to the editor as a below-the-belt attack by the spouse of a business rival.

In full fact, though, Susan Bauer had drawn the ire of this contingent earlier in the year with a brief note on her personal blog praising an "egalitarian" book by Christian author John Stackhouse, *Finally Feminist: A Pragmatic Christian Understanding of Gender*. The book argued that the Apostle Paul's restrictions on women in Titus 2 were a case of accommodating the prevailing culture of the times so as not to alienate potential converts, but that it left openings, through the example of "exceptions to the rule," that allowed a path to greater gender equality in time as God worked through society to change that culture with human agents.

These were familiar fights for Bauer. She and husband Peter had both attended seminary at Westminster, a school that broke away from Princeton to pursue a more orthodox path, and which has since become known for producing theologians and pastors with strictly patriarchal or complementarian conceptions of gender roles in the church. Michael McVicar noted the role of Westminster in the rise of Rushdoony's ideas, as the seminary graduated a number of Rushdoony disciples that "turned Calvinism on its head." Their influence has been charged with leading to a number of church splits over a revived devotion to Reformed theology and the prioritization of gender issues. But even before Rushdoony, said McVicar, Westminster had a reputation for turning out smart but very problematic people, at least from the perspective of the mainstream, "mainline" old denominations.

While the Bauers were at Westminster, they were part of a Presbyterian Church in America congregation, the conservative alternative denomination to the liberal Presbyterian Church (USA). There they witnessed a number of the key "new Reformation" issues play out in front of them.

"We loved that church. At first. But the last year that we were there, in 1991, the Church spent the entire year arguing whether women can read Scripture aloud. They finally decided that women could read Scripture if they weren't in front of the congregation, so as not to give the appearance of their having teaching authority. I said to Peter, 'This is what Pharisees do—hedge around what's important for Scripture with nonscriptural lines.'" The Bauers didn't consider the issue of what women can do as a central church issue. "So we left and decided to church plant. I feel like we're still very theologically conservative, but I think we've gotten a lot more socially liberal—though I don't like those terms—as I think has most of our seminary generation."

But for years Bauer recognized that many of her readers were socially conservative Christians, and she was hesitant to provoke them by speaking her mind on social and gender issues. She didn't act until 2003 when, after three sons, she had a daughter. Then she worried, "What will this child see in how her mom talks about these issues? How will the church treat her?" Bauer's convictions were far from radical—she finds both abortion and homosexuality immoral—but even acceptance of Stackhouse's tepid feminism made her suspect. "I figured I'd get some flack," she said, "but I didn't realize how dramatic it would be."

A good number of the Bauers' contemporaries, both from Westminster and other conservative seminaries, had not in fact liberalized, but had deepened in their convictions on gender. After Bauer's review of *Finally Feminist* came out, there was a roar of condemnation, starting with a chorus of homeschooling mothers' blogs warning that Bauer's books would lead unwitting homeschooling families astray if people read them without realizing she had subversive feminist sympathies. The din reached the pillars of the Reformed leadership, with movement heads such as Al Mohler, Ligon Duncan, and Rick Phillips lambasting what they saw as Bauer's betrayal of the cause. The Council on Biblical Manhood and Womanhood (CBMW) charged that Bauer "is undermining biblical authority by holding her current position on the gender issue."

The homeschoolers criticizing her, said Bauer, "assign words an almost magical power to corrupt" and feel very strongly that you must protect your child from the "wrong written words." They advocated a boycott against Bauer's books. The Reformed theologians warned—in a particularly frustrating argument that Bauer countered when the battle reached the pages of *Christianity Today,* the preeminent publication in American evangelicaldom—that accepting this book placed Bauer on a slippery slope, opening the door to accepting gay rights, abortion, and other such "abominations." Such was the risk of arguing that the Bible's rules could be understood as culture-bound and conditional in other cases.

But this literalist standard seems to be limited to questions of gender, Bauer argues, seeing that many of the Reformed theologians who argued against Stackhouse and her were bringing unacknowledged cultural and nonscriptural baggage to the fight. "They tend to be very sophisticated when reading Scripture about where it fits in to its original context, except when it comes to women. Then they're not as eager to look to the context."

This, for Bauer, is where it comes back to Westminster and the quiet, decades-old promotion of Reformed ideas within the evangelical church. "Reformed people, at bottom, have a high regard for Scripture, marked by careful exegesis of the written word, as that is how God communicates with us—through the written word. So always in Reformed circles, there's a debate about when we can say the surface meaning of Scripture isn't what Scripture is actually saying without undermining the authority of Scripture. What's at the center of it is the fear that we won't have a clear way to understand what God is saying to us."

. . .

Though the patriarchy, complementarian, or biblical manhood and womanhood movement is a cross-denominational phenomenon, Reformed theology, or Calvinism, has done a great deal to mainstream the ideas throughout the conservative Christian church at large. And while neo-Calvinist Reconstructionists claim themselves to be the faithful Reformed heirs of Massachusetts Bay Colony Puritanism, Reformed theology encompasses a far broader and more popular Christian tradition than such far-right factions.

Reformed doctrine is summarized as holding to the five points of Calvinism known by the acronym TULIP: total depravity, unconditional election, limited atonement, irresistible grace, and perseverance of the saints. But it's also distinguished by the general sense that "life is religion" and that God is invested in and concerned with all aspects of a Christian's life. It's a short step from this general understanding of living one's faith to the politicizing, neo-Calvinistic insistence, common among evangelicals over the past thirty years, that God intends His people to champion "Christian" social causes and to live their lives in accordance with a conservative biblical worldview.

In 1993, two years after Susan Bauer's church was torn over the question of women reading Scripture, a thirty-three-year-old Al Mohler came into leadership of the Southern Baptist Theological Seminary. His appointment came on the heels of the conservative revolution within the Southern Baptist Convention, when a small, organized band of conservative activists, led largely by CBMW board member Paige Patterson, plotted a gentle coup, a takeover through leadership assignments, and effectively changed the face of what had been considered a moderate to even liberal denomination.

Upon Mohler's presidency, he promptly enforced a doctrinal test on the seminary's moderate faculty, requiring them to pledge adherence to the Westminster Confession, the seminary's official confession of faith and a seminal document of Reformed theology. With this move, Mohler cleared the school of dissent and almost cleared entirely the ranks of faculty: only four of more than one hundred professors stayed on. Today, Mohler's seminary produces a steady army of Reformed pastors and Christian leaders who are disseminating a Christianity that is far more concerned with doctrine and far more Puritanical—and that in fact frequently calls itself Puritan—than the emotional evangelicalism that has swept the country.

Though Patterson and his fellow SBC revolutionaries didn't speak of the need for a new, or rather, a return to old, gender politics as an explicit reason for the conservative takeover of the denomination, it was certainly an auxiliary goal. "It was a matter of strategy that we focus on the prior question—the reliability of the Bible—first. If we established the Convention's commitment to the reliability of the Bible, that would in turn take care of many questions we had, including gender roles." Cementing the notion of Christ's authority over all spheres of life and the authority of His Word meant establishing the concept of biblically ordained authority throughout a Christian's life: "We're always under the authority of Christ," explains Patterson. "And if [a woman] chooses to marry, she must accept that role and be under the authority of her husband. It's a question of whether we take the Bible seriously or not." It's understood within the vast swath of Christianity that Patterson represents that one follows the other.

During the takeover, then–SBC president Tom Ellis spoke to the Pattersons and other denominational leaders about adding an article on the family to the denomination's statement of faith, Baptist Faith and Message. To that end, they established a study committee including Dorothy Patterson and Richard Land, president of the SBC's Ethics and Religious Liberty Commission since 1988, to write the article. The resulting document called for husbands to sacrificially love their wives and for wives to submit gracefully to their husbands' authority: the same declaration that 2008 presidential candidate Mike Huckabee signed on to in 1998, causing a media flurry over the idea of "wifely submission" when his candidacy gained strength.

Academic apologists for the growing evangelical emphasis on headship and submission, such as W. Bradford Wilcox, a sociologist at the University of Virginia and author of *Soft Patriarchs and New Men: How Christianity Shapes Fathers and Husbands,* argue that in practice, the doctrine creates a benevolent patriarchy that domesticates men into responsible husbands and loving fathers. Wilcox suggests that while evangelical women may indeed take on more housework as a result of submission, the trade-off is worth it, particularly for women of color—on whom Wilcox focuses—for the good work patriarchy does to fix the "weak link" of family life that men have become since the sexual revolution: becoming fathers without following traditional obligations of the role. Such "neotraditional," "religious family men" as form the new patriarchy, writes Wilcox, "especially more conservative ones—combine elements of the new and the old in their approach to family life. They are more likely to have unequal marriages and to take a strict approach to discipline; but they are also more emotionally and practically engaged than the average secular or nominally religious family man." To Wilcox and his fellow travelers, this indicates that women's embrace of patriarchy is the preferable path to family security.

"A soft patriarch is also seen—by himself, his wife, and his children—as ultimately responsible for the welfare of the family. In practice, however, his authority is more symbolic than real. In other words, he is given the gift of symbolic leadership by his family in return for an expectation of practical and emotional engagement in the life of the family."

But Wilcox's insistence that patriarchy leaders don't really intend a power imbalance is belied by the force and frequency of their focus on hierarchy and their sense of the chain of command as a time-proven structure. Noting statistics on domestic violence that show that church-going evangelical men are among the least likely groups to abuse their wives, Wilcox explains to me that family and church members provide important "checks" to keep patriarchy safe for women, reproaching husbands who are domineering rather than service-oriented, "who are behaving badly, or who are not meeting congregational standards for good family life." He acknowledges, however, that evangelical men who don't attend church regularly—a group that biblical womanhood advocates suggest should be largely left to their ways—are among the most likely spousal abusers, a situation of seemingly little recourse for many women.

In some ways, the renewed focus on patriarchy is an older movement. A British publication, *Banner of Truth,* began republishing key Reformed documents and Puritan literature in the 1950s in the belief that the best of Christian literature had been allowed to fall into oblivion, taking with it its certainty. Today, taking advantage of a larger pool of potential converts through the Internet, *Banner of Truth* publishes original articles on favored Reformed subjects, such as wifely submission to male headship. Geoff Thomas, pastor of a Reformed Baptist church in Aberystwyth, England, and a great promoter of Puritan literature and sensibilities, argues for the necessity of wives' complete submission to their husbands in that they're representatives of the faith. In one of his numerous *Banner of Truth* pieces, "Wives Submit to Their Husbands," published on the site in 2005, he writes:

> If a woman does not honour her husband and is not loving toward him, if she is independent and defiant toward him, she proclaims this as the church's response to Christ and thus attacks God's Word. A wife's behavior toward her husband either makes the Word of God more attractive or else makes it an object of contempt. In other words, the reason why wives are to submit to their husbands is not because they are wonderful guys who deserve it. The reason why you submit is because your Lord Jesus Christ deserves it. Out of gratitude to him, for all that he has done for you, you submit.

That this happens to be a very convenient state of affairs for men—exacting obedience of Christian women to make the lifestyle attractive to others—is something that wives should ignore, to avoid the risk of blaspheming an all-sovereign God whose plan surpasses understanding. If God is using women's submission to unworthy men as an advertisement for the power of the faith to a skeptical public, that is their role to play. It's a clear-cut extension of John Piper's description of Reformed theology, resting on the sense of a truly all-powerful God and the dire need for obedience to him, or what other commentators call "high-commitment Christianity."

It's also a highly masculine Christianity, following historical Christian apologists such as author C. S. Lewis, an orthodox Anglican well admired by Reformed Christians, who worshipped a distinctly "muscular," untamed, and sword-bearing Jesus. It also follows current leaders such as Mark Driscoll, head of a booming countercultural—in more ways than one—Seattle megachurch, who boasts that he could never worship a Jesus he could beat up. This coincides neatly with the recognition of church growth leaders that in order to attract men, the power holders in society, back to the pews, religion had to offer them something. To begin with, a

Jesus that they can't beat up; at "higher commitment" levels, a marriage structure that prizes male authority and anoints husbands and fathers as earthly representatives of the divine.

In a 2006 interview with *Christianity Today,* a young star Reformed pastor, Joshua Harris of Maryland megachurch Covenant Life Church, who came to homeschooling fame with the publication of his 1997 treatise on courtship, *I Kissed Dating Goodbye,* described his conversion to Reformed theology as a romance: falling in love with the heartiness of doctrine. "Once you're exposed to [doctrine], you see the richness in it for your own soul, and you're ruined for anything else." This is what he sees in many young evangelicals, who read books by popular Reformed theologians like Piper, Grudem, C. J. Mahaney (who preceded Harris at Covenant Life Church and tapped the young pastor for leadership), or R. C. Sproul, Sr. and begin to deepen in their Christianity. "[Hearing someone say], 'You know what, it's not about us, it's about God's glory, it's about his renown.' Now I don't think most kids realize this, but that's the first step down a pathway of Reform theology. Because if you say it's not about you, well then you're on that road of saying it's not about your actions, your choosings, your determination." And if it's not about you, or your husband and what he deserves, but about what God deserves, it becomes easier to demand obedience of gender guidelines as well.

Harris is the son of Greg Harris, an early leader of the homeschooling movement in the Pacific Northwest—a surprisingly strong branch of the movement—and a compatriot of men like Doug Phillips and Sproul, Jr. Joshua Harris's book on courtship is a favored item at homeschooling conventions, and his younger brothers and sister are following in his footsteps—in gender-appropriate ways, of course. His two younger brothers run the popular "Rebelution" blog, where they conducted a high-trafficked "modesty survey" asking Christian teen boys to rate what clothing is and isn't acceptable for a Christian girl trying not to cause her brothers in Christ to "stumble." They also launched a countrywide youth tour promoting their mantra, "Do Hard Things." In 2007 and 2008 they were chosen to run the "Huck's Army" blogging campaign for Republican presidential candidate Mike Huckabee. The younger Harris sister, far less in the limelight, runs her own blog on biblical femininity, a junior sister in the thriving biblical womanhood blogosphere that is filled with today's mothers of the movement.

As Carmon Friedrich, a homeschooling mother of ten in Northern

California's rural Gold Country, as well as a friend of Vision Forum and the author of a popular women's blog, Buried Treasure Books, tells me, "It becomes a very small world when you share these convictions."

But not so small these days. If there is such a resurgence in Reformed theology as appears and as *Christianity Today* assumes, it makes sense in the context of the evangelical megachurch boom, not in spite of it. This was Friedrich's own path—becoming a Christian through the evangelical Young Life group and later attending a mainstream evangelical church with her husband. Both eventually craved more of the daily doctrine, the rules for life, that Reformed theology provides. Today Friedrich, though a member of a local Baptist church, describes her theology more in terms of the Reformed pastors of various denominations that she reads, such as Mohler, Sproul, John MacArthur, and John Piper.

"We used to believe that Jesus was coming back any day now, and all that stuff," Friedrich tells me, referencing her former evangelical, premillennial/dispensationalist beliefs—the "rapture-ready" theology of Christians who believe that Jesus will return in the near future in order to establish his one-thousand-year reign on earth—a position Reformed believers define themselves against. Reformed believers know it is up to them to establish a godly order closer to the Kingdom before Christ can return. And for this to happen, rules matter.

"This life isn't all that there is," says Friedrich, "and that goes back to my evangelical roots, and I'm grateful for that. But after that, they flounder a bit. Especially in not emphasizing that this life and the next are both important. God cares about how we conduct our relationships, how we vote, how we raise our children, about the art that we create. We need to know what God wants us to do and apply that. That's something the evangelical church was missing—they forgot totally to talk about what was going on in the rest of our lives."

But in fact, Reformed theology often follows such an introduction. Mark Driscoll's Mars Hill Church, rated the eighth-most-influential church in America, relies on the fixtures of "emergent" or "seeker"-oriented ministries, such as countercultural groups like Bikers or Skaters for Christ, to attract its young, urban congregation. But churches like Mars Hill, which espouses a deeply conservative theology, recognize that such outreach ministries are meant to be transitional, introducing a person to Christ where they are, then easing them into more serious study and graduating them to traditionalist doctrine—in Driscoll's case, to a doctrine that places substantial weight on gender, submission, and a wife's role in marriage. Or, in the parlance of the faith, a move "higher up and deeper in," as C. S. Lewis described the idea of a maturing Christian commitment in his gospel-based Narnia fables. For as many churches as operate on the mission of bringing new believers into the fold with an evangelical fervor and love for Jesus, there is a second set of missionaries —either within the more established ranks of that same church or in a more doctrine-oriented church to be found "deeper in"—gradually convincing believers to eat more substantial meat of the faith and leading them into conservative doctrine on marriage relationships, submission, and obedience in all things to God.

CHAPTER FIVE

Titus 2: Submission and War

Beyond the Holy Spirit, there's a practical mechanism for effecting this sort of graduation from mainstream evangelical practice to the conservative gender doctrines of Reformed faith: through the myriad Bible studies, women's, mother's, and family ministries, "parachurch" organizations, and publications that have proliferated across the Christian landscape. Though they may engage in purist rivalries within themselves and against each other, these groups operate with such minute doctrinal differences that the combined effect of their voices is as a steady drumbeat, teaching Christian women to submit. An umbrella term for many of these ministries is "Titus 2" mentoring or training groups.

Many narratives about the genesis of the American Christian right begin with Francis Schaeffer, variously described as a fundamentalist or neo-Calvinist Presbyterian pastor, author of a number of books, including *A Christian Manifesto,* and creator of the film series *Whatever Happened to the Human Race.* Schaeffer is widely credited with rousing the apolitical giant of fundamentalist Protestant voters to action against secular humanism—an opposing religion, in Schaeffer's description, that could not be squared with a Christian worldview—and to an even greater degree, against abortion, urging Christians to be "salt and light" to the culture at large, as the Bible instructs in Matthew 5:13–16. At a time when antiabortion activism was seen as the province of the Catholic Church—damned idolaters in the eyes of a good fundamentalist—Schaeffer counseled an interfaith cooperation that transcended doctrinal differences. He promoted "cobelligerency," the ideology that informs today's formidable (though incomplete) united religious right front, particularly the evangelical, Catholic, and Mormon alliance against reproductive freedom, women's and gay rights, and church-state separation.

To Carmon Friedrich, Schaeffer's influence on American Christianity was to make Christianity a full-time faith again. When young people would go to see Schaeffer during the 1960s, full of questions about what was going on in the world, Schaeffer would explain the biblical view, the Christian foundation for all the things that were happening. He told them it was the faith of the great men of history that accounted for their accomplishments, whether in art, music, economics, or politics, and that it was God's unseen hand turning the wheel of history. Articulating a difference between evangelical and Reformed churches, Friedrich says the idea that Schaeffer planted was that, "God cares about more than whether we give Christian tracts to our neighbor. He cares about our home, our marriage, what we do, what work we do. That's something the evangelical church was missing. Schaeffer showed us how to do that. We don't compartmentalize that way anymore. His ideas are starting to filter through—you can see it in debates about what men and women are supposed to be doing." In the decompartmentalized view of Christianity lived every minute, God cares equally about prayer, faith, prolife activism, and the particulars of domestic life.

A character in this narrative lesser known outside of evangelical circles is the woman standing beside Schaeffer: his wife and trusted help-meet, Edith Schaeffer. Edith was the indefatigable hostess of Schaeffer's American expatriate community in Switzerland, L'Abri (meaning "Shelter"), a training ground and experiment in radical Christian living. She is also an author whose most durable contribution to the culture wars are two of her seemingly most apolitical books: *L'Abri,* a memoir of her role in her husband's ministry, and what became, perhaps unintentionally, a landmark book for proponents of biblical womanhood, *The Hidden Art of Homemaking.* Interestingly, the latter book's original title was simply *Hidden Arts*—evoking a broader range of artistry in the "feminine," domestic realm—but in reprinting, the title was restricted to housework, possibly reflecting the movement it inspired and the generation of antifeminist writers who saw the book as an alternative to the women's liberation movement blooming across suburbia and the country at large.

These women found in Edith Schaeffer the counterpart, the warm heart, of her husband's call to Christian political action, one frequently summed up in a truism that today's antifeminists, patriarchalists, and complementarians like to repeat: "As many people were brought to the Lord through Mrs. Schaeffer's cinnamon buns as through Dr. Schaeffer's sermons." Women's work in the home is their own most important ministry, they mean, and though domestic and supportive, it is as critical as men's leadership role in the Great Commission and in the eyes of God.

Mary Pride's homeworking manifesto was not only inspired by Schaeffer, but she even credits two books by Edith and Francis as key to her salvation. The impact the Schaeffer family had, Pride says—through the parents, children, and now grandchildren (save son Franky, who criticized the Christian right in his 2007 book, *Crazy for God*)—in calling Christians to the arts and politics was due to their obedience to God and their fidelity to God's family order. It was the comforts of the home environment Mrs. Schaeffer created, her hospitality, and her good cooking that convinced pilgrims visiting L'Abri to sit at her husband's feet and absorb his new political theology. The way home, Pride says, is to follow Edith Schaeffer's model and be a homeworker, submitting to and building up your husband and making the home your ministry rather than searching for God's work outside your home. "What a day it will be when all God's women return to homeworking and every wife has a church in her home."

The cinnamon bun anecdote is also a promise of power, similar to the old adage about the hand that rocks the cradle ruling the world—another favored verse for antifeminists—directed at a group that claims to want none and which advocates revolution through the forfeiture of any claim to authority and self-determination. Though it seems odd to outsiders, the faithful might recognize this paradox as a particularly Christian one: that you sacrifice yourself to gain the world; that true freedom comes through abject submission and obedience to authority; that the meek shall inherit the earth.

John Piper echoes this, arguing that women's challenge is to influence their husbands spiritually, through "fearless tranquillity and holiness and prayer." Prayerful women, he writes, are using their God-ordained power over men, and this enables them to "exert far more power in this world than all political leaders put together." For those unmoved by rote Christian platitudes about the power of prayer moving mountains, Piper offers practical information as well—consider the power women wield through the way they raise their daughters and sons. Though this too is an offer of delayed power and reward, vindication through posterity, it's one that has caught on.

It's a theme that Pride inhabits thoroughly in her crusade against feminism. In this war, women's call is to echo their role in life: as help-meets, as servants, submissive to the authority above them. "Submission has a military air," she writes in *The Way Home*. "For the greater good, the soldier is subject to his commanding officer, even if he disagrees with him."

> This generation is in danger of forgetting that the Christian way of life is still a war. We have strong enemies—the world, the flesh, the devil. We also have a commander in chief, Jesus Christ, who has created a winning battle strategy. Jesus is the one who assigns roles and goals in his own army. And Jesus, through the Holy Spirit, has said that wives are to willingly subject themselves to their husbands.
>
> When the private is committed to winning the war, and is willing to subject his personal desires to the goal of winning, and is willing to follow the leader his commander has put over him, that army stands a good chance of winning....Submission, then, is dedication to God's interests (the war). You work for your head's best interests in obedience to God.
>
> When we stop looking out for our own interests (which is what feminism and careerism are all about) and start looking out for those of Jesus Christ (which is what biblical submission is all about), then his kingdom will start making some progress.

These truths, Pride and the ranks of complementarians argue, were too generally accepted to merit mention several decades ago: they were the commonsense rules for life followed by most men and women, conservative Christians and otherwise, across the country. What happened in between they blame not just on the rise of the women's liberation movement, but on a previous generation of women abdicating responsibility by failing to follow the guidelines of Titus 2, the Apostle Paul's instructions to his disciple Titus on how to govern the lives of his early Christian community on the island of Crete. Among those rules is the instruction that older women spend their days training younger women to love, submit to, and obey their husbands so that the word of God will not be blasphemed. The mention of blasphemy is interpreted variously by conservative theologians, some of whom argue that, since early Christians were a religious minority, Christian leaders were determined that their family order be unimpeachably proper, giving outsiders no cause to speak badly of the new Church. Other theologians more bluntly declare that unsubmissive women are such an outrage to the Lord that their disobedience is as blasphemy.

Edith Schaeffer has written that a family is a "perpetual relay of truth," and Mary Pride seized on this metaphor to accuse her mother's generation of dropping the baton, of failing to instruct Pride and other women who came of age during and after the feminist revolution in the ways of biblical womanhood, who instead forsook homework for "wicked ways." Pride, a dedicated scorner of the "expert advice" modern parenting guides dispense, rallied the women of her generation to make up for lost time and pass on literalist Titus 2 wisdom to tomorrow's mothers and wives. "God intended motherhood to be a relay race. Each generation would pass the baton on to the next. But the baton has been fumbled. So it's our job—yours and mine—to pick it up. We have to do more than follow in our mothers' footsteps. We have to go directly back to the Bible ourselves, taking nothing for granted, and rediscover the lost art of mothering."

This call, though neither Pride nor Schaeffer named it as such in the early 1970s or '80s, is now recognized across the Christian community as a demand for Titus 2 ministries: ministries, including blogs, books, clubs, women's retreats, and one-on-one mentoring relationships, dedicated to rediscovering the lost arts not just of motherhood but of cleaning, cooking, homeschooling, and, particularly, submitting in wifehood.

In an institutional take on the calling in August of 2007, the Southern Baptist Theological Seminary in Fort Worth, Texas, announced the formation of a new university curriculum and bachelor of arts degree in homemaking developed by the seminary president and his wife, Paige and Dorothy Patterson. The program, available only to women and targeted at the wives of pastors-in-training, pairs Bible and literature studies with twenty-three hours of biblical womanhood instruction, including seven hours of meal preparation and nutrition; seven hours of "textile design and clothing construction"; and three hours each of instruction in "general homemaking," "the value of a child," and the "biblical model for the home and family." Other, "more intimate" topics, unsuitable for mixed-gender classrooms, are also covered, Paige Patterson told me.

The program is intended to strengthen family life, the decline of which Patterson blames on the cessation of university home economics programs, but he also hopes it can turn around what he sees as a nightmare forecast for American academia: today's sixty-forty gender imbalance of women outnumbering men in American universities, which Patterson fears is a foreshadowing of a future intelligentsia dominated by women who have abandoned their families for careers.

But, Patterson says, he also means war. "We're preparing [our women] to do battle with the feminist culture."

The response to the new curriculum from individual advocates of biblical womanhood across the Internet was surprisingly cold: what comment is it on the culture, they sniffed, that a *university* should need to teach those things that Titus 2 *women* were meant to?

Today, in the name of honoring God's word on women, or at least this conservative interpretation of it, hundreds of ministries and publications are weaving a whole-cloth alternative to women's liberation that begins and ends with women's submission to men. As the Virtuous Woman blog, one of hundreds of Christian womanhood blogs dedicated to propagating biblical womanhood, describes its mission: "So many women today were not taught how to run a household efficiently while in the care of their mothers. God gives guidelines for how a virtuous woman lives. Proverbs 31 is an empowering look at the role of women. Not only is a virtuous woman righteous in the Lord, but she is a loving wife and mother, a smart shopper, a seamstress, a gardener, a good housekeeper, and trains her children with wisdom. Her husband appreciates her and can praise her to his associates and friends because she is worthy of praise."

ABOVE RUBIES

But before them all, and in contrast to Edith Schaeffer's "accidental" women's ministry, there was Nancy Campbell.

In Primm Springs, Tennessee, a point in a web of barely paved country roads southwest of Nashville lined by hay bales festooned with American flags and notices to "Vote Yes on 1 to Protect Marriage," I met one of the grande dames of American Christian womanhood, Nancy Campbell, author of books such as *Be Fruitful and Multiply* and *The Power of Motherhood* and the self-titled "editriss" of the internationally distributed *Above Rubies* magazine, a missive of "family encouragement" for women seeking to become more virtuous mothers and wives. Campbell sees her magazine, with a readership of one hundred and twenty thousand, as a Titus 2 ministry, and as such she is perhaps one of the first women of the post-1950s era to have picked up the "dropped baton" of female training.

The title of Campbell's magazine points to another portion of Scripture popular with conservative Christian women, Proverbs 31, an exhaustive delineation of the proper spheres of feminine activity. A woman who excels in the catalogue of Proverbs 31 virtues is praiseworthy, a boon to her husband, and valuable "far above rubies or pearls." And *Above Rubies,* which frequently features an assortment of Campbell's children and grandchildren in various tender moments of motherhood, exists to glorify women following their "natural high calling." Articles cover topics such as "Dressing for My Husband," "The Beauty of Homemaking," "Where's My Apron?" and "Raising Missionaries."

When Campbell started printing the magazine in 1977, she says she was seeking to fill a void in encouragement to women who resisted the lures of feminism and careers. Having just given birth to her sixth child in rural New Zealand, Campbell, like many women who would become conservative leaders, says she felt bereft of guidance and encouragement in her stay-at-home life and determined to provide it herself for other young mothers living a homemaker's life. She started from scratch and eventually went on to mentor thousands, leading women back to hearth, home, and the proper honor of their husbands.

When I drove onto Campbell's Tennessee property a trio of dogs led me up the driveway, trotting lazily up a dirt roadway to an attractive house undergoing construction on one corner of a ranging plot of land. As I parked, a pair of blond toddler boys appeared at my car door and led me to the house, bidding me to enter through a curtain of plastic flaps into the mudroom Campbell uses to store back issues, and finally into a grand open workspace where two teenage girls, interns sent by their mothers for training, smiled up at me from a pile of readers' letters they were sorting for print.

Though over the phone Campbell's voice sounds almost as lilting and formal as a parody of the Queen Mother—Campbell came to southern Tennessee with her husband, Colin, a Pentecostal pastor, by way of Australia, by way of New Zealand—and the smiling portrait of her and Colin that graces the masthead of each issue gives the impression of a slightly dotty old aunt, in person she is far more formidable. A handsome, tall, and slender redhead in her sixties, Campbell stood with immaculate posture in a floral, mid-calf skirt and sandals—the dress of a high school English teacher with poetic sensibilities—as she received me upstairs. Upstairs is the "living" portion of their two-story house, a cocoon of soft carpeting, peach paint, and ample-enough couches to host her six children and thirty-two grandchildren, all of whom emigrated to the Nashville area between ten and fifteen years ago. Her sons, who brought the popular Australian Christian rock band the Newsboys to great success in the United States, continue to work in Nashville's Christian music industry, as did her daughters before they married and dedicated themselves to building homes and rearing their children in the Tennessee countryside.

On the cover of a 2006 issue of *Above Rubies,* Campbell published a photo of her three daughters, Pearl, Evangeline, and Serene, as well as a daughter-in-law, Monique, all holding their latest offspring—four babies apparently born within weeks of each other—at arm's length, a bounty of chubby blond offerings to the camera. The young mothers stood before a thicket of mossy trees glinting in spring sunshine, wearing bohemian crocheted sweaters, thong sandals, and baggy cargo pants. Their hair fell loose to as low as their waists, and their mouths were open in laughter: an image better suited to commune-living earth mothers than stern fundamentalists.

Other covers offer similar scenes, family and children shots with a heavy preference for soft-focus close-ups of wispy-haired, gently pretty women adoring newborns cradled in their arms. One cover features a blond toddler boy, a Christian back-to-the-land farmer's son from Tennessee, wearing overalls and a yarmulke, head-butting the Wailing Wall in Jerusalem—a somewhat baffling image until explained by the story within, that of an eleven-child family that moved to Israel as a "fulfillment of biblical prophecy" and were greeted as kindred spirits by the Orthodox Jewish community because of their large family. It was international proof, they explained, of their love of the same God. This is a returning focus of Campbell's—convincing Christian couples to be abundantly "fruitful" in their offspring—but the first step toward that is returning women to their rightful roles as helpmeets and keepers at home.

"I think humanists set out to undermine marriage, motherhood," she said, "not just by promoting careerism. Really the first thing was the undermining of man, of manhood, with 'what do we need a man for?' and 'who's going to submit to a man?' Let's get out of that. Goodness me. Encouraging women to not ever come into any submission to a man, and to do their own thing, and to have a career and put their children in day care, and to get out and be themselves." As Campbell spoke of the eroding influence of feminism and humanism on traditional family life, her voice became gruff and Americanized, taking on the gritty accent of a hard-living film noir newspaperman, rattling off the facts of a sad case. When she returned to describing biblical living, her voice softened back to a syrupy drawl. "All that," she said, meaning all that independence and doing your own thing, "sounds very wonderful, but it doesn't work in the long run. It only brings heartache, the weakening of the family, and it has wreaked havoc on marriage and homes. So we don't have that strong family unit that we once had in the nation. There are many who do have that, but many don't because they've been taught against it by the education system. By the time you get through college, a young woman is really brainwashed against the biblical understanding of marriage and home and motherhood."

The biblical understanding, of course, is that men and women are one, united, and equally important in the eyes of the Lord. But within that understanding, the first created human, Adam, has authority—demonstrated by God's choosing him to name the animals and to in fact name Eve when she was taken from his side to be his servant and companion. So a woman is to submit to that leadership, and a man is to love his wife as he loves his own body, as Christ loves the church, for she is his body, after all.

" 'She is flesh of my flesh, bone of my bone,' said Adam. 'She shall be called woman, because she was taken out of me.' " Campbell repeated the oldest story with starry-eyed wonder. "Adam recognized that, of all the animals, she was not a new creation. Every single thing God created was new creation—the stars, the sun, the moon. Adam and the animals were dust of the earth. Eve wasn't. She wasn't made from dust. She was not a new creation. She was not some independent, new creation who could do what she liked. She was part of man. Out of man. Made for man."

LIBERATION THROUGH SUBMISSION

But woman, being what she is, cyclically fails to accept this knowledge, mourn Campbell and her fellow Titus 2 mentors. They see a darker story in Genesis as well, that in the beginning, there was Eve, and Eve had a feminist heart. Her particular sin nature was to rebel, as Lucifer rebelled, against God and the authority He'd put over her: her husband, Adam. The original sin is gendered, as they see it, and feminism is the nature of women's original sin: an inclination to disobey, to subvert authority, to rebel, to not submit. And it was through her rebellion, and Adam, with his particular sin nature, rebelling by failing to lead his wife and allowing her to lead them into sin, that paradise was lost. In some tellings of the story, feminism is not in Eve, but is the serpent itself, whispering in Eve's ear. This is what Raymond C. Ortlund, Jr., imagines in *Recovering Biblical Manhood and Womanhood,* a feminist devil enticing Eve with visions of the world beyond Eden. "This tree, Eve, is your only chance to reach your potential." There in the garden, the first man and woman allowed a reversal of sex roles that gave Satan his opportunity: the snake "struck at Adam's headship," and therefore God's order, through the naïveté of Eve. Uprooting gender roles, this lesson explains, is the way that Satan always strikes at God.

Many books in the canon of biblical womanhood start with Eve because, until the past few decades, the fundamentalist and evangelical church understood one of the lessons of the Fall to be that women, daughters of Eve, were more easily deceived than men, and that therefore they should not be entrusted with overmuch authority. Or, more darkly, if not more easily deceived, more intrinsically wicked and likely to rebel.

P.B. "Bunny" Wilson, a popular speaker on Christian women's issues and author of *Liberated through Submission* and "Pruned to Bloom," describes God's post-Fall curse on men and women as an eternal sitcom, millennia of *Honeymooners* acting out the battle of the sexes to a drum-roll and laugh line: "When God cursed Eve," Wilson riffs, "it was almost as if he said to her, 'OK Eve, you want to be the boss and make decisions? When you leave this garden, you will always want to control and lead the course of your husband's life. But he will rule over you instead.'" Likewise Adam, whom Wilson depicts as a layabout who'd vastly prefer to lounge on the couch, will have to get up and lead.

Wilson's jokey representation is anomalous, for two reasons. First, for its theology: most Titus 2 authors reject the depiction of wifely submission as part of the curse, God's punishment for Adam and Eve's disobedience, but rather point to Eve's creation as a helpmeet as proof that submission was part of God's plan before the Fall. To argue otherwise would open the door for women to claim, as some dissenters do, that

Christ dying for their sins should clear the slate for this sin, and punishment, as well. But secondly, the anomaly is in Wilson's levity over what most Titus 2 authors see as a serious sin issue. Failure to submit to God's appointed authority, the husband, is failure to submit to God. And rebellion against God is not a charge to be taken lightly, because, as even Wilson reminds, 1 Samuel 15:23 warns Christians that "rebellion is as the sin of witchcraft." And witchcraft, Christian women will be reminded, is punishable in the Bible by death.

Martha Peace, an author of several books on biblical womanhood and Titus 2 ministries as well as a "Nouthetic counselor"—a neologism coined by her mentor, Jay Adams, describing a distinctly conservative sort of biblical counseling that forgoes psychological training, theories, or ethics boards (bastions of liberal ideas) in order to instruct women to solve their problems through strictly biblical means—warns against rebellion in *The Excellent Wife*. "If you disobey your husband, you are indirectly shaking your fist at God. You are saying in your heart, 'God, I don't care what you say, I'm going to do this my way!' When you rebel against your husband's authority, you are grievously sinning."

Peace is like many prominent Titus 2 teachers in highlighting her own transformation from egalitarian "full-blown career feminist"—which, in biblical womanhood literature, generally means having once had or desired a career outside the home—to submissive wife and labels her redemption "the taming of the shrew."

At a podium in the center of a Sunday school building on the wide-ranging campus of the First Baptist Church of Jonesboro, Georgia, an eight-thousand-person megachurch in a green suburb southeast of Atlanta, Peace, wearing a dark blazer over a floor-length floral skirt, told this story again. Speaking before nearly 120 women, attendees to the church's Women of Purpose event series, in a hall spacious enough to host its own midsized congregation, Peace was flanked by embroidered church banners—shields, birds, and crowns (all the women in the room "wear crowns" as daughters of the King of Kings). She recounted a laundry list of "I'd just be happy if…" demands she'd made on her husband before she was saved at thirty-three.

She'd have "been happy," Peace mocks her past self, if they got married, if they had a child, if they had a second child, if they moved home from the German military base he worked at to Georgia. Her husband acquiesced every time, and thirty years later, Peace mimicked his "okay" in the dull, crushed monotone of TV's browbeaten husbands. Around the room several dozen women laugh at the depiction of a familiar setup: the tyrant wife and her henpecked husband. Peace told the story with the informality of long repetition. Her audience received it with nearly as much familiarity, as even those unfamiliar with Peace, one of the founding mothers of "biblical womanhood," and her work understood the peculiar brand of salvation narrative she is reciting. It's not just a salvation of the spirit in finding God, but in realizing God's intentions for Christian women. And salvation, in particular, from the deceptions of the egalitarian, feminist worldview that has stained them as surely as original sin.

The recitation of sins is also a necessary starting point for the sort of submission doctrine Peace has taught, through women's Bible studies, speaking events, and a number of books wildly popular among a certain evangelical readership, over the past fifteen years. That is, that Christian women are instrumental in turning the church at large away from a worldly flirtation with egalitarianism. The common starting point of this argument is the sort of illustration Peace delivers of just how bad things get under feminism. In Peace's own biography, she depicts a direct slide from a run-of-the-mill demanding wife to a career-worshipping, anxiety-ridden, adulterous, substance-abusing "feminist" whose pursuit of personal fulfillment was so reckless that she nearly left her marriage and plotted taking her own life.

This "taming of the shrew" rebirth, from "wild thing" to "excellent wife," is a coinage that's been picked up by some of Peace's conservative Christian protégés around the country as her brand of women's ministry—part Bible study, part Titus 2 mentoring model, and part antifeminist book line—has shaped a generation of Christian women.

Today Peace, a reserved but youthful-looking woman with short, dark brown hair and a nearly unlined face, is at sixty-one the author of five books on Christian womanhood, including *Becoming a Titus 2 Woman, Attitudes of a Transformed Heart, Damsels in Distress, Tying the Knot Tighter,* and her first and most popular, *The Excellent Wife.* The latter is the sort of book that some conservative churches dispense to women congregants who approach them with marriage complaints and that women's Bible study groups across the country continue to use as curriculum thirteen years after its publication.

And lest the nightmare scenario Peace tells of her early, unsaved life seem like any old preconversion hedonism, Peace warns that it can happen to disobedient Christians as well. "'All things work together for good, to those who love the Lord,'" Peace explained to me, referencing the promise of Romans 8:28, that God is personally tending to the prayers of His flock. But there's a hitch: "'Those who love the Lord' are born-again believers. And they're obedient. Otherwise the Bible says you're at enmity to Him. You're his enemy." The prayers of Christian women will not result in all things working together for good until those women learn to obey.

But getting to this stage of obedience requires some groundwork, the sort of deepened commitment to authority and doctrine that complementarian theology is based on. And this is what Peace talked about to the Women of Purpose at Jonesboro First Baptist, a number of whom were independently studying *The Excellent Wife* in separate Bible studies. "Our sole purpose in life is to glorify Him," Peace said, "and we do that when we submit to His sovereign command. God has decided, decreed, how we may best give Him glory, though our ideas of that and God's are sometimes two different things."

"Being sensible" is a problem for women, writes Peace, one that God has known all along, since the moment Eve sinned. This is why God passed his instructions for wives down a long line from Paul, to Titus, to the generations of older women instructing the younger wives how to be godly. "It's common for young Christian wives to rebel against home life as her primary ministry, and to want to pursue other careers of ministry work. It's the older women's role to help her understand her priorities better."

Those priorities include anticipating a husband's desires as well as asking for explicit instruction. Among some purists, it means submitting a list of daily activities to one's husband for approval and following his directions regarding work, going to church, clothing, head covering and makeup choices, as well as what a wife does with the remainder of her time. Sexually, it means being available at all times for all activities (barring a very limited number of "ungodly," "homosexual" acts).

But in even the most lenient of conservative Christian circles, it means accepting that a husband always has "the burden" of the final say in a disagreement between the couple. Following that authority structure strictly, some Titus 2 mentors advise instituting an "appeal process" that a wife can use in emergency situations, but which she may not abuse for the sake of her own whims. If a husband still disagrees, the wife is to submit to his desire, unless, in a few specified exemptions, he is asking her to sin. Her husband is the representative of God in her life, and as such, by serving him, she is really serving *Him*, her Lord Jesus Christ. And, Peace writes, not only is her husband God's representative, but also, on earth, His voice; if a wife appeals her husband's decision and is denied, says Peace, "Her husband's answer (unless he is asking her to sin) is God's will for her at that time."

But as a lifestyle, being a submissive wife means a number of other things, too. It means learning to be content with and grateful for your lot in life rather than seeking to improve your position through unbiblical means, such as getting a job. It also involves redefining love so that it is not a feeling but a choice that women make day after day. Beyond being an immature, lust-based emotion that can never be truly satisfied, the idea of a love based on feelings, romance, and attraction, says Peace, is a secular deceit. Feelings-based love, Peace writes derisively, is like the proverbial pony children always hope for and never receive on Christmas morning. Feelings, she declares, "are always somewhat disappointing. Just as I never received the pony I longed for, most women are never recipients of the romance that they desire." But, she continues, "As you change your thinking, your expectations will change."

Under this setup, women, once they've pledged themselves to a husband, have no excuse to leave by saying they've fallen out of love: falling out of love in this definition becomes an act of volition, a choice to give up on one's husband. It's a deceptively retrograde argument—on its face too reactionary and self-denying to seem like a persuasive argument to modern women. But it's also an argument that contains enough truth for many couples that have lasted through rocky years to convince them of Peace's unusual extensions of that commitment: a biblical love that is "unconditional" in the sense that it binds a woman to her husband forever, "even if the other person never changes," and requires her to continue showing him love as a responsibility to God. "Choosing love" in Peace's way means following a very particular set of rules.

A submissive wife understands that, as the Bible commands that husbands and wives have authority over each other's bodies, she owes her husband enough sex to satiate his appetite so that he is not tempted by another woman. In this way, a woman withholding sex from her husband is not only defrauding him of that which is rightfully his but is inducing him to sin.

Nancy Cobb and Connie Grigsby, coauthors of *The Politically Incorrect Wife,* also counsel women to focus on their behavior rather than their feelings, loving their husbands as their obligation to Christ (a focus on love as duty that gives men little credit or emotional satisfaction either beyond the weighted benefits of patriarchy). The payoff for women who obey properly is described at the end of Cobb's and Grigsby's book as a deeply sensual, almost erotic scene of union with Jesus: the fulfillment of all their stifled and postponed emotions and longings as they finally meet the man whose emissaries, their husbands, they've long served. "Press on! An inheritance from the Lord awaits you," they write. "Can't you hear the trumpets sounding? The heavens applauding? Can't you imagine the misting of your eyes as they meet the sweet soft gaze of His? Can't you sense the swelling of your heart and the joyful singing of your soul as He wraps his loving arms around you and says, 'Well done'?"

This is the reward of a wife who has served Jesus through serving her husband, and it is emblematic of the more mainstream evangelical versions of the Titus 2 teachings, which offer storylines of divine romance to carry home the same message. In this vein are Stasi Eldredge's *Captivating: Unveiling the Mystery of a Woman's Soul,* which steels women to be courageously vulnerable "real women" who battle for their relationships by expressing their feminine frailty and which simultaneously warns them that only Jesus can heal their broken hearts, and Shannon Ethridge's *Every Woman's Battle* (a companion publication to the bestselling men's book against sexual temptation *Every Man's Battle*), which focuses on women's purity and biblical sexuality.

While men's sexual purity is tied to fidelity and their abstention from pornography, Ethridge writes that women's sexual purity requires a more thorough internal purge: taking all thoughts "captive to Christ" by refusing to fantasize, masturbate, or entertain negative thoughts about their husbands. Honoring Jesus (whom Ethridge thanks as "the lover I've longed for all my life") through women's sexuality means "overcoming disappointments to keep their connection with their husbands healthy"; spending more time ministering to their husband's sexual needs than they spend on church activities; refusing to compare their husbands with other men but instead changing the "measuring stick" of their marital expectations and desires until those desires match up with their reality. Adultery, Ethridge warns, includes not just a physical or emotional affair, or even fantasy, but also self-gratification and "wishing for something better." A woman of "sexual integrity" instead chooses to love her husband as he is and places his needs above her own, in the bedroom and beyond. She doesn't do anything so physiologically unfair as demanding sexual parity but rather "shows that [she isn't] a scorekeeper but a cooperative team player" by being available for "a quick fix" when her husband "needs a sexual release and [she doesn't]."

The godly wife, Peace agrees, understands that the idea of fair play or equality—in sex or daily living—is more than just feminist heresy; it's also an idol to be repented of. Women set up a number of idols, says Peace, placing such importance on their desires that they are willing to sin—through anger or bitterness or uncontentedness—in order to get them. These idols are no golden calves but instead are ubiquitous modern demands for a partnership: "how her husband behaves or treats her...being treated fairly, having a hurt free/pain free life, having your needs met" are all common idols.

The most pervasive problem Peace sees is women being uncontent "with what God has given them." This, she says, is where older Titus 2 mentors should focus their efforts: "admonishing" and "energetically urging and warning" women to do what's right and to be grateful for what they have—ostensibly a description of Peace's own work as a biblical counselor.

While a common critique of mainstream Christian culture is its wholesale adoption of secular pop culture, made over with New Testament lyrics, the Christian counseling movement that Peace comes from doesn't just seek to provide a Christian gloss on normal counseling but to use that counseling for God's glory. For those coming from a fundamentalist reading of gender roles, that means counseling women by transmitting the theology of headship and submission. While Peace, unlike more extreme biblical womanhood teachers, says she's counseled numerous women to leave abusive husbands, up until the point of physical danger, her advice is singularly informed by her keen sense of women's failings: as nags, as gossips, as malcontents ungrateful with what they have. If women consider themselves night owls, she writes, they should begin following Proverbs 31 and rising before their husbands and children to prepare them breakfast. They'll soon find that they're too tired to be up reading novels late at night. "Women are not 'night people,'" she declares. "They are lazy and selfish." Such erasure of personal idiosyncrasy for the rigid demands of biblical wifehood is only one way that what comple-mentarians speak of as a "heart conviction," adopted for the love of God, becomes a lifestyle of binding rules.

Being biblically submissive is how wives act as "living sacrifices" for Jesus, Peace writes; it is a "fruit" or demonstration of their salvation. The implication is clear and frightening to Christian women who take their spirituality seriously: if they are not demonstrating these fruits, whether or not they are actually saved comes into question. A truly saved woman, Peace means, would feel led by Jesus to appropriate actions and behavior. And, if veiled eternal threats aren't enough, Peace adds an earthly exten-sion that many conservative congregations follow: a man with an unsub-missive wife should be considered unfit for church leadership since his wife's lack of submission proves he isn't in control of his own house.

Peace balances the damning charge that being unsubmissive is evi-dence of a woman lost to God with the suggestion that these fruits of salvation can be cultivated. She recommends teaching younger women to memorize and recite Scripture—Corinthians on love in particular—as well as to practice speaking in a "soothing tone of voice" until they've perfected a gentle, soft tone with which to address their husbands. "You may feel silly at first," writes Peace, "but if you want to be godly, you must be trained!"

The keystone of that training is in Peace's series of thought-control exercises: an endless series of charts pairing "right thoughts and wrong thoughts," "unbiblical and biblical responses," and sinful, unloving thoughts, with godly, loving thoughts about one's husband. The purpose is that women train their minds out of negative reactions toward their husbands, their head. When you're tempted to think, "I don't love him," Peace commands, think instead, "I may not feel love for him, but I can choose to love him and the feelings will follow." When he acts horribly and does not show you love as Christ loves the church, mentally respond by thinking that while he may be a complete failure before God, you don't have to be. Rather than lamenting a sexually demanding husband who won't leave you alone, thank God for a husband who desires you. The importance of changing one's basic thoughts, writes Peace, is that a wife's hurt feelings lie at the beginning of a slide from disappointment to anger to bitterness to an end point of rebellion. To avoid the last phase, disobedience, women must keep themselves from dwelling on hurt feelings. To this end, Peace suggests women keep a "log of bitter thoughts" and turn the log into a before-and-after chart of biblically wrong and right thoughts. After they've transformed their thoughts, wives must destroy the record of their unhappiness so their husbands don't come across it and be hurt. In this way they destroy a second time emotions already sublimated into "God-honoring" thoughts; it is a double denial of self.

· · ·

In the early days of the women's liberation movement, before marches and policy campaigns, many women were gradually politicized through protofeminist "consciousness raising" (CR) or "rap" groups, where their private disappointments and complaints resounded with the experiences of other women, and where they grew to see their personal unhappiness as part of a widespread, systematic oppression. Gloria Steinem wrote that such groups were "the primary way women discover that we are not crazy, the system is." With roots in the civil rights movement, women's CR groups were the inspiration for the often misapplied mantra, "the personal is political" (often misinterpreted as a call for purist identity politics) in discussing issues as mundane and seemingly apolitical as beauty standards, housework, sexual satisfaction, and depression. As Kathie Sarachild, a feminist leader of the 1970s, described consciousness raising to a 1973 women's movement convention, CR wasn't a mere stage in feminist development but a part of its radical core, constantly challenging women to examine the question, "who and what has an interest in maintaining the oppression in our lives?" and to not stop at that recognition but to translate that knowledge into action. Originally, the methodology of CR was simple and powerful: going to women's own history and everyday lives, pooling their experiences, coming to insight by recognizing or "naming" their oppressors, and then graduating to political resistance and action. Sarachild told the convention:

> We made the assumption, an assumption basic to consciousness-raising, that most women were like ourselves—not different—so that our self-interest in discussing the problems facing women which most concerned us would also interest other women. Daring to speak about our own feelings and experiences would be very powerful. Our own rising feminist consciousness led us to that assumption by revealing

that all women faced oppression as women and had a common interest in ending it.

If the feminist movement grew from the dissatisfaction voiced when women met together to discuss shared problems and recognize common oppression, the "counterrevolution" of women rejecting feminism and returning home intends to separate such gadding, "idle" wives who grew dissatisfied through the malaise of 1950s and '60s suburban life, return them to busy work lives within the home, and rebottle their unhappiness for either transformation into "right, biblical" thoughts through Martha Peace's charts or for consecration to God, for whom no lament is too small or prayer inconsequential.

Barbara Hughes, a contributor to the collection *Biblical Womanhood in the Home,* expresses the imperative of women capturing their thoughts and holding their tongues. "When I hear women whining about their husbands' faults to friends, and I catch myself speaking to my husband in tones that don't sound honoring, I want to shout, 'Stop! Stop yourself, Barbara! Think of the consequences!' Our attitudes and words are teaching the next generation."

Martha Peace bluntly suggests that it helps not to talk too much. "If you continue to talk long enough, you are likely to say something you should not have said. It is so easy to overstep the bounds of what is right."

For Courtney Tarter, writing for the Council on Biblical Manhood and Womanhood, the answer is casting off an old, stubborn sin.

> Our problem lies in the fact that there is no one righteous and we are all feminists at heart. My "recovery" from feminism is not about learning how to bake pies or a decision to be more feminine (though these are important and helpful things), it is about repentance. Repentance of my desire to control and to raise my fist against God's created order. Only through repentance and faith in Christ am I, or anyone for that matter, able to renounce rebellion and submit to the Lordship of Christ.

Remember, she says, "With the curse came the promise. Feminism was, and will finally be, defeated when the Seed"—that is, the children of Christians, the godly seed—"crushes the Serpent."

Or, as Nancy Leigh DeMoss, host of the Little Rock–based radio program *Revive Our Hearts* and editor of *Biblical Womanhood in the Home,* unselfconsciously declares, this "is a revolution that will take place on our knees!"

"You don't have to be a damsel in distress," said Peace to the women attending the Women of Purpose dinner at First Baptist Jonesboro. "God has already ordered your steps and has a perfect plan to accomplish His will in your life." Around the Sunday school hall, over plates of chicken and salad, dozens of women's heads bent—not yet in prayer but instead over the margins of their event programs, where they were taking notes.

CHAPTER SIX

Titus 2 in Tennessee

Just as the varied worlds of conservative evangelicalism fall along a spectrum, from kingdoms such as the Southern Baptist Convention to the individual fiefdoms of independent churches and even smaller home churches, Titus 2 ministries span biblical womanhood teachings, from large-scale, feel-good young women's conferences offering marriage tips to didactic fundamentalist study groups that actively, and tangibly, punish its wayward women for falling out of line. These aren't so much warring worlds as graduated steps. As with most diversity on the religious right, this is not the fracturing of the movement that pundits unceasingly predict but rather a sign of strength and sophistication, of a body fit enough to allow, and then absorb, dissent.

So it is with putting Titus 2–type wife mentoring programs into practice. There's no single way to "do" Titus 2 ministry. It's less a matter of receiving membership into an official club than an illustration of where you fall along the continuum of conservative biblical womanhood.

It's fitting then, that I passed through several different counties of wife mentorship as I drove from Nancy Campbell's house in Franklin Falls, some forty miles southwest of Nashville, past Debi and Michael Pearl's No Greater Joy ministry in Pleasantville, to Cumberland Camp in Clarksville, in northern Tennessee. I was going to an "Apron Society" mentoring event put on by the Titus 2 ministry of Traci Knoppe and Sylvia Britton, two friends who combined their online ministries in 2006. The journey took me from Campbell's mix of airy gentility and fierce demands for obedience, past the Pearls' backwoods fundamentalism, and into the welcoming arms of the ladies gathered at the Titus 2/Christian

Homekeeper (T2CH) weekend retreat, which was to focus on hospitality as a Christian woman's calling and wifely submission as a gentle but undeniable fact of marriage.

Along the back roads connecting these worlds, the cool October air was sweet with smoke from the tobacco-curing barns that lined the roads and puffed into the sky. The shoulders of the roads were lined with broken brush, perhaps kindling bundled for the curing fires. During weeks when the barns are smoking, the local schools empty dramatically, the children home sick from the smoke.

Along the way, contemporary Christian radio, old-timey gospel stations, and Fox News talk radio dominated the airwaves. The contemporary Christian stations promised that donations to the station are "donations to Him"; the old-time gospel hosts discussed cults and hawked vintage homeschool materials, such as the *New England Primer*; and a local Fox affiliate shock-jock interrupted his theory on a local rape case (that the alleged victim, a high school student, was just covering up her sexual promiscuity to her parents) in order to tell a female caller to try back at another time of the month. They were flavors of on-air conservatism as varied, and connected, as the different styles of biblical womanhood being taught.

Clarksville, where the T2CH retreat-goers met at the campgrounds of a local church, proclaims itself the "Gateway to the New South." But there, among the new subdivisions spreading outside town at a reasonable ninety thousand dollars per prefab house, the old South still stands, barely: skeletal barns quietly decay at a remove from the road; roofs sink low on their supports over the porches of closed country stores; an abandoned gas station that shut its lights off when gas was ninety-nine cents for a gallon of regular squats on a weedy parking lot, the fuel price still looming like an epitaph on a twenty-foot-high billboard above the store.

As I approached Cumberland Camp itself, where the weekend Apron Society retreat would be held, I drove down a maze of back roads devolving from highway to country road to one-lane to dirt and finally parked atop a hill next to the cabin dorm where the ladies' retreat attendees would stay. Across the driveway from the cabin was a yard-sized miniature golf course with zodiac signs inexplicably marking the holes.

I walked past the cabin down a long path of large-stone gravel that curved toward the dining hall on the lower level of the camp. Women's laughter wafted out of the building. Inside, the women sat around empty, or nearly empty, Styrofoam plates with the remnants of lasagna (served in an industrial-sized disposable aluminum pan) and iceberg salad, playing get-to-know-you games. On a buffet line was a Styrofoam bowl of Dove chocolates—the "bonbons" alluded to in the planning materials for the event, a sarcastic jab at how the women imagine the world derides stay-at-home mothers as lazy, soap-opera-watching housewives who eat sweets all day long.

To introduce the two groups of women attending—members of Sylvia Britton's local ministry in Clarksville and a vanload of Traci Knoppe's church sisters who had come down from St. Louis—the women interviewed each other on the pertinent details of their lives: their husbands, their children, their self-identified professions—mostly homemakers—and whether, if money were no object, they would hire domestic help or clean house themselves.

This last bit bore the mark of Knoppe, an easy-smiling, country-pretty woman with a redhead's freckled complexion below hair gently darkened to light brown, who interrupted her teachings on homekeeping with self-deprecatory one-liners about her lack of domestic prowess: her favorite thing to make is reservations, she'd repeat with a laugh. This levity is to assure us that it doesn't take a Martha Stewart to be a godly wife, but rather a combination of biblical role models: yes, part Martha—the scriptural Martha, that is, who served tirelessly—but also part Mary, Martha's more spiritual sister, who sat at the feet of Jesus to learn and was praised for her holiness over Martha's dutiful service. The two sisters represent a set of competing demands that continue to perplex Christian women.

Knoppe also punctuated her conversations with snippets of sarcastic pop wisdom from talk show host Dr. Phil: "How's that working out for you?" or "It's all about you, isn't it?" She admired the pop disciplinarian to the extent that she wished he'd "get right" on spanking—Dr. Phil, unlike Dr. Dobson and many conservative Christians, is not a proponent—so she could unequivocally recommend him as a Christian leader. Knoppe's fondness for Dr. Phil hinted at a nervousness and sadness that occasionally broke through her cheer with frank admissions about an unwed, homeless pregnancy she had experienced at sixteen that had "given

her a heart" for unwed moms and crisis pregnancy centers. But the sentiment of her quotation was intended for all of her disciples that weekend:
for Christian women, it's never about you.

The last question on the get-to-know you questionnaire was on the
women's favorite Bible verses, and, when I admitted myself unsaved, I was
promptly adopted for instruction and conversion by Erin, a moonfaced,
twenty-three-year-old Tennessee Baptist wife a month away from delivering her first child. Erin, despite her impending maternity, had a young
girl's instinct for ingratiating herself with teachers, raising her hand read-
ily to tell the class the eight traits of a Titus 2 woman. She explained
to me the allure of faith, "the peace which passes understanding," with
the help of one of Knoppe's party, Kathy, a broad-shouldered, mothering
Missouri woman in her fifties, with white hair in a pixie crop and a fondness for punning evangelical T-shirts: "Take a walk…with Jesus."

The dorm was a divided cabin, each side fitted with a row of bunk
beds and dressers and separated by a central toilet and shower area—a
camp for adults who wanted sturdy shelter against the surprisingly brisk
Tennessee autumn. I shared my side, the near-empty, spillover side, with
just two other women from Britton's church: Jo-Jo, a friendly, heavy,
middle-aged woman with walking difficulties, and her charge, Joyce, an
ebullient twenty-three-year-old African woman, another young wife several months pregnant, who was quick to entertain the assembly with tales
of her exotic upbringing as the daughter of an African "chief."

In the mornings, the sink top was a jumble of curling irons and eye
shadow, not the picture of unadorned feminine modesty that outsiders
might expect. Modest in dress they might be—though Beth, Britton's
much-loved daughter-in-law, a gentle and intelligent beauty, had arrived
in a pair of sleek, tan knee-high boots—yet they rose early every morning
to curl, dust, spray, and line, even at a rural retreat, only amongst themselves, before piling into one of several minivans to be taken the quarter
mile down the hill to the dining hall.

After breakfast, Knoppe, wearing overalls and a brown T-shirt pro-
claiming "All I need is love and chocolate"—a message she says some
of her stricter friends in the Christian blogosphere would find blasphe-
mous—lectured on hospitality. Not hospitality in the *Southern Living*
magazine-spread sense of the word, with its slightly beribboned and
deep-fried version of *Better Homes and Gardens* standards, but hospitality as an expression of Christ's love and a mandated part of Christian

life. Demonstrating hospitality as a Christian offering, therefore, doesn't depend on a fine house or expensive refreshments but rather a loving heart. Knoppe recounted a failed episode of "practicing hospitality on her guests" when the food got burned and the air conditioning broke. "I was really Martha about it," she recalled, meaning Scripture's Martha, "but 'love covers a multitude of sins.'" For this reason, because hospitality is so dear to God, the things that keep women from offering hospitality, like prideful embarrassment over a humble home, or simply too much clutter and junk, need to be taken on as impediments. The point is offering hospitality without complaining, not as entertainment or a prideful showcasing of one's home but as God's way to extend love to strangers—if your husband agrees that you can invite them home—or simply to your own family. "That's what we're doing when we serve our families: offering hospitality."

Knoppe has six children, three grown adults and three young children, reflecting two marriages and a reversed tubal ligation, but she counts seven, to include her last, stillborn baby, whose death was followed by a string of "female problems," including preeclampsia, postpartum depression, gestational diabetes, fibroids, polyps, chronic inflammation, and ovarian cysts, which ended in a total hysterectomy five years ago. Through all these problems, and through a gastric bypass surgery that Knoppe lists on her Web site's profile among "things to know about me," Britton has helped counsel her and hold her to accountability as a woman's leader through her Titus 2 Web site, "Traci's Cottage." Knoppe has run the ministry since 1996, mentoring women about organizational skills, child-raising, or sometimes having mentees come over and watch her housekeeping routine, as the women had never been taught to properly clean their houses before.

In 2005, Britton and Knoppe combined their parallel ministries into a nonprofit with a board of directors and plans for future women's conferences, a self-help manual for Christian homemakers, a monthly e-zine, and an online store. But unveiled at this conference was their really grand scheme: the launch of a nationwide network of small Titus 2 clubs banded together under their umbrella organization, the Apron Society Coffee Club. The apron would represent their service, and an older woman's service in particular, as something evocative of grandmotherly wisdom; the "coffee club," like the references to bonbons, was something of a joke—poking fun at the idle "kaffee klatsch" women of the Southern women's group the Red Hat Society. Together, the groups could raise funds or collect clothing for antiabortion crisis pregnancy centers, Knoppe's favorite cause, and individually, they could train women in basic housekeeping and wifehood tasks that their mothers might not have shown them.

Britton, a mountain woman with her short, slightly round body sensibly clothed in jeans, clogs, and a green and orange paisley shirt, with a white braid falling to her mid-back and a wide, kind face trenched with laugh lines, offered her own shortcomings as a hostess to the assembled women, sitting in rows of semicircled fold-out chairs in a conference room adjacent to the dining area. The women were divided almost evenly between younger women in their twenties and middle-aged "older" women. From time to time, people asked questions or exchanged their own "hospitality" mishaps: Erin's first attempt at cooking dinner—spaghetti and tomato sauce—for her husband during their honeymoon and his heartbreaking rejection of it as different from his mother's; Joyce's attempts to share the gospel with a fellow student by inviting her for dinner and being repeatedly stood up with a full dinner in the oven.

This isn't quite what Britton and Knoppe meant, though, and Britton gently guided the conversation back to her story, some years ago when she and her husband attended a fellowshipping church in Galveston, Tennessee, and were called upon by "the church starter people," Scott and Angela, to become small group leaders and host a meeting in their home. At the time, Britton and her husband's home was "old and ugly but ours," with gouged woodwork and chipped paint. Attending the training session for small group leaders at Scott and Angela's house, Britton became cowed: the couple and their home were impossibly glamorous, with a wraparound porch and a swing, no clutter, and children neatly dressed and tucked into public schools. "Like *Better Homes and Gardens,* country decorating at its finest." Britton imagined if she had this home, she could do anything the Lord asked her to, but in her own low-rent house, she felt she had nothing to offer.

But as Britton was doubting her own capacity to be a hostess for Christ, "God spoke to Scott and told him, 'This one right here.' So Scott asked me what was wrong. I told him I was overwhelmed by what it took to be a small group leader. Then during the devotional, he asked us, 'What makes you grumble when you have to show hospitality in your home?' He called on me, but didn't fuss on me. He just stopped me at the door on my way out later and told me, 'I know this is really eating at you, Sylvia. The reason you don't want people in your house is called the sin of pride.' I didn't have anything to be proud about, but he said that's just it. 'God calls it the pride of life.'

"So I just bawled. What else can you do but bawl, repent, when someone points out lovingly your sin? How did it get so complicated that I'm jealous and envious of this palatial home? Scott and Angela just cried with me. 'God's got us in a different place than you. God provided this house, the job we needed to pay for what we have, and said, fill it with God's people.' They're using what God gave them. That's their path. Remember Jesus has a job for you, in your home. It may not be like this, mine, Traci's, but he's given you a job. Don't limit Him. He might not give you missionaries or anything that glamorous. God has a work for you that's different from anyone else. You've got to trust that he's going to give you the grace to do what you need to do."

The message of course is contentedness as a demonstration of faith and a discipline of self-abnegation present in all facets of the homemaker's life. The difference, Britton explains, is between hospitality, which focuses on your guest and needs only those things which Jesus sought and provided—a listening ear, a safe place to rest, food, and love—and entertaining, which is focused on one's self: *your* clean home, *your* fancy meal, *your* fine furniture. Even more so, these things are applicable to your own husband and family. "It doesn't really count as obedience if you're swearing at each other before the company comes over. So practice on your family: set the table, light the candles, fix yourself up, and use the good china. God will bless you, you will grow confident, you'll open doors and let people in and serve them with a smile."

But though she preaches that all things are possible through God, and a humble home is beautified through love, Britton tells another story to demonstrate the necessity of diligent housekeeping, grace notwithstanding. While newlyweds in West Virginia, she and her husband attended dinner at a friend's house, memorable more than two decades later for the state the house was in when the hosting wife arrived late, with grocery bags in hand, garbage in the kitchen, and dishes in the sink. The stress the other woman felt being unprepared was shared by all and made the event a hospitality failure. Likewise, in women's own homes, clutter and overwhelming cleaning projects can hinder a woman's service—her ministry—to her family.

This is how Britton and Knoppe transition from the biblical mandate to show hospitality irrespective of one's situation to the softer mandate that women be properly prepared to host: a woman's failures in the kitchen or in housekeeping are nothing so frightening as the sin of pride that keeps them from serving, but they are impediments to showing hospitality nonetheless. Unremedied, the problems make guests uncomfortable, and so interfere with the task of Christian women to spread the gospel through their welcoming homes.

And so, Titus 2/Christian Homekeeper urges its disciples to better prepare themselves for the lofty goal of hospitality with the very earthly practice of cleaning their closets. And every spring and fall, Britton and Knoppe organize a top-to-bottom housecleaning series among their readers, who undertake the project across the country in tandem, following Britton and Knoppe's tips. Donate or throw away a good portion of your clothes, Britton advised. "You don't work outside the home, you don't need as many clothes." Get papers and sewing projects out of the living room and into storage bins. Stock up on easy refreshment options such as off-brand cookie dough rolls that can be decorated and thrown in the oven at a moment's notice if the preacher stops by for a surprise visit. Thus prepared, when the occasion for hospitality arises, Britton warned the women not to become offended when the men and women separate into different groups. "It's how God intended it," she said, and also a great opportunity to learn from other women. "Go home and make some cookies," Britton said, distributing handouts for cookie recipes. "There's no excuse."

· · ·

After lunch on Saturday, we walked through the woods around Camp Cumberland to gather flowers and leaves for a "home arts" project in flower pounding. The path winds along a quiet Tennessee brook bordered on the other side by a farmer's pastureland. His cows and bull milled on the other side of the water, occasionally raising their heads to stare at the slow-moving line of Christian women picking their way at a snail's pace down the rock and dirt road in order to accommodate the older and less-mobile mentees. Sometimes the cows took a few steps into the water as a tentative, uncertain challenge, sometimes they bellowed; the women giggled and appraised the threat they posed—the bull looked lazy—and kept walking.

Erin walked by my side, her eight months' pregnancy slowing her considerably, so that we lagged behind all but the oldest women at the retreat. She stopped frequently to catch her breath and hold her stomach, which protruded from her petite frame dramatically; the baby, all the women agreed, had dropped. At times, Erin's mind also seemed to wander, and she trailed off dreamily in midsentence while lecturing me on the fine-hair differences between Calvinist or Reformed Baptists and Arminian Baptists like herself and her brethren at Clarksville's Free Will Baptist Church, spiritual home to a number of the local women attending the retreat. "The Holy Spirit's got her again," the other young women teased Erin when she drifted away, her mouth slightly open and her eyes focused on middle distance as conversation continued around her.

She drifted back to warn me that her brand of Baptists believe Christians can forfeit their salvation by free choice, as had her husband's co-worker, who had enjoyed the blessings of salvation but decided that it was just too much work. In one sitting, while his wife sobbed, he told their children that Santa, the Easter Bunny, and, most frightening of all, Jesus, were none of them real. Erin shook her head.

A lot of things with Erin came back to her young husband's authority, and she named his accomplishments and opinions and background as frequently as she discussed her own. Her husband, Nate, was the son of a Christian principal and worked in computer technology. At the altar they'd shared their first kiss. Now they lived in one of those reasonably priced new developments, and Erin planned on staying home as a housewife and mother to as many children as she happened to have. She doesn't believe in birth control, and she stopped seeing a gynecologist who offered her contraception during a pre-wedding exam.

In all this talk, Erin paused occasionally to tell me I really should get saved. In a way, she acted—and rightfully so, by the rules of the relationship—as a Titus 2 mentor to me. She was younger than me in years but older in the gospel, and therefore a spiritually mature mentor. When she remembered this position, she instructed me: faith is a discipline. God's voice is still and small, not a firestorm or anything like that. The Holy Spirit is like a conscience, but not quite. You grow to recognize it. Satan's voice is the one that tells you to do wrong. And Satan, reliably, would never tell you to do something good, like give a stranger money or food or the Word.

Mostly though, Erin liked to talk about herself. She was delighted I'd been to see Nancy Campbell—an amazing woman, she told me, and an even better cook, known regionally for her Middle Eastern, vegetarian fare. Throughout the weekend, Erin vied for the attention of Knoppe and Britton—she was still a very young woman to be indulged—and was quick to compare herself to the other young married women in attendance, offering the details of her wedding dress and cake.

When we'd gathered enough flowers for pounding and returned to camp proper, several of the cows had beaten us there, wandering around the swing sets and slowly climbing the hill toward the dorms. The pastor was called to alert the farmer who owned them. Inside the dining hall we arranged our flowers on small squares of linen, covered them with plastic wrap, and pounded them with hammers. The banging was overwhelming, its echoes ricocheting back and forth around the hall, and those women waiting to pound covered their ears with their hands. When it was their turn, they let loose with surprising force. Under the plastic wrap, the juices of the flower petals and leaves bled onto the fabric, staining it with a natural dye. The women studied each other's poundings—largely unsatisfying attempts, with the bright yellows of dandelions translating to the linen as a brown, pulpy mess. But the lesson at least was clear: decoration, like hospitality, is within everyone's realm, wherever that may be.

Afterward, Erin was tired, and she drove us both up the hill to the dorm in her sedan, bearing a "W '04" bumper sticker and an assortment of McDonald's debris. In the dorms, she lay down in the cot next to me and turned on her side, covering herself with the miniature fleece throw she toted around all weekend as part of her pregnancy prerogative, and smiled hazily at me, open-eyed, until she eventually fell asleep.

Before dinner, we gathered again in the dining hall for another art project: creating a bracelet of twenty-four strung imitation pearls with gold clasps and centerpiece. The pearls represent the virtues and attributes of the ideal Christian wife, the Proverbs 31 woman. It is a lofty vision of perfection that generates the most complaints from women visiting the T2CH Web site, and many have asked Britton, "I don't understand why God would expect us to have all these virtues, these twenty-four virtues."

"I'm in my forties now," Britton countered. "I've been reading the chapter since I was in my twenties. The main thing I've learned is that the virtues are like a string of pearls: they're priceless, very valuable. We don't awake one day to say, today's the day I'm going to be that perfect Proverbs 31 woman. No, it's one pearl at a time. I'm a Proverbs 31 wannabe, not a completed Proverbs 31 woman telling you to be like me. You've got to work on it and practice." Around the room, we strung the plastic pearls on double strands of clear plastic wire. Beth, Britton's sweet-tempered daughter-in-law, sat at her side, helping fit wires into clasps for the rest of us to string. Beth and Britton had beaded before, and Beth worked as her mother-in-law's assistant, quiet and soothing, always ready to help.

"Some women don't start on their strands until they're older," said Britton. "It blesses my heart to see Erin, Beth, and Joyce working on getting these virtues, these pearls, on that strand. In Joel, God promises to restore the years the locust has eaten. God will work at bringing those virtues into your life, just like that bracelet. You string those pearls by doing the important things in being virtuous women: read your Bible, stay in the Word, pray, fellowship with the Lord and other believers. That's what it takes to be a vibrant, beautiful Christian woman, to be a beautiful strand of pearls."

We finished our bracelets and Britton led us in prayer, that we may be the women God wants us to be, that He's prepared us to be.

·   ·   ·

Ideally, Knoppe told me, there wouldn't be a need for retreats like this because Christian heritage would be passed down from Christian family to Christian family; women would learn what they needed to know from their mothers, grandmothers, and aunts. "Now we have to rely on the church to do it," she said, meaning the church at large, the Body of Christ teaching its own.

"A lot of younger women have a hard time understanding submission. There are Christians who take it to an extreme level, but the basic truth is the same. Man is ultimately responsible, when he stands up before God in heaven, for how he ran and managed his family. We women are responsible for how we were as helpmeets. We're not supposed to be wearing the pants to the elbows, like a lot of women do. We're equally intelligent and capable of doing the things that men do, but that doesn't mean we have to or that we should." This is a common rejoinder of biblical womanhood advocates, often professional activists themselves, and often addressing women serious enough about their doctrine to be accomplished students of Scripture in their own right: they acknowledge women's equal capacity, but they suggest that women lay their abilities aside with their pride as a living sacrifice fit for their Savior.

To demonstrate this truth, Knoppe and Britton showed us *Little House on the Prairie* episodes. This is also something of a joke in homeschooling circles, which have so idolized Laura Ingalls Wilder and the wholesome prairie life depicted on the '80s-era TV series that some feel forced to deny that they're basing their lives on the show. Others disapprove of the series for not going far enough to reclaim the culture and for harboring latent feminist messages of self-sufficiency. The episode Knoppe and Britton screened is indeed an instance of women doing it for themselves—harvesting a crop of wheat during a surprise storm because the men had left for town to find work. The message isn't that they're capable, though they are, but that, while the Wilder women are off harvesting wheat, "out doing the men's work, who was there doing the work that they, the women, needed to get done? All these circumstances where women have to work, and have to do things, even today that are maybe not ideal. We're not so hard-line as some," Knoppe said. "If you have to switch roles for a while because your husband got laid off or gets sick, there's nothing wrong with that, but it's not ideal."

The need for reinforcing that message, said Knoppe, comes from what she sees as a feminist devaluation of housework—one of the most common accusations of secular and religious antifeminists alike. "Men are identified by what they do, their jobs. That's the way they are. God designed them that way. It's no great mystery. Since the feminist movement, women all ask each other, 'What do you do?' But it's okay to be a stay-at-home mom." Knoppe imagined that instead, the many and varied skills stay-at-home mothers need intimidate some women into taking up a more finite career. In the past, the skills needed in the home "would have been taught down the generations, but it was left off. We're trying to bridge that gap. There are a lot of women coming home because they've been out there, they've struggled, and they're just not able to do it all. And they realize, if I'm not able to do it all, and you have children, your choice is going to be your children. That's what we're here for: come home, and here's what to do when you get there."

On the last night of the retreat, the pastor of the church that owns

Cumberland Camp took us on a hayride, pulled not by horses but a hefty piece of farm equipment. We got ready in the cabin, bundling layers against the October night chill, then climbed into Knoppe's van for the commute down the hill. Squeezing in, one of the younger women, Amy, a ruddy-faced redhead who kept up a cheerfully self-effacing commentary on her own Proverbs 31 status—"There's that servant's heart!"—beckoned Beth with playful seduction. "Come a little bit closer, you're my kind of girl," she sang. From the front seat, Knoppe called back, "Miss Amy, Miss Beth! We're not that kind of women's camp!" The van erupted in titters.

We sat on hay bales in the bed of the farm trailer and Erin covered my legs with her fleece blanket. She began telling Beth and Amy a story about the way she saw a "hoochie" girl dressed in town. Beth, across from us, laughingly chided Erin, "You speak to your husband that way?" Erin was immediately chastened, explaining that her language became "ghettofied" at a pre-marriage part-time job at a Clarksville Build-a-Bear franchise, but that normally, she'd never say such a thing. On the hayride, the young women talked about nearly normal gossip: stories about weddings and bridesmaid mishaps, speculation about whether or not Jessica Simpson's father is really a man of the Lord. We sang Sunday school songs as we bumped hard over the dips and bumps along the dirt road perimeter of the camp.

After the hayride, at a farewell night bonfire, I stood close to the fire with Erin and Beth. Beth talked about getting "prayed up" for her upcoming move to the woods, when her husband, Britton's son, then finishing police academy to be a ranger, graduated and she would become a homemaker in an isolated forest cabin with a reputation for being haunted. She'd miss the live music scene of the area, of which she'd been a peripheral part through her husband's former job at the Gibson guitar production plant in Nashville. Beth herself played and sang some, and her taste ranged far beyond the slim offerings on local contemporary Christian music radio. While Erin listed her favorites among the top Christian pop talent of the moment, Beth talked about Lucinda Williams and began to sing a bar from her favorite CD before reddening and stopping, flustered. She was trying to describe the melody of "Righteously," one of Williams's huskier songs, where she growls to a lover that he needn't prove his manhood to her, but Beth could only remember one line: "When you run your hand all up and back down my leg, get excited and bite my neck, get me all worked up like that." "That's terrible, I can only remember that line," Beth said, and blushed and smiled into the fire.

In the morning, before Knoppe and her Missouri crew packed up the van for the trek back to St. Louis and the local women returned home, she and Britton distributed gift bags: Amish cookbooks and homemade jars of tea. A final speaker, Joyce DeFow, a rotund missionary's wife in her sixties wearing a gigantic flowered muumuu, glasses, and an amber necklace, described hospitality in the jungles of inner Hawaii, when her husband spread the Word there years ago. It was a tale full of Dr. Livingstone–like moments of interaction with the natives as well as the central message to women who weren't so fortunate as to be married to adventuring missionaries: "The best place for evangelism is in your home. Being hospitable is one way we can serve the Lord, but first you need to learn to have a servant's heart. Then watch to see the people coming through."

It being Sunday, we had church in the chapel. We sang some songs together: "Change My Heart Oh God," "The Servant Song," "I Am a Woman (Called to be a Servant)," and "We Are an Offering." After completing the last, Knoppe and Britton told us they hoped we understood that's what they'd been talking about all weekend. Knoppe's friend Kathy, whose husband was laid up and unable to work, leaving Kathy to scrape together a living for the family with a part-time church administrator's salary, rose to sing solo a song that she introduced as Knoppe's favorite, "Lay It Down." In a trembling alto over swelling taped instrumentation, she sang a familiar message: to lay your burdens at Jesus's feet, to "let go and let God," to lean not on your own understanding but put your trust in Jesus. Listening, Knoppe sobbed quietly in the front row. "Lay it down," Kathy repeated in a stage whisper, her tall body swaying as the taped music resolved to a close and, with a click, shut off.

CHAPTER SEVEN

No Greater Joy

Debi Pearl is the author of *Created to Be His Help Meet,* a controversial entry into the biblical womanhood library, as well as cofounder, with her husband, Michael, of the No Greater Joy ministry in Pleasantville, Tennessee, an Amish enclave in the western corner of the state where the Pearls, with their rootsy fundamentalism and Michael's shaggy beard, are often mistaken for the plain folk they live among. "Sister Kathryn," Pearl writes me when I ask her to expand upon the lessons of her book, which calls wives to new depths of devoted service,

> This week a dear old friend, I will call him Jon, whom we had not seen in many years, came to visit us. Jon needed to talk—no counsel, no fellowship, no questions or answers—he only needed to talk. He had recently lost his life-mate, his best friend, to cancer. As I sat listening to Jon, watching his sad face as he told of his wife's last hours on earth, I could see that he dearly loved her. He told of the great lengths he went to to try to save her life, his struggles with the doctors for not being honest with her concerning her impending death, her pain and her vain attempts to recover, and then, toward the end, her pleading with him to let her go. He fell silent after a while, and in the dim evening light we watched as his expression of emptiness and loss suddenly changed into peaceful joy and finally gleeful amusement.
>
> Finally he broke the silence, his face growing red, his hand covering his mouth as if to stop himself from speaking, but it bubbled out anyway, "You know what she did, just like maybe, four hours before she died? It's really embarrassing, but I just have to tell it. There she

was gasping for breath, a tube sticking out of her nose forcing air into her fluid-filled lungs, full of cancer, and she calls me over to her and says, 'Honey, let's make love.'"

Jon crossed and recrossed his legs as he cackled with laughter, "The last thing I had on my mind was sex. I didn't think I could even do anything with her in that shape, plus I was afraid somebody would come into the room and think I was some kind of pervert, attacking a dying woman."

So he made excuses, "Honey, I might pinch your breathing tube and nurses are coming and going. We might get caught."

He said she laughed and teased, "Now, come on…you have never turned me down…let's make love."

My husband and I sat spellbound watching and listening to our bereaved friend as he replayed their final moments as man and wife. He laughed, wiping away tears of joy, and after a pause he said with great conviction, "Man, she was some kind of wife. I was so blessed."

He never finished his story, so we never knew if, well, you know. He told us what he needed to say and then he left. As my husband and I lay in bed that night we talked and laughed at Jon's consternation. We grew quiet and thoughtful as we considered his intense loneliness. I silently wept in my husband's arms as I thought of the possibility of one of us being left alone without the other. Then we slept together in each other's arms, more thankful than usual. But during the night I awoke and thought about Jon's wife. She put his needs before her own pain and even before her very breath, right to the very end she wanted to serve her man. I turned over in the bed and began to pray, "God help me to be that kind of woman."

There's a lot in that story that bears the mark of the Pearls, two un-likely owners of a publishing business that earns close to one million dollars a year on a handful of titles that have become favorites among homeschoolers. Michael Pearl, a reclusive bear of a man with a notorious aversion to media, or, as his children have told reporters, any "situations in which he will be censored," is pastor to a small church, Pearl's Church, located on his own property. Its several dozen congregants include many of his own family. But the Pearls' reach is far broader through their inter-net ministry and collection of self-published books on fundamentalist family life. Michael Pearl has said that a sixth of the three million homeschooling families in America use his materials, most of which focus on a strict, corporal punishment–based method of not raising, but "training up," a "whineless" child: what the Pearls cite as a Bible-based method that employs tree branches and PVC piping or plumbing supply line to impress upon children the imperative of obedience.

To Train Up a Child, the Pearls' first book, has sold more than half a million copies, though its popularity is lately clouded by the book's alleged connection to the 2006 beating death of a four-year-old adopted boy in Tennessee, Sean Paddock. His adoptive mother followed the Pearls' advice of switching and spanking children into submission starting in infancy, when parents are instructed to tempt six-month-old babies by placing off-limits toys just out of reach and to swat the infants with a small tree twig if they reach for it. (Parents should always use an implement, such as rulers, branches, belts, or plumbing line, since hands, the Pearls write, "are for loving.") In a passage frequently quoted since Lynn Paddock's attorney blamed the Pearls' book for the child's death, Michael Pearl writes, "These truths [about child training] are not new, deep insights from the professional world of research, [but] rather, the same principles the Amish use to train their stubborn mules, the same techniques that God uses to train his children."

The Pearls, of course, distanced themselves from the death and other reported—sometimes self-reported—accounts of abuse, though one of Michael Pearl's sole comments to a local paper was the dismissive estimation that, of the thousands of families following their teachings, "the chances of one of them committing a crime is pretty good." His Web site does feature a more scathing "millstone award" section, condemning abusive parents who discipline their children in contradiction to Jesus's admonition in Matthew 18:6, which reads, "But whoso shall offend one of these little ones which believe in me, it were better for him that a millstone were hanged about his neck and that he were drowned in the depth of the sea." But Michael's unabashed promotion of switching children has led to boycotts of homeschooling magazines that publish No Greater Joy advertisements, and British homeschooling groups have protested a Pearl speaking tour due to their methods.

Though Michael's child-training materials are what introduced the outside world to the fundamentalist phenomenon of the Pearls, Debi Pearl's writings and women's ministry have had almost as deep an impact on the homeschooling community. Debi's son has credited her with the financial success of the ministry, and *Created to Be His Help Meet,* Debi's first solo book, sold one hundred-fifty thousand copies in its first fourteen months of publication. In many ways, the lessons of the Pearls' child-training books are evident in her wife-training manual as well, which a number of women I spoke to cited as inspiration for turning their lives toward biblical submission and motherhood.

But Debi departs from the conventional wisdom of other biblical womanhood manuals, offering a flavor of submission darker and more sexual than her suburban sisters. This is largely an expression of shaping the message to a different audience, a more rural, working-class, "Old South" church than that ministered by Martha Peace and Nancy Leigh DeMoss. The message is the same, but with Pearl, blunter and crueler.

Women who don't submit to their husbands in Debi's wifehood gospel, organized as a series of "Dear Debi" letters with Debi's withering replies, aren't just upsetting the heavens but are setting themselves up for worldly destruction as well.

A woman who writes to complain that her husband's TV-watching is exposing the family to bad influences is warned that the social circle for divorced women with children is painfully small and that the job they'll be forced to take will leave the kids in the hands of a fornicating baby-sitter. Other single mothers, Debi suggests, end up with bad haircuts and cheap clothes, pooling resources with other divorcees and becoming lesbians; they live in fear of eviction and violence from their exes and are only courted by men who aim to molest their children. When they get breast cancer, Debi writes, there will be no one around to care for them, and it's all because they got high and mighty about the TV. "Listen to me, young mother. Do not play the fool. You don't know how bad it can get."

In her own marriage, which came about after Debi told her then-pastor Michael that she'd like to give him babies, Debi describes her own submissiveness being tested on her honeymoon, when she angered and bewildered her twenty-five-year-old husband by questioning the expensive cut of meat he wanted to buy for their dinner. Michael, she writes, "had never had a woman question him about how he was spending his money," and he looked at her "as if he were trying to remember who I was and why he had put himself in a position to be criticized." From then on, Debi resolved to adapt herself completely to her husband, whom she gushingly describes as "Mr. Command Man...strong, forceful, and bossy." When Michael throws a bag of garbage at a dumpster and, missing it, strides away, leaving his wife to pick up the trash, she chooses to view this as an endearing insight into the proud male psyche and a fair exchange for not being "trashed by her man" instead.

In practice, Debi's submission involves "reverencing" one's husband —pointedly the "active verb" form of the word, as reverencing, like love, "is not first a feeling" but something you do, "a voluntary act." That means keeping an eye on his dinner plate and jumping up with enthusiasm, not resignation, to refill his cup with "the quick, carefree swing of your body [indicating] your delight to be engaged in serving your man."

A wife's sexual duties consume a great deal of Pearl's teachings, leading off with her responses to two letters from men writing to No Greater Joy charging that their wives weren't giving them enough sex. One man writes that his wife's complaints of sexual pain and exhaustion are leading him to temptation by other women—and that his telling his wife so had only upset her more; another announced that his wife's reluctance was making him consider castrating himself so that he wouldn't be forced into adultery. Unlike Debi's scathing responses to her female readers, her replies to the men's letters are wholly sympathetic. To the wife of the first man, she commands, "Wife, it is your God-ordained ministry to your husband to be his totally enthusiastic sex partner, ready to enjoy him at all times. To do less is a grave error." Of the latter, she cries that his wife's sin is a "staggering" blasphemy and shows she has "NO FEAR" of God. "Never, never, never be guilty of such a grave sin," she tells other readers. "God grants the marriage partner full access to his spouse's body for sexual gratification. And remember," she adds, for unenthusiastic consenters, "indifference is unwillingness."

Women, writes Pearl, should see sex as their ministry to their husbands, and as such, one that doesn't require their interest, pleasure, or fulfillment—that is a "hedonistic," self-absorbed approach to sex. Instead, women should view it as "a selfless act of benevolence.... She need only seek to fulfill her husband's needs." As such, menopause is no excuse to Pearl, but rather a disingenuous excuse for denying God's commands.

The flip side of the Pearls' stringent requirements for a wife's "sexual ministry" to her husband is their demand for unimpeachable sexual purity around all others—which goes hand-in-hand with an expectation of sexual availability once owned. They require wives to dress and behave modestly among men to whom they do not belong, lest the sight of their bodies tempt other men into "thought" or "sight" adultery. Pearl recounts the complaint of a young man disgusted with his friend's wife for "dressing so godless," that is, wearing clothes that have aroused him. She was no "little hidden treasure," as he'd have his own wife be, he wrote with disgust.

The lack of men's responsibility or culpability for their own actions and the acceptance of male "urges" as irresistible forces of nature is the understructure of Christian modesty movements and their secular counterparts: seeing women's bodies as almost supernaturally perverse and corrupting. It's in this way that the Bible's Bathsheba, raped by God's chosen son King David, becomes a scriptural villain, responsible for her own violation and everything that followed from it, including David's murder of her husband, because she bathed where David could see her.

Such twin convictions about sexual duties and sexual purity, Pearl argues, should be seen as the fruit of salvation, that is, something a Christian woman would do if she were really saved. "If you are God's child in more than just name," Debi warns in a potent accusation to a devout believer, "you will be led by the spirit of God. If God is not leading you consistent with his word, then you must face the fearful truth that you do not have that spirit indwelling you."

This is a frightening charge to many Christian women, for whom being out of step with God is an abandonment far worse than the grim divorce scenarios Debi Pearl paints. It's just such fears Debi taps when she offers the most damning indictment a fundamentalist can lay on a woman: to call her a Jezebel, a woman more reviled than any in the Bible but the whore of Babylon. Jezebel, a biblical queen and prophetess, wielded authority through her husband and son to turn Israel away from God to paganism, and for this, she was killed by her servants, her corpse left to be eaten by dogs.

In modern fundamentalist parlance, a Jezebel is a woman who contradicts biblical injunctions against female spiritual teachers and who attempts to usurp authority over men. As illustration, Pearl cites the saga of a particularly "spiritual" woman in her church—using the term in condemnation of wives who strive to be godly in ways counter to their husbands' wishes. Pearl's "Jezebel" was sinning by attempting to be the conscience of her "carnal" husband. "When a woman attempts to live for God contrary to his word," Pearl warns, "her spirituality is equal to witchcraft, because she is attempting to 'divine' the will of God in total disregard of his clear written words. God calls such a woman 'Jezebel.'" In time, the disobedience of the woman in Pearl's church led to what Pearl sees as God visiting her with "madness" for attempting to force her husband to submit, culminating with a surreal scene at the church when the woman accused her husband of having affairs with numerous female congregants. All of the woman's fellow church members began singing loudly in order to drown out her accusations. "What can wash away my sin?" they sang, "Nothing but the blood of Jesus," until they could force the woman from the church.

Other Jezebels abound, Pearl says, in the female-dominated spheres of spiritualists, palm readers, fortune-tellers, witches' covens, Christian cults, and more generally, women teachers in the church and laywomen who attempt to lead their families. All are embodiments of the same sin: women who "believe they are doing what is good for the family" but are instead undertaking a "religious act driven by rebellion" because they are deceived.

"This is why God has so carefully taught us ladies to observe and maintain our roles as helpmeets. It is why we must implicitly trust God's judgment as to our duties, regardless of how we feel. God gave us a careful and stern warning as to what women would become in the last days. The prophetic picture of this woman is now in full array. It is the spiritual Jezebel, who is the exact opposite of a helpmeet, that is the death knell of the most noble institution on the earth—the family." Biblical women, Pearl commands, must "learn to hate all that she is."

For this reason, the Pearls caution against women becoming too involved not only with women's church groups and fellowships, but also with close friendships with other women at all, as the intimate bonds of friendship can lead to "spiritual masturbation" and a dangerously heightened sense of spirituality. This, in turn, echoes the restrictions on female relationships that other Titus 2 ministries codify. "There is a grave danger in becoming emotionally dependent on other women. Too many times I have seen this lead to something abnormal and sick. Your husband and God should be the ones to whom you turn for emotional support and intimacy.... Seek to serve your family by tying shoestrings, reading them books, making sweet love with your husband. These are the things God counts as important in knowing and loving him."

A woman's neediness in isolation, they insist, is itself particularly appealing to her husband—the loneliness that builds from a day alone at home "awakens" her husband's desire.

Of course, this isolation and dependence can lend itself to abusive situations. And while the Pearls condemn wife abusers as they do abusive parents, Debi Pearl emphasizes that a woman in a relationship with a controlling man must learn how not to upset him and "how to speak and conduct yourself in a way that will maintain your physical and emotional safety and eventually win your husband."

This extreme interpretation of 1 Peter 3:5, which promises that godly women can bring lost husbands to Christ through their submission, is illustrated in Debi's account of the story of "Sunny," a sweet-hearted young woman in her church whose husband tried to kill her with a knife while she was pregnant with their third child. Debi counseled her to leave him forever if she must. But better, Sunny should wage an all-out campaign to win his heart by refusing to bring the stories of his abuse to their church or her family again, reverencing him by keeping his "flaws" hidden. Sunny's disclosure of the abuse, Debi writes, had only exacerbated the situation, enraging her husband more. When she stopped telling others of the violence and began instead publicly praising him, he was brought to Christ.

"When God puts you in subjection to a man whom he knows is going to cause you to suffer," she writes, "it is with the understanding that you are obeying God by enduring the wrongful suffering." God's mandate that men lead and women follow is so important, says Pearl, that it must be followed even to the point of allowing some abuse. It's a stark statement about how little the complementarian insistence on marital reciprocity—a balanced equation of the wife submitting because her husband loves her as Christ loves the church—actually means. With an honesty for her implications that her more genteel colleagues lack, Pearl insists that for women, marriage is martyrdom, whether through the sacrifice of friends, interests, and pride or through a more literal death of the self for the sake of the principle.

CHAPTER EIGHT

Submission and Abuse

Jocelyn Andersen's husband, an associate pastor in their Baptist church, held her hostage for twenty hours in their Kansas house while she bled from a near-fracture of her skull inflicted by his foot. While she lay on the floor, he ranted about women who want to "rule over men." While Anderson is a happily smiling brunette in more recent pictures, the photographs taken after she escaped from captivity show her face a swollen canvas for blue-black welts.

This tie of abuse and the doctrine of wifely submission led Andersen to write about her experience in her 2007 book, *Woman Submit! Christians and Domestic Violence.* In it she argues that headship and submission teachings in the church exacerbate volatile marriages, provoking husbands with anger problems to be further unsatisfied with their wives' "disobedience" and, more dangerous yet, command women to stay committed to harmful partnerships.

"Christian women often feel compelled to stay in marriages because of submission teachings and turning the other cheek. Rather than offering resources and alternatives to battered women, [pastors and religious leaders] have often advised women to return to violent homes and be 'better wives.' Men today are still being assured that God ordained them to rule over their wives, and women are still having it pounded into their psyches that their place is to submit to their husbands regardless of the circumstance."

This last emphasis on wives' passive responses is especially potent combined with the common conservative Christian emphasis on 1 Peter 3, which asserts that wives should win their husbands through their chaste and meek behavior. "If leaders would spend only a fraction of the time they spend trying to teach women how to manipulate their husband's behavior through submission, teaching men how to control themselves, who knows how much tragedy could be avoided."

Instead, as Andersen documents, the emphasis among Christian leaders on women's submission goes far beyond the grassroots patriarchy movement and is voiced at the top of Christian media empires. Dr. James Dobson, founder of Focus on the Family, the Colorado-based parachurch family ministry that is large enough to rate its own zip code, has a long history of spreading this take on domestic abuse to his audience of 220 million Christians reached through seven thousand stations in 160 countries. In the 1980s, Dobson announced on his radio program that some wives seek abuse for the "moral advantage" that a black eye gives them as a "martyr" in the relationship, or conversely, to justify an exit from the marriage when divorce would otherwise be unbiblical. That argument, of women goading husbands to violence to win the "prize" of bruises to display in church, went unchanged more than a decade later, in 1996, during a republication of Dobson's book, *Love Must Be Tough*.

John MacArthur, a leader of the Reformed movement and pastor of a California megachurch, Grace Community Church, allows for women to leave their husbands for a limited amount of time "while the heat is on," but only with the intent of returning when the violence has cooled—and with care not to provoke further abuse, as wives, he argues, often cause their own injuries by desiring to rule over men. More recently, in June 2008, Southern Baptist seminary professor of theology Bruce Ware told an audience at a biblical manhood and womanhood conference in Denton, Texas, that women were frequently abused because they rebelled against their husbands' authority and sought to have their own way, rather than submit.

For battered Christian women already in a dangerous situation, Andersen tells me, this advice from pastors is doubly dangerous. "A Bible-believing woman very likely wants to be in the will of God. I needed to know what His will was for me. But if they receive the advice that His will is for her to submit, that's dangerous. In some cases they'll tell her she can't leave at all, though that's rare. They'll tell her, 'If you walk away, you'll be sinning, and if you remarry, you'll be committing adultery.' Most often, they'll tell her to leave until the pressure is off, then to go back home. But everyone with a lick of sense knows that, in a violent marriage, the heat is never really off. Everything can be fine one minute, and the next minute, you're dead."

"How carelessly these two men," writes Andersen of Dobson and MacArthur, "along with many other evangelical leaders, deal with the lives of women. Christian wives appear to be simply expendable in the name of good, solid, patriarchal, male supremacist theology." A devoted evangelical, Andersen tells me she didn't make the charge lightly, but prayed over it and finally determined that some counsel is so uncaring as to warrant anger. Sending women back home into danger in order to maintain a "fierce defense of male position in the evangelical church" makes women "simply expendable in the arena of male supremacy." Indeed, when Andersen sought help from a variety of pastors and licensed counselors, she was told that she had trained both of her husbands to be abusive. Teachings like these, she says, are more pervasive still. She points to guides for military chaplains—ministers to a very large and conservative flock in all branches of the armed forces—that warn them to mind the teachings of submission and headship when dealing with spousal abuse since advising divorce or legal intervention may run counter to scriptural calls for wives to submit.

Andersen also considers that the focus could have a market motive. "It's no secret that there are more women in church than men—if not true on the rolls, then true in reality. Women tend to be more active than men, and it's been suggested that women are more spiritual. So it doesn't surprise me that the move is on to make churches more appealing to men. But it's Jesus Christ that churches should be concerned with, not making themselves more appealing to men."

Having grown up in the Southern Baptist Convention, Andersen tells me that the teachings of submission aren't a new fad or introduction to worship but part of the spiritual structure of the church. "It wasn't elaborated upon, it was just 'submission, submission, submission.' The teaching was always there, it was always a part of my life and my spirituality. You don't really question it until it gets too extreme." Though the SBC moniker is easy Christian shorthand for doctrinal diligence on conservative issues like marital roles, Andersen emphasizes that it's little different from other evangelical churches on this issue. "What's ingrained in the evangelical mindset is that men were given authority by God and women need to submit to be in the will of God. Even good men, who'd never beat their wives, they like that power. Who wouldn't?"

Following publication, her book was criticized by a number of Christian leaders. She was turned away by the head of one prominent Christian literary agency who said that they wouldn't publish the book unless she withdrew her criticism of Dobson and Focus on the Family. In an interview on Christian radio, Andersen was sharply chastised by Rev. Jesse Lee Peterson, a black minister who runs an eponymous radio show, who argued to Andersen that men needed to defend themselves from controlling women, and that was when battering occurs.

Peterson's race points to a corollary issue of domestic abuse cases among women of color, and his statement echoes a number of old controversies. In the early years of second-wave feminism, many black feminists criticized the movement, feeling torn between standing with white feminist "sisters" and black family members and husbands, sensing that the frequently more privileged white feminists were asking them to turn against their male partners in the fight for racial equality. From the other side, this could also explain the vigor and ferocity of the patriarchal Peterson's attack on a black Christian woman who became a prominent symbol of Christian domestic violence, Juanita Bynum, a popular Pentecostal televangelist and "prophetess" whose estranged pastor husband, Bishop Thomas W. Weeks III, beat her badly during an attempted reconciliation meeting in the summer of 2007.

Bynum, whose ministry to women has revolved around submission and personal chastity, is a leader in the neo-Pentecostal movement, which is marked by a focus on self-improvement and prosperity gospels over social justice issues. It's the same trajectory the broader evangelical movement took away from poor people's concerns in the 1960s into obsession with personal morality in the 1980s. Within the black church, the movement has been electrified by celebrity pastors such as Bishop T. D. Jakes, founder of the Dallas megachurch Potter's House and a leading mainstream black voice for the idea that women find freedom through submission in marriage. As a prophetess and preacher, Bynum in particular focused on issues concerning women and sex. One of her most popular sermons was "No More Sheets," a call for single women to abstain from premarital sex—a common enough Christian message. The other side of that message Bynum delivered as well: once married, women are obligated to be totally sexually available to their husbands, asking their husbands whether they are pleasing to them and fulfilling their "covenant vow" of marriage to treat their husbands as "a wonder when you know he ain't."

After the news broke of Weeks's abuse of Bynum outside an Atlanta hotel, as well as rumors that Bynum had accused Weeks of being gay and having inappropriate relationships with men in his church, Bynum declared a new commitment to fighting domestic violence in her ministry. While some churches reportedly responded by condemning Weeks and asking him to step down, patriarchal Christians focused on Bynum. Jesse Lee Peterson attacked her with particular force, demanding to know "her role in the altercation" and denying that Bynum is a godly woman. "It's impossible for a God-fearing woman to exploit her marital problems for personal gain and publicity. Juanita Bynum's comments and actions prove that she's an angry, out-of-control woman. God wouldn't have her discard her marriage in order to promote the domestic abuse issue or any other phony cause."

Andersen sees little difference between Peterson's message and those of more prominent ministers. Messages like these reach a vast audience, delivered through Focus on the Family or through the influential Moody media empire, which has broadcast Dobson and MacArthur as well as Christian psychologists Dr. Frank Minirth and Dr. Paul Meier, who blame women for domestic violence on their radio counseling show. "These aren't people only some Christians know about or little pockets of fundamentalists. Almost every evangelical has been exposed to them," Andersen says. "The scope and influence of their ministry is huge. And the message that's ingrained is huge."

But Andersen hasn't left the church. Though she's moved to Florida, remarried, and now attends a nondenominational evangelical church, she doesn't see the root of the problem in patriarchal biblical literalism but rather in a perversion of the Bible's real story. In Andersen's retelling of the story of the Fall, Adam is the world's first abusive husband, demonstrating his abuse by betraying Eve in front of God after they'd *both* eaten the apple, telling God, "It was this woman you gave me that led me into sin." Adam, like other abusive husbands, Andersen says, blames everyone but himself. In tattling, Adam turned his wife over to death, for God had told them the penalty for eating the apple was death. The patriarchal order that stretches back to Genesis, says Andersen, was not the intended order but a consequence of sin. And it's one repeated ever afterward as men rule over women and women react according to a biblical version of battered wife syndrome that Andersen calls the "Eve syndrome": spending their lives hoping to transform their husband's character and his betrayals and to restore their pre-fall bliss.

"Everything that we read in the Bible isn't from heaven," says Andersen, explaining why the Eve story should be read as the history of a man sinning against his wife rather than the theological grounding for continued patriarchy. As much of a stretch from literalist readings as this is—and an argument Andersen's critics would surely find heretical—to Andersen, it's a necessary revision if she is to keep her faith. As a devoted, conservative Christian whose love of God is the most important relationship of her life, the alternative is a heartbreaking choice, the same choice that Al Mohler noted, "between two unavoidable options," seeing the Bible as an inerrant guide for gender relations or a document corrupted by fallible human hands. As Andersen poses the question, "The crux of the whole issue is: is the God of the Bible a chauvinist God, and is the Bible a sexist book?"

·   ·   ·

Of course, unhappy wives of the submission and patriarchy movements don't always suffer something as blatant as terrorizing physical abuse. Jodi Jett describes a less dramatic story of early marriage and a lonely, gray resignation to what she imagined was her fate as a woman stuck forever in the wrong relationship.

Jett, an austerely beautiful thirty-one-year-old with a thoughtful face framed by light brown hair, was fifteen when she was saved. She'd attended church all her life with her family, starting at an Assemblies of God body in Missouri and then a charismatic evangelical church when they moved to Kansas, but for her family, religion was "more of a social thing." "My mother's spirituality was more about loving people," Jett says now, fifteen years later, after having left the faith following her mother's death. But at the time, she didn't consider her mother spiritual or saved. Not as Jett and her sister were spiritual and saved, under the mentorship of a pair of dynamic youth pastors who visited their church on a regional youth ministry circuit. Once saved, Jett felt it her duty to become a leader for her classmates. She aspired to save the entire school, attended a minimum of three church services per week, and became president of her high school's Christian club—some of the tasks that she felt her spirituality required and that earned her what she called "Jesus brownie points."

"Christianity was like a treadmill. You have to keep going; you always have to increase because if you're standing still, you're backsliding. Everything was about God, every thought. I remember going to the bathroom and thinking, was I doing this for God?"

Jett is today a physician's assistant who works for two New York City–based reproductive-health community-outreach initiatives, manning mobile units to offer health care throughout Brooklyn neighborhoods. She's also something of a local presence on the New York bar-band circuit—a talented singer and rock guitarist who had a small following in New York before the normal obstacles to professional music careers (business complications and anticipated deals that failed to solidify) dampened her enthusiasm. But on her existing CD, which now she only gives away, Jett has a low alt-country alto that matches her reserve and her tendency to weigh questions slowly before answering.

"In any field, there are catch phrases. In ours, it was a lot of talk about desires of the flesh versus the spirit. Anything of the flesh was bad. Any desire I had for myself was bad. That was materialism, not a desire of the spirit. But 'dying to the self,' becoming so separated from yourself and your own desires, is terrible." Hoping to kill her fleshly desires, Jett absorbed the lessons of her mentors, that godly self-sacrifice in relationships took the form of submissive women following the leadership of men.

"It was constantly discussed how God was the head of church as man was the head of the household. It was easy to buy into because the man had to lead and provide, making it seem more like there are roles. I don't just have to submit; he also has to provide, so there's an exchange there. But the expectation for righteousness is just as great for women. If women didn't submit, they'd be looked down upon, considered rebellious, in rebellion against God."

In retrospect, after counseling, Jett sees an early abusive relationship with her father—physically, emotionally, and, in her older sister's memory, sexually—as "the perfect setup to be perfect Christians. Whatever we did, we had to do it right for him. Whether giving him backrubs or getting him food. So when I became a Christian, it felt so right because I was doing what I'd always done, but now I was being rewarded and loved for it instead of punished."

For all her training, Jett wasn't at first ready for marriage. At eighteen she wanted to go directly into missionary work—a common vision for Christian women hoping to tie their gospel mission to a life of excitement and travel. Jett's mother, however, had grown up with the stories of her own mother, who lived through the Depression with eight children and an eighth-grade education, and who had been forced, during the leanest years, to send some of her kids away to be cared for by wealthier relatives. She insisted that Jett should never put herself in the position of needing to depend on a man for income. And so, out of biblical obedience to her parents, Jett compromised by going to Oral Roberts University in Tulsa, Oklahoma, a Christian college named after its charismatic televangelist founder. Women at Oral Roberts had to wear skirts or dresses, and for the semester she remained at school, Jett remembers the whip of wind against her legs in the dead winter on the prairie. Most women weren't there for long but instead came to school with the hope of meeting "pastor husbands." The joke was, "married by spring or your money back."

Jett didn't stay past the first semester herself, even though she didn't meet her husband on campus. Rather, she met him one dissatisfied Sunday when she was forced to visit a friend's church—an inferior church by her standards. Jason was the preacher's son, and shortly they began dating.

"I guess we felt like we were in love," says Jett. During her first weekend at Oral Roberts, Jason drove down from Kansas and proposed. "I think he felt like he had to grab on to me. I said yes mostly out of feeling bad for him. I couldn't come up with a strong objection, so I went along with it." Jett was eighteen at the time. She attempted to postpone the wedding, which was scheduled for December of her first year in college, but Jason delivered an ultimatum: marry him and return to Kansas or break up. "I submitted," says Jett.

At the altar, Jett says, "I had it all figured out. I remember thinking, life is going to be boring because I know how it all goes." The pastor marrying them spoke for forty-five minutes about the need to evangelize. Jason muttered, "Shut up," but the pastor, partially deaf, didn't hear him. Jett figured that if someone was saved at her wedding, that would be a good thing.

Promptly after the wedding, the relationship soured. "I think we fell out of love when we got married," says Jett. On their honeymoon, in a cold cabin in Oklahoma, Jason had control of the couple's finances and refused to spend the money to rent a VCR so they could at least watch movies. They ended the honeymoon early, and Jason almost immediately stopped going to church. Though Jett continued school at Kansas State, switching her intended major to medicine with plans of becoming a medical missionary, Jason pressured her to drop out and work to add more money to the couple's budget.

Jett stayed in school. "I felt that was a higher calling. I thought, he may be my boss, but God is his boss and God's over him." As they settled into unhappily married life, Jason wasn't particularly authoritative, but did whatever he wanted to. He bought himself a thirty-five-thousand-dollar car while Jett drove a used beater, and he told her to spend less money on food and not to buy her sister a birthday present. Jett donated blood to buy her sister a present, and when she took out student loans, Jason used the money to buy new golf clubs.

"I felt like this was my role. I made this mistake, I married the wrong person, and now I have to live with this forever. I was prepared to be miserable forever. It was a very lonely time." Three years after their marriage though, Jason had an affair and told Jett he wanted to "date other people." Jett moved home, and Jason asked her to continue giving him her paycheck. One day he came by and apologized, and he asked Jett to take him back.

"I didn't want to go, but I felt like I had to." They moved to Nebraska to follow a job offer for Jason, where once again, after four months, he cheated. He came home crying that she would never forgive him. Jett assured him she would forgive, and when he admitted the affair, she "automatically" told him it was alright. "I was obligated to forgive him," she said, echoing the wisdom of Titus 2 mentors: if Jesus can forgive our sins, there is nothing a wife cannot forgive her husband. The sin, rather, would be on the woman for holding on to her anger. When Jett tried to bring the issue up the next morning, Jason shut the conversation down, reminding her she'd promised to forgive him completely.

They settled back into an unhappy routine: Jason stayed out late and then came home expecting sex when Jett was asleep and "half-conscious"; she still felt it was her duty to comply. The housework became her burden entirely, around both work and school. Once she tried to challenge this and left dinner dishes in the kitchen sink for Jason to do. She waited a week for him to clean them, until the dishes were covered with maggots and had to be cleaned before company came that night. After that, Jett says, "I knew that it was my duty."

Eventually, Jason decided he wanted the marriage to be over, and Jett moved out, shortly relocating to Long Island, where her mother and her now-step-father, Jason's father, were church planting. Jason followed her, halfheartedly pursuing reconciliation. "I remember thinking, I hope he doesn't go to counseling like I'd asked, because then I'll have to take him back." Jett was sad for two weeks, then suddenly, overjoyed. She felt that God had decided to give her a "second chance," a morally defensible exit from her marriage since it hadn't been her decision to divorce. "It felt like a gift."

A year and a half later, Jett's mother died in a car crash, when a speeding highway patrolman collided into her car. At the funeral, Jett had an urge to protect God, to assure herself that it wasn't His fault, but by the following May, on Mother's Day, she hated Him. It was easier in New York for her to "fall off the map" of her old church fellows, who would call to check on her spirituality and the state of her walk with God; she was eventually cut off from her Christian friends as a backslider.

"A lot of relationships were severed: to hang out with someone spiritually not right with God, that could rub off on you. Most people didn't really care about me. They loved me in that role."

Though Jett, at twenty-three, began to slowly adopt a secular lifestyle—getting drunk for the first time at Fire Island, dating, suddenly being aware that she "had rights again"—the lessons of a lifetime of submission died hard, and in a therapy session with an unscrupulous counselor, she was nearly taken advantage of when the psychologist told her to have sex with him as a cure for her depression. "I responded like a rape victim, though I'm not. I thought it was my fault. It's taking a long time to think differently."

CHAPTER NINE

The Small World of Vision Forum

Among fundamentalist churches that have long held to biblical literalism, patriarchy, like politics, is local, and there is a new insistence on enforcing biblical commands through the authority of the local church. Phillip Lancaster is a former Army chaplain and Presbyterian minister as well as founder, in 1993, of *Patriarch* magazine and author of the Vision Forum book *Family Man, Family Leader,* which argues for a men's movement that transcends the cheap emotionalism of the Promise Keepers and focuses less on sentiment than on obedience and duty. Lancaster promotes a Christian men's movement of "abiders" who "abide in Christ" by obeying His commandments and harkening to the "good old days" not of the 1950s but the 1700s, before industrialization came and upset the balance of men in the fields and women at home. Barring such an unattainable return, Lancaster calls for a more disciplined Christian men's movement, which doesn't rally stadiums full of weekend prayer warriors but will guide the church back into an orthopraxy that rebukes sinning members for gossiping, chastises husbands for their wives' immodest dress, and excommunicates adulterers. In the either-or battle of feminism vs. patriarchy—and you must choose one or the other, Lancaster warns—husbands must be vigilant commanders of their houses, keeping track of whom their wives and children speak to, what books they read, what television programs they watch, what music they listen to, what they eat and spend money on, and when they wake and go to bed.

"This system is especially good for Mom," Lancaster writes, "who is relieved of a great burden God never meant for her to bear. She was created to help her husband and carry out his decisions. She was not meant to make the big decisions and enforce them on the children." Women should cultivate an attitude of respect for the leadership of all men, though they are only accountable to their husbands, and display that respect by judging carefully whether or not they should speak in mixed-sex crowds, understanding, as Lancaster's own wife does, "that when she speaks it means a man does not have the opportunity to speak at that point, and she doesn't want to grasp the reins of the group."

Among prominent men of the patriarchy movement such as Lancaster, many roads lead back to Vision Forum and its founder, Doug Phillips. Through Phillips's publishing house, Web site, catalogue, Vision Forum special events, and the year-round calendar of homeschooling conferences, he has assembled a stable of writers and fellow-travelers who focus chiefly on his message of patriarchy, submission, and large families. Some existing leaders, he partners with; some smaller writers, he brings to larger audiences; and some public personalities, he helps create and mold from scratch.

Carmon Friedrich explained to me how she became a part of this small world through the invitation of Phillips. Several years ago, Friedrich, a sharp writer with a libertarian sensibility who considers herself an autodidact, self-educated through her library card, began writing her tongue-in-cheek "Prairie Muffin Manifesto." She was responding to the online mockery of her and her peers' lifestyle as "baby machines." She was afraid that her readers, especially the younger girls reading for guidance in growing up to be Titus 2 women, would be discouraged from biblical womanhood. The name itself had a more loving genesis, though even this held a pointed barb at egalitarians; it was taken from the nickname of R. C. Sproul, Jr., for his wife, his "Prairie Muffin," in honor of her prolific motherhood and domestic prowess. Following the identity-politics strategy of reclaiming hurtful labels, Friedrich decided, "If you call me a prairie muffin, I'll be a prairie muffin. This is what a godly woman stands for." And it's not just the "denim jumper-wearing, *Little House on the Prairie*–worshipping baby machines who never trim their hair or wear makeup." She proceeded to tabulate "what a godly woman stands for" in an ever-growing list, currently consisting of forty-nine items, of Prairie Muffin traits: biblical literalists who apply the Bible to their lives; helpmeets to their husbands' goal of dominion; owners of aprons; willing mothers to as many children as God gives; "fiercely submissive" wives; modest dressers who aim to please their husbands with their appearance; soft and gentle talkers who don't gossip or raise their voices at their spouses; feminine warriors who raise their weapons of spoons and children against the serpent and understand that, counter to feminist mantras, well-behaved women do indeed make history, if slowly, and will eventually turn the world right-side up.

Friedrich herself, a petite woman with a youthful, freckled prettiness that makes her look far younger than her forty-plus years, doesn't restrict her wardrobe to the denim jumper that stands as the centerpiece of homeschooling stereotypes. She tells me she will even wear pants occasionally when she practices with the .357 her husband bought her for Mother's Day. She wants me to understand that biblical womanhood is fiercer than its critics may imagine.

Friedrich's contributions to the movement go deeper than ironic relabeling. She's introduced a level of serious theological debate to an Internet community often mired in saccharine, lightweight posts on home life, modest feminine wear, and acronyms like DH, DD, and SAHM (Dear Husband, Dear Daughter, Stay At Home Mom). Friedrich instead frequently leads her readers into more serious right-wing scholarship, posting essays on the pertinence of sixteenth-century theologians such as John Knox, current fundamentalist intellectuals such as Gary North and John Piper, and religious right leaders operating in the secular world, such as Allan Carlson, head of the Illinois profamily think tank the Howard Center: hearty intellectual sustenance for the thinking far-right woman who has chosen to live a submissive life at home. As a connoisseur of patriarchy's teachings, both religious and academic, Friedrich isn't surprised by the dovetailing of so many men from different disciplines arguing for masculine authority. She sees it as God's sovereignty directing different people in different spheres to work on the family. "There's a great Martin Luther quote, 'Whatever the pressing issue in your time is, that's what you need to be addressing.' In his time, it was the Roman Catholic Church. Today it all stems from what people believe about men and women."

Her writing and "manifesto" in time attracted the attention of Doug Phillips, who wrote asking if he could call and speak to her and her husband together. He told them that he appreciated Friedrich's writing and invited the couple to come as his guests to his first film forum for conservative movies in San Antonio. Friedrich went with her oldest children and received a press pass to cover the event for her blog.

In San Antonio, Friedrich met Jennie Chancey, coauthor of the Ladies Against Feminism blog. Stacy McDonald, author of *Raising Maidens of Virtue* and a former editor, with her husband, of *Homeschooling Today* magazine, had also recently gotten in touch with Friedrich to write for them. In time, Friedrich began copyediting and proofreading for Vision Forum; she later graduated to editing with her work on a collaboration between Jennie Chancey and Stacy McDonald.

The collaboration, the fruit of a long relationship between the authors' families and the Phillips clan, was another Vision Forum project, the 2007 book *Passionate Housewives Desperate for God,* which promised to take on the twin threats to happy housewifery of feminism and the "subversive" sitcom message that housewives are desperate and liable to temptation. Chancey was a one-time coworker of Doug Phillips at the Virginia-based Home School Legal Defense Association, where she met her husband and the father of her eight children, Matt. A Virginia native with an Austen-esque style—pale, rose-cheeked skin, upswept dark hair with flowing tendrils, and dresses that she sews herself and markets under her own brand, Sense and Sensibility—Chancey is an avid proponent of courtship over dating. That is, that a prospective suitor should apply to a woman's family before approaching her. Her family should approve of him and his family approve of her well before she ever knows she's on the market, in the name of protecting her vulnerable heart. Only upon parental approval all around may the suitor pursue courtship with the goal of marriage. In the story of her own courtship, Chancey writes of the romance of having her future planned around her by her parents, her suitor Matt, and Matt's family. Chancey's stepfather, Ovid Need, a widower whom Chancey's mother married after her first husband died, runs a Christian courtship service as well as a Baptist church in West Virginia, and he speaks on the topic at conferences. Chancey, who graduated from a Christian college and writes for her own blog as well as for Vision Forum, nonetheless argues against college for women, offering the example of her life—growing up devout, going to Christian college, deciding that she'd pursue a career, and then repenting of her "feminism" and returning to her parents' house—as a picture of the dangerous subversion of pious homeschool daughters away from home.

Stacy McDonald, a mother of ten and another veteran of the patriarchy and submission movement, also has family ties to the Vision Forum circle of friends. Stacy's husband, James McDonald, is the Reformed Presbyterian pastor of Providence Church in Peoria, Illinois, as well as creator of *Patriarch's Path* magazine, a popular homeschooling publication of the 1990s. James McDonald is also a founder of a new Presbyterian denomination, the Covenant Presbyterian Church, formed in 2006 to advance biblical inerrancy and what they call "family-integrated worship." One of their candidate churches, Reformed Family Fellowship Church in Chelsea, Alabama, is the spiritual home of the Chanceys, who host worship meetings for the congregation in their home.

Chancey and McDonald's book, despite its promises of revolutionary new thinking about homework, is much the same as other Titus 2 books: heavy with military rhetoric, noble calls for a return to the domestic sphere, and reassurances that drudgery is a figment of the mind, not the real state of household affairs. More than other writers perhaps, the "fresh vision" of McDonald and Chancey emphasizes gratitude to their husbands for helping relieve them of the burden of decision-making or the busywork that they would focus on if left to their own devices to prioritize their days: "slaves" to their "own whims and wishes."

Like Debi Pearl, they warn against female friendship. "Today's wives are told they cannot expect their husbands to be their best friends or to meet all of their needs," write McDonald and Chancey. "We are encouraged to seek out women friends who can share our woes, listen to our marital problems, and commiserate over the difficulties of bringing up children. Of course, there is a place for relationships between women, but these cannot be based upon gossip, family disloyalty, shared bitterness, or unwholesome intimacy."

"Unwholesome" friendships, they warn, can lead to feminism, and in particular, the whitewashed feminism of the modern church: one all the more dangerous for its "beguiling cloak of Christianity," which obscures its core rejection of submission and hierarchy. "One cannot be a partial feminist any more than one can be 'kind of pregnant,'" the women argue. "Once conceived, it is only a matter of time until the labor pains begin giving birth to rebellion against God's created order." Such rebellion is fleshliness, secularism, carnalness: being of the world, not its light and salt. Christian wives who allow their inherent feminist sin natures to rule will soon be enslaved to corporate America, and enslaved to themselves, as they struggle to avoid servanthood to a loving husband—a fool's bargain.

Lest the doctrine of antifeminism come across as all stick and no carrot, the leaders of biblical womanhood are quick to blame feminism for the modern "superwoman" character who haunts gender-issues stories across mainstream media: the working mom who can effortlessly "do it all" without breaking a nail. In an impressive co-option of their enemy's terminology and critique, Chancey and McDonald argue that it's feminists who hold women up against this unattainable ideal, making housewives look dowdy and incompetent. They go so far as to blame feminists for impossible beauty standards, seamlessly conflating what they see as feminist pressures for women to work outside the home with advertising and beauty industry ideals that feminists have long protested. Ironically, both McDonald's Web site and a wide array of feminist blogs wrote admiring posts about the same recent advertising campaign that highlighted the Photoshopped alterations that went into "perfecting" even the faces of cover models.

The critique, in both cases, is likely more a response to materialism and capitalism, which itself has co-opted women's liberation rhetoric ("Who says you can't have it all?") in the service of selling pantyhose and long-wear mascara. But "materialism," to conservative Christians, doesn't mean corporate greed and commercialism but rather is code for secularism and socialist leanings. So biblical womanhood happily misses the forest for the "You've Come a Long Way, Baby" sloganeering and blames women's liberation for the variety of pressures and insults to women that exist in modern media.

And the message is resounding with Christian women. Sheri Muma, a North Carolina mother to seven children (including five adoptees) who was raised on the mission field in Nigeria, tells me that "feminism is definitely at odds with how Christian women are called to live. Feminism is a lie. No matter what they tell you, you can *not* have it all—at least *not* all at the same time! You may be able to have a career, you may be able to have children, you may be able to maintain a good relationship with your husband, but if you try to do all these at one time, something simply has to give."

"Submission is actually very freeing to me," Muma continues. "I can rest in the fact that my husband is wrong....I rest because I trust God with my husband! I trust that either God will change Tom's mind, or God will deal with him when he finds out he was wrong. Or it could possibly be that Tom is right and I am wrong."

. . .

Increasingly, Doug Phillips and his followers are moving to higher-tech modes of transmitting their message. At Vision Forum's San Antonio Independent Christian Film Forum, a weeklong academy in film and video for Christian homeschoolers that began in 2004, Christian filmmakers screen new productions and vie for a grand "Jubilee" prize for the best new film. The winners of 2007's Jubilee Award—ten thousand dollars cash and a golden statue of a father standing behind his son, hands on the boy's shoulders as the son looks through a camera—were the Gunn brothers, Colin and Euan, two Scots who are thirty-three and twenty-six years old, respectively, separated by half a continent and an ocean, but who have still managed to win two Vision Forum competitions. Their first win was for *Shaky Town*, a documentary blaming San Francisco's gay population for its earthquakes, but the crowning prize came for their take on feminism: *The Monstrous Regiment of Women*.

Colin Gunn, a short, nearly bald man whose remaining crown of hair is cut stubble-close has a lilting voice and easy laugh. He lives in Waco, Texas, with his wife and their five children and works long distance for a California computer animation company. His brother, Euan, works at a bank in Scotland. Their Christian documentaries are a labor of love that don't pay the bills.

Colin Gunn, like many Vision Forum friends, attends an orthodox Presbyterian church with his wife, Amy, the conservative heart behind his work. It was Amy Gunn, a lifelong Christian and Texas native, who impressed on him the need for a documentary about biblical womanhood and the scourge of feminism.

She told him of the indignities she and her homeworking peers experience while walking their broods of children: they are stared at and laughed at, subjected to mocking questions about the size of their families like, "What about the economy?" Homeworking women's real and perceived slights at the hands of a "feminist" culture—though this again lays blame for mainstream culture's dismissal of women's labor in any realm at the door of the feminist movement that sought to recognize and compensate women's work in and out of the home—are a well of resentment the movement eagerly taps, turning male advocates of patriarchy into valiant defenders of persecuted stay-at-home mothers and submissive women into bold revolutionaries. "The movie is a defense for my wife's sake, and for women like her," Gunn tells me.

In defense of women like his wife, Gunn and his brother turned to the example of one of their countrymen, the sixteenth-century Scottish Protestant reformer John Knox, who railed against the reigning Catholic queens of his time for their persecution of his fellow Protestants. Knox, considered the founder of the Presbyterian Church, distilled his hatred of Mary, Queen of Scots, Mary of Guise, and Margaret Tudor into a misogynistic treatise, *The First Blast of the Trumpet against the Monstrous Regiment of Women,* from which the Gunn brothers borrowed the title of their movie.

Gunn's easiness and laughter is a stark contrast to the atmospherics of his documentary, heavy on dirgelike hymns, church organs, and ominous filmic segues tying feminism to all manner of fantastic evils. The cast of the film is all female since some of the truths of the film are too sensitive and threatening to come from the mouth of a man, according to Gunn. Alongside Vision Forum favorites, such as Jennie Chancey, Stacy McDonald, Denise Sproul, and Carmon Friedrich, are several ruling matriarchs of antifeminism: F. Carolyn Graglia, author of the scholastic attack on feminism *Domestic Tranquility: A Brief Against Feminism*; Mary Pride; and anti-ERA crusader Phyllis Schlafly, who tells the young would-be homemakers in the church that most of the jobs out there are tedious and boring anyway.

Narrated by Amy Gunn, *Monstrous Regiment* argues that "Christians can't be egalitarians. We believe in hierarchy and inherent authority." The monstrous regiment of women in John Knox's time, however, has been replaced by a new foe to Christianity: feminism, derived from statism, derived from Marx. In this way, Chancey tells the Gunns, even feminists are serving a man: Karl Marx. "Marx and Engels knew that you can't bring a culture, a nation, into subjection until you've destroyed the Christian family with the father as its head," Chancey explains through a voice-over as the circle-and-cross women's symbol slowly morphs into a hammer and sickle, the sickle bearing a row of jagged, menacing teeth.

"We don't apply the term 'monstrous regiment' to all women—we're very much for women," Colin tells me. "And we're not saying that every woman is a monster, or even that every feminist is a monster. But there are aggressive women, like Hillary [Clinton], who have achieved office, when it should be a real question whether women should hold office." But Colin means a point broader than the particular issue of a female president.

Lamenting that 7.8 million more women vote in America than men, the Gunns declare, "America is now indicted under this verse, Isaiah 3:12. 'Children are their oppressors and women rule over them.'" Women ruling over men in the home or the nation is a biblical curse, a judgment from God; America is a cursed nation. Hillary or no Hillary, the Gunns say, today women already are ruling over men through the unbiblical exercise of women's suffrage. "The men of the suffrage era were willing to abandon their dominion role in that they were willing to give up half of their electoral power to women. The Nineteenth Amendment can be seen as the point in American history when the fathers ceased to sit in the gates as representatives of their families' interests. Individualism and self-interest would now be the approach to the ballot box."

Beyond antifeminist celebrities, *Monstrous Regiment* included the testimony of "Jane Doe," a former military cadet whose face was blurred in the footage of her interview, discussing sexual assault in the armed forces and speculating, under what appears to be coaching by the interviewers, that women serving in the military might cost lives. Upon her saying so, the camera cuts to a slow pan over a military graveyard while taps play. "Death is a significant outcome of feminism," Amy Gunn's voice-over intones before the film transitions to a graphic segment on abortion, featuring a video of either a late-term abortion or a stillbirth, as well as the testimony of Carol Everett, a former abortion clinic worker who now runs an antiabortion organization, the Heidi Group, and claims that before her salvation she aimed to convince schoolgirls to have three to five abortions each before they turned eighteen.

All of these deadly "outcomes" are the result of unbridled equality, Amy Gunn announces, and she tallies the progressive losses that demands for equality will incur on women's lives with a graphic of a disappearing family of stick figures: "Maybe feminism told you that your children were a burden. For the sake of some money or a career or even some free time, you missed out on some or all of the children you could have had." The children figures fade away. "Maybe feminism taught you egalitarianism. You couldn't submit to a hierarchy, so you tried to usurp your husband's authority. You tried to control your husband, you belittled him. You certainly didn't submit to him." The husband disappears. The house disappears when women listen to their inner voice and leave home for work. Finally, the woman herself vanishes after feminism's "fearless sexual ethic" objectifies her and leaves her feeling used. It's a literal interpretation of the mainstream message of abstinence movements: women's worth is contained in their sexual purity, so that having too many partners debases them; they become worthless, nonentities whose value has been so corrupted that they're seen to have erased themselves.

Instead, the Gunns suggest, as the somber music is replaced by an up-tempo chorus, women should return home and have children—more children than the feminists. The Gunns chart the offspring of ten prominent feminists against the progeny of their ten antifeminist commentators and compare the might of the various camps: sixty antifeminist children to a mere seven descendants of women's lib. "As the monstrous regiment seeks empowerment," they explain, "true influence is given to the faithful wife and mother who obeys the Lord. Matthew 5:5: 'Blessed are the meek, for they shall inherit the earth.'" The movie closes with Amy Gunn welcoming her children home with hot chocolate and kissing her newborn baby's brow. "I may not look, to a feminist, like a liberated woman," she tells the camera, "but freedom for me hasn't been won by ballot box or protest or convention. True freedom means freedom from sin, freedom from the curse, freedom from condemnation, and freedom from feminism....As women we might find that when we look for liberation, it quite surprisingly comes to us through a man." There is a pause. "Jesus Christ."

CHAPTER TEN

Life in the Garden

On January 23, 2005, Doug Phillips, who's not just president of Vision Forum but also pastor of a small San Antonio "home church," Boerne Christian Assembly (BCA), read aloud to the congregation of around 125 homeschoolers a notice of disciplinary action against two of his sheep, Jennifer and Mark Epstein, respectively forty-two and fifty-one years old, congregants at BCA for almost five years. First, Phillips explained the biblical grounds for the authority of the church and of himself as its pastor to discipline its members, described in the Bible as a protection for the congregation to help sinners and hold believers accountable, to rein in unruly members, and censure heretics. Such discipline, said Phillips, "is one of the marks of a true gospel church."

Phillips then explained the purpose of the discipline: to show love to the unrepentant, thereby restoring the sinner to right relations with Christ; to maintain order in God's house; to shield other believers from the bad influence of members resisting the authority of the church; and to serve as an example—"a reminder to saints everywhere"—to fear God and be wary of the state of their hearts and the deeds their hearts lead them to.

Then Phillips launched into the specifics of the case against the Epsteins, who had been called to church an hour early that day in order to read the notice before it was presented to the congregation and to decide what they would plea in response to the charges brought by Phillips, his wife, Beall, and four other prominent couples in the church. These ten church fellows declared that the Epsteins, through their troubled marriage, were in serious sin and rebellion against God: Mark, for his anger, violent temper, and frequent threats of divorce, but worse, Jennifer, for her complaints and gossip about her husband to the Phillipses and other church members, provoking her husband and making public accusations about his violence toward his family, her "discourteous and rebellious manner," and her refusal to obey the orders of the church leadership to behave in a more submissive, reverent, respectful, and loving way toward her husband.

Furthermore, Phillips told the congregation, despite Mark's plea that he spare Jennifer the humiliation of this disclosure, Jennifer was continuing to upset her husband due to an old sin: an adulterous affair that she had engaged in—and concluded—fifteen years before, in 1990, a year before both Epsteins found Christ. The affair had resulted in a child, who was given up for adoption; during the pregnancy, both Mark and Jennifer were saved and became dedicated Christians. But this sin, committed preconversion, was admissible, Phillips said, because Jennifer had not completely repented of it. Mark was perhaps unloving and lacked proper leadership in his home, but Jennifer was rebellious and unsubmissive to the authority of both her husband and her church, which had tried to direct her in greater humility and submission. And she showed a lack of repentance for numerous sins; she failed to acknowledge sins that the Phillipses and other church leaders brought to her attention, including the adultery, rebellion, and a "heretical" denial that she was a constant sinner in her marriage.

The Epsteins, Phillips declared, were to continue attending BCA, but with the understanding that their brothers and sisters at church could only interact with them with "confrontational encouragement to repent." The Epsteins were not to join their brethren during the post-church "pot-providence" (for God's provision isn't luck to the truly faithful) fellowship meal, nor were they to enjoy the Lord's Supper while the other congregants took communion. The BCA disciplinary action document counseled the Epsteins to humble themselves and seek God "while He may yet be found." If the Epsteins didn't repent within six weeks, they would be excommunicated.

After the charges were read, the couple was given an opportunity, courtroom-style, to "plead guilty" or "appeal" the action. Mark pled guilty. Jennifer, long embattled with the church leadership over her marriage problems and the blame that she felt was laid at her door, appealed, and in a rare instance of a woman being allowed to speak in the BCA church, was permitted to rebut the document she'd first read only an hour before. Feeling her impromptu defense lacking, she later sent an exhaustive fifteen-page defense first to the ten members who had voted on her discipline and then to the entire congregation.

On January 30, the Epsteins ate lunch in their truck while the rest of the church had a meeting and shared the fellowship meal inside the church buildings. Jennifer, in photographs, is a round-faced brunette whose short, graying hair curls gently away from her face in wisps. Mark is a stern-faced military man who holds himself with the discipline of his twenty-year career in the Army, where he met Jennifer. Two of their three children, Natasha and her brother Joshua, then sixteen and ten, went back inside the church after the meeting to eat their meal—bean pizza, an Epstein favorite—as they weren't under discipline. "It was a very cold Sunday," says Natasha. "The atmosphere was very charged, very different. I knew something was going to happen. Everyone came by and said 'hi' to me, but I felt like a leper. You could tell they were thinking, oh, there's that Epstein girl, stay away from her. Her parents are being shunned."

That's a retrospective realization, though. The Epsteins didn't realize they were in fact being shunned until Jennifer came inside with a gift for a baby shower for a woman in the church who'd had triplets. The mother refused the gift. When Jennifer, confused and hurt, went inside to find her children, everyone she encountered began backing away from her, and then, inside the building, the whole congregation turned their backs to her.

The following Saturday, when Jennifer's letter apologizing for saying "hurtful things" about the BCA leadership and "for responding when I should have kept quiet," but pointedly not apologizing for the accusations Phillips had brought against her, had reached the entire congregation, BCA called an emergency meeting of all the other church families. The next day, the Epsteins went to one of BCA's two sister churches. When they returned that night, they found an e-mail from 8:15 in the morning, shortly before they would have normally left for service at BCA, informing them that they were excommunicated from Boerne Christian Assembly and barred from all church grounds: the implication to the Epsteins being that a public humiliation had been intended by the church leadership, who would have turned away them away at the door. Within a week, the community that had become the replacement for the Epsteins' extended family—their actual relatives lived far away—and that had constituted the children's sole social network for five years disappeared from their lives. The Epsteins, according to the excommunication e-mail, would henceforth be treated "as heathens and publicans," the despised tax collectors and petty contractors of ancient Rome.

"It was like all my family had died. I don't think people can understand how bad that feels," says Natasha, an affable, baby-faced brunette whose post-BCA life shocks her mother, full of friends and boys and parties. "To this day, almost three years later, if I were to see someone from BCA, I'd be in tears. After all those years, and all those memories, how could they just kick us out and never call or care?"

· · ·

Jennifer speaks hesitantly, pausing frequently before answering, a timidity at odds with her online persona—a sharp-witted if somewhat martyrly writer who has continued shaping her BCA defense in a controversial blog and who signs her personal e-mails with self-assured fighting words: "For those who come behind me." She grew up in central Oregon, in Salem, Bend, and, later, Portland, where her parents still live. They were serious, rule-oriented Baptists, and their church, a Christian and Missionary Alliance church, was very concerned about its list of off-limits activities, which included drinking, smoking, and playing cards. They were the kind of Baptists, a generation of comedians riffed, who worried that "fornication might lead to dancing." At eighteen Jennifer rebelled and left the church for the world, wary of all religion and especially the legalistic brand she'd come from.

She joined the Army to become a nuclear/biological/chemical weapons specialist at twenty-one, telling the recruiting officers that she wanted money for college and she wanted to go to Germany. There, in 1985, while training for the position, she met Mark, a strong, mustached military man, then thirty-two. Mark was a field tester for new recruits. He was so impressed with Jennifer's "low crawl," she says with a little laugh, that he wanted to meet her. Four months later, the couple eloped on a "Darling Denmark" vacation tour, but they continued living what she now describes as "wicked lifestyles" as unbelievers for ten years.

Something she doesn't bring up on her own, but which is buried in the documents surrounding the Epsteins' excommunication, is the assault that figured into Jennifer and Mark's decision to marry. When Jennifer had been at the Army base in Germany for just a month, in a company of more than one hundred soldiers that included only two women, she was gang-raped by four nineteen-year-old soldiers she had agreed to have a drink with. After one drink—a nominal amount for the twenty-one-year-old Jennifer, who says she's always had a high tolerance for alcohol—she passed out. When she awoke and went to the bathroom, her bra and underwear were on inside out and her body was covered with marks. When she returned to the barracks to get her things, the soldiers were looking over Polaroids they'd taken of the assault.

Mark, whom Jennifer was seeing casually at the time, tried vainly to get the company commander to discipline the soldiers; he felt an old boys' network interfered with the process. Failing progress with their commander, they tried to take the complaint to higher levels of the military but were turned down and threatened with being sent to different posts. "Mark said, 'Let's get married so they can't make us separate.'"

From the first day of the marriage, Jennifer tells me, Mark accused her of cheating on him and having an affair; a year and a half into their life together, he told her that "he didn't wanted to be [her] friend anymore." At the three-year mark, Jennifer did have an affair. "It seemed natural, after being told for so long that I was cheating," she says. After about five years on assignment in Germany, years sometimes marked by tensions and fights caused by Mark's jealousy and anger, the couple was transferred to Fort Carson in Colorado Springs, which was then beginning to blossom into the spiritual center of the evangelical world it is today. Mark, who was nonobservantly Jewish, found Christ first. Six months later, Jennifer was saved too. Mark says that he thinks God saved him when he did deliberately: a week before he found out about Jen's affair with a fellow soldier, whose race and religion—a black man who may have been Muslim—would later become fodder for accusations made against Jennifer online. During this time, Jennifer realized she was pregnant. Mark made preparations for divorce and attempted to have the Army prosecute Jennifer under its rarely enforced adultery prohibition, a charge that could have resulted in a court martial and dishonorable discharge. "They knew I was pregnant and that I'd been gone for several months, so it wasn't Mark's," Jennifer says. She decided to leave on her own.

In desperation, Jennifer began reading a study Bible she bought in a local bookstore. Though she'd begun volunteering at a crisis pregnancy center that promoted adoption rather than abortion, she agreed to have the abortion Mark wanted her to have in the hopes that it might save her marriage. While they were on their way to the abortion clinic, Mark stopped at Fort Carson to talk to the chaplain. He came out an hour later, persuaded that Jennifer should deliver the baby and give it up for adoption instead.

Mark agreed to continue living with Jennifer, and the couple renewed their wedding vows. They were sent back to Germany for a honeymoon period in both their marriage and their newfound faith, joining a close-knit military church in the Assemblies of God, a Pentecostal denomination not known for its formality or insistence on doctrine, in which Natasha was free to wear Daisy Duke shorts and tank tops. The family felt a sense of ease and belonging they'd never known. "That's really where we learned about love," Jennifer remembered. "They do love really well."

After another six years, the Epsteins were transferred to Fort Sam Houston, in San Antonio, Texas. They joined a Southern Baptist megachurch, Alamo City Christian Fellowship, with three thousand members. Jennifer's convictions began to conservatize and rigidify—she thought there was too much unbiblical, humanistic content in the Sunday school classes for her children and saw too many congregants leading shallowly Christian lives—leading her into conflict with her more moderate pastor.

As an adult Sunday school teacher, she began teaching submission and headship doctrines to her class, and she approached the pastor about integrating the children's Sunday school classes into the rest of the church. Jennifer's complaint, though she didn't know the terminology behind it at the time, echoed that of "family-integrated church" advocates. Proponents of family-integrated churches see the separation of the young from their parents during church services as a damaging "age segregation" that undermines the centrality of the father-led family as the basic unit of the church and a "holy institution" ordained by God; this separation, they assert, can run counter to the religious lessons parents wish their children to learn.

Such family-integrated churches are another of Doug Phillips's projects, advocating and networking family-integrated congregations through his Uniting Church and Family conferences and his National Center for Family-Integrated Churches. The latter is an organization of five hundred churches devoted to the same principles, which include keeping all ages together throughout the full church service and full-family communion, where a father receives and distributes the family's share of the Lord's Supper. Many of the member churches are committed to Phillips's larger "new Reformation" mission as well. Today, Jennifer Epstein argues that the collection of churches Phillips is organizing looks "more and more like a new denomination every day," a charge that finds support in the numerous conservative churches that go into internal conflict when congregants attempt to introduce Vision Forum teachings.

When Jennifer sought to integrate children's Sunday school classes into the rest of the church, her pastor at Alamo City replied that no changes were forthcoming and that perhaps they should look for a more formal church. Jennifer continued to see hypocrisy in the congregation and began, she says, "to expose it" to the rest of the congregation. When they'd been there nine months, the Epsteins were asked to leave.

"We didn't know exactly what we were looking for. But I knew that it wasn't right that my kids were torn away from me every time I walked in the doors. And we wanted to be with people more concerned with personal holiness and with living God's words. Every Sunday we'd visit different churches, but nothing came close to feeling right. For some reason, I got the thought in my mind that we should go to a home church," she says, meaning the sort of nondenominational churches or communities that believers, often very conservative believers, set up within their homes in order to create a godly alternative to what they see as lax church standards. "I began asking everyone I met about it, at my homeschool group, in the grocery store. Finally, a friend of a friend told me about BCA." But when Jennifer asked BCA if they could visit—standard etiquette for fundamentalist churches that function more as closed membership clubs than open-door evangelical churches—BCA said no. "I was ready to join an Amish church and only wear gray or tan dresses," she says, so desperately did she want to be around a higher standard of morality than that she saw at Alamo City.

In retrospect, three years after excommunication, Jennifer thinks the very rigidity and discipline of the church is what appealed to her, shaped as she'd been by years of fidelity to military order and, before her brief rebellion, her rule-oriented Baptist upbringing.

"I crave structure," she writes. "I'd been in churches where they just 'let the Holy Spirit lead,' and we never knew what was going to happen from week to week." Jennifer didn't like the "touchy-feely" boundaryless sensibility of such spirit-led congregations. She'd thrived under military discipline, memorizing long lists of rules and regulations, willing to submit to such authority, she says, as long as she understood the reasons for the rules. That this need to understand the rationale behind regulation indicates a desire for dialogue and debate more than a readiness to submit seems evident in the wake of Jennifer's experiences at BCA, where she attempted to grapple intellectually with the logic behind the rules as she had in the Army. But at the time, her desperation for the "perfect church" compelled her to seek the holiest body she could find.

Natasha is blunter: "It was a safe haven. A way for us to escape from our lives."

Six weeks after Jennifer called BCA, she tried again. This time BCA welcomed her. The next Sunday, the Epsteins arrived at Boerne Christian Assembly forty-five minutes early, prepared, Jennifer says, to follow any necessary rules: drab clothing colors, wide dresses, no makeup, even a head covering if that was the cost of admittance. What they found instead was a congregation happily mixed between such Mennonite-style devotion to modest dress and women who wore makeup and even occasionally pants. Indeed, Beall Phillips was painting her nails when the Epsteins arrived at the Phillips' home church. Beall, a pretty, fair-skinned blonde in her early forties with a wide smile and casual bearing, met Doug working at their college paper, and she has edited a collection of poems for women for the Vision Forum catalogue.

She greeted the Epsteins with a number of questions: Did they homeschool? Were they members of the Home School Legal Defense Association? Had they heard her husband speak?

"Apparently most of the visitors came to hear this famous man," said Jennifer. "I didn't know that there were any famous homeschoolers."

After a four-hour service, the families gathered together for an all-day fellowship, sharing a pot-providence meal, the children playing together in grassy fields till five or six in the evening. The Epsteins felt they had found a spiritual home.

It was the fall of 2000, and BCA was just over a year old; it was attracting a growing membership, including a high percentage of military families such as the Epsteins. The fellowshipping, or "one-anothering" as Doug Phillips called it, was wonderful and nonjudgmental at first: on the Monday following their first BCA service, the Epsteins were invited to a special event where a BCA friend would be demonstrating the lessons of the Sermon on the Mount by breaking a wild horse. Jennifer showed up to the event in shorts and a tank top, and although all the other women in the congregation were in long dresses, no one chastised her.

Even in the first happy year of their membership, when the congregation was growing rapidly, there were expectations of the lifestyle members would adapt themselves to. Jennie Chancey came as the Phillips' special guest to address the women of the church on the dangers of sending their daughters to college. Instead of traveling far outside the authority of their parents, Chancey argued, young women should stay at home and serve their fathers until they married. Jennifer protested, beginning a pattern of dissent at BCA. How would the women know enough to homeschool their boys, she asked, if they were only educated enough for their other duties as mothers? It was a reprise of a familiar homeschoolers' debate concerning the age at which it becomes inappropriate for a mother to continue teaching her son, as her having instructional authority over her son after he attained manhood may be unbiblical. Chancey told Jennifer that someone else could teach the boys algebra.

Women were not allowed to speak in the church, a requirement that Jennifer believes began as a loose guideline but in time ossified into a rule so steadfast that women had to rely on their male family members or other male congregants to say anything in church: to announce a prayer request, to walk to the front of the church to receive communion for the family, to introduce an out-of-town visitor or family member attending the service. After the service, the men would discuss Phillips's sermon in a semidemocratic roundtable fashion that Phillips proudly describes to outsiders. The women listened.

Beyond listening, the church women followed the roles that church women traditionally have: serving and cleaning up after the communal meal, girls helping care for the young children of church mothers, attending frequent baby showers for women in the congregation, and refining their understanding of wifely submission through weekly women's discussions. If disagreements arose in the women's Sunday afternoon meetings, they called in the men, who resolved the problem while the women sat silently beside their husbands. It was a radical change of life. Jennifer had desired just that.

"I had previously thought that maybe I was the only person in the world who was concerned with holiness," writes Jennifer on the blog she began in late 2006 in order to tell the story of her excommunication and "expose Doug Phillips's Ecclesiastical Tyranny." Over the next six months the blog, Jen's Gems, would swell in popularity, receiving three hundred and fifty thousand hits in its first eight months, collecting eleven thousand comments and, at its peak, landing in the top seventy of more than nine thousand other WordPress blogs. Jennifer thinks the blog's appeal was tied to the spread of the patriarchy movement among conservative churches, sparking debates about the theology and sometimes splitting churches as believers felt compelled to choose one side or another. Jennifer's story encapsulated many of the arguments being fought across the country.

"Once I started attending BCA," she continues, "I realized that I didn't even begin to meet their standards of holiness." She started the family on a regimen of catching up with their brethren by listening to hundreds of hours of Vision Forum tapes, sometimes three or four sermons or messages a day: on patriarchy, submission, and the godly way to be a Christian family. After each tape, the Epsteins would discuss the message. "If we agreed that it was biblical, we would cry and repent and make major changes in our family…[Sometimes] that meant three or four major changes in our family a day." Among the changes were an ever-tightening dress code of no pants for Jennifer's daughters but only dresses and skirts. No sleeveless shirts. No dating, no college, no working outside the home, no celebration of Christmas (considered a pagan holiday by BCA; 2007 was the first Christmas the Epsteins celebrated in seven years), and generally no independent time for children away from adults—a mixed blessing, as Natasha now feels comfortable socializing with all age levels, although the rule was intended partially to curb the negative effect of children influencing each other to disregard their parents' rules.

At the one-year mark, Jennifer says, the church changed. The church itself moved further away into San Antonio, requiring an hour commute for many of its members. At the same time, Phillips's speaking engagements for national homeschooling events increased dramatically, and several of the other church elders split off from BCA in an amicable division, starting other churches that would form, with BCA, "the community": a trio of sympathetic sister churches consisting of BCA, Living Water Fellowship, and Faith Presbyterian. BCA also decided to develop a church doctrine: "purposing" (in a peculiarly Vision Forum grammar) to "establish a local church committed to the wedding of orthodoxy and orthopraxy; one which will seek to take captive every thought to the obedience of Christ, and to strive to build strong families, to train men for leadership; to affirm women in their biblical roles as wives, mothers, helpmeets," in order to better take on the "Satanic conspiracy to annihilate the Christian family."

The men read and either approved the statement of doctrine or left: half departed, Jennifer estimates. The half that remained was not the group that accepted makeup and pants but the faction that "wanted lots of rules," she says. "So legalism grew as time went on. In my life as well. I started doing things in my life with the right spirit, but over time, I started thinking that everyone else should be doing these things. The same thing was happening with other members. Some women would take other women aside for wearing pants and tell them what a sinner they were."

Around the same time, Doug Phillips, Phillip Lancaster, and R. C. Sproul, Jr., wrote an article detailing the "Tenets of Biblical Patriarchy": a definitive exposition of the lifestyle they'd been advocating. The tenets affirm that God is masculine; that God created gender roles, including the authority of the father; that the family fits into a disciplinary order within the church; and that women and men are to exercise dominion through their proper spheres, through fruitful procreation, and through homeschooling their children as agents of God's kingdom. Reading through the list, Jennifer found most of the tenets acceptable. But she thought that the spirit of the new laws tended in the same legalistic direction as had the church, becoming more extreme as a matter of solidifying doctrine.

"He'd say woman is created as a helper, a keeper at home, and lots of Christian women would agree. But then what he would start to say is that the only reason women were created was to be helpers to their husbands. The slight attitude change makes it more extreme." It could almost be seen as a commercial decision for Vision Forum, which competes in an increasingly lucrative field of homeschool publishing as the homeschool community grows and emboldens its message to retain readership.

One of the "new" things that Phillips began preaching was the idea of a multigenerational family dynasty, a "two-hundred-year plan." "This plan," Jennifer recounts scornfully, "is that his children will train up their children to train up their children—twelve per child—so that in two hundred years, you have all these people following your vision. In four generations, you'd have 780 people or something. So that makes you, what, king? For most men, probably it starts as a desire to obey God and to see the roles fulfilled that aren't being done right in the typical church. But as you get into it, it gets more and more extreme. For women too. I talked to a lot of friends and the consensus is that women are frustrated about men abdicating their roles: they didn't lead, they didn't show Christ's love for their wives. Patriarchy provides that. It starts out with good intentions, good details, but then you add new details, new rules, and before long, it becomes something else, a system."

Jennifer still holds to this argument years after her excommunication: patriarchy is the ideal but Phillips and his followers aren't practicing it correctly. They were teaching the women to submit before teaching the men to love. She argues that patriarchy, when it's done right, in a heart-driven, grace-inspired way, makes women want to submit to their husbands because their husbands lead the way, by loving them as Christ does, not because it's a system imposing a set of rules from without. In truth though, it was an operating system that Jennifer encountered when she first came to BCA, embodied in an ornate set of rules to follow, which she recognized when she started her family on the program of taped Vision Forum messages. But through the eyes of new love for her adopted church, this body of rules seemed like an inspiration and challenge rather than dogma.

So over time, Jennifer noticed the existing rules tighten. Women who had spoken briefly during BCA church services stopped talking. And the "heart" conviction of submission increasingly meant observing a list of proscribed behaviors. Many women weren't allowed to drive, but if they were allowed, they certainly could not do so at night (a circumstance that complicated many evening baby showers). Likewise, the meal sign-ups for women helping to ease the cooking load of sick wives or those with newborns—a level of community support that is a major draw for many women in tight-knit conservative communities—became a bureaucratic ordeal on the scale of organizing a public school field day, as a church full of women had to seek their husbands' permission before signing up for meal duty. Submission was still described as a wife's voluntary display of love for God and her earthly lord, but increasingly, it was an expectation that came with heavy penalties for noncompliance.

Outside this realm of patriarchal teachings, Mark Epstein, who in 2002 reached his twenty-year-mark of Army service, was being eased out of the military due to medical problems with his neck and vertebrae, on which he'd had three surgeries. This severance of his Army ties, combined with what Jennifer sees as Phillips's vision-heavy but impractical patriarchy sermons, exacerbated the anger problems that had marred the Epsteins' early years of marriage, and Mark began behaving erratically and threatening divorce. Jennifer approached Beall Phillips for counsel on submitting to an angry man. Try harder, Beall told her. One Sunday, when Mark was threatening divorce, Jennifer approached Phillips after church, explained the severity of their breakdown, and asked if he would intercede.

Phillips immediately began to challenge Jennifer, she recounts, "'Are you being submissive? Are you trying to win him without a word? Do you have a gentle and quiet spirit? Do you obey him?'" When Jennifer answered that she was trying her best to fulfill these roles, Phillips approached Mark at his car, and, according to Jennifer and Mark, asked him whether Jennifer was "a nag," "a dripping faucet," or "disrespectful," "unsubmissive," "rebellious," and "churlish."

Mark told Phillips that, yes, Jennifer was all these things. Phillips arranged a meeting six weeks later for the Epsteins, the Phillipses, as well as another church couple, elder Bob Welch and his wife. There, Jennifer says she was interrogated about the details of her adultery thirteen years prior. According to Jennifer, Phillips called her a "whore" and a "Jezebel." Beall Phillips, Jennifer charges, concurred. (Phillips and Vision Forum's press secretary Wesley Strackbein refused to comment on the Epstein affair beyond an online notice they posted on a BCA Web site, but associates of Phillips who defended him as surrogates online have denied that Phillips called Jennifer a "Jezebel.")

Phillips told Mark and Jennifer that they would not be permitted to receive communion—the first time they were barred from communion—until they satisfied BCA's leadership that they were in compliance with a set of accountability guidelines for their marriage. Mark was to control his temper and not threaten divorce. Jennifer was to desist from speaking ill of Mark to third parties, to never "question, contradict, criticize, correct, or end-run any communication or decision by Mark, to Mark, or to anyone else," and to examine herself for unconfessed sins against Mark. Phillips gave Mark his cell phone number and Beall gave Jennifer hers.

Jennifer tried to demonstrate her repentance for the affair, writing a letter to Mark in which she apologized for hurting him with her infidelity and swore that the assault she'd suffered in Germany was nonconsensual. Moved by the letter, Mark showed it to the Phillipses as demonstration of Jennifer's repentance, and the Phillipses, the Epsteins recalled, cried while reading it, agreeing that it demonstrated Jennifer's fully repented heart. After another terse group meeting and a meeting between just Phillips and Mark in the fall of 2003, communion was summarily restored.

The restoration didn't last long. By August of 2004, tensions had again risen to a breaking point between the Epsteins, culminating in an episode of road rage where Mark swerved in and out of traffic at one hundred miles per hour, terrifying Jennifer and the children. When they arrived at BCA, Jennifer told her church brethren that Mark had just tried to kill the family. She was chastised for breaking her accountability guidelines by speaking ill of Mark, and when the couple met with the Phillipses six weeks later, Phillips laughed at Jennifer's characterization of the episode and her complaints that Mark was becoming physically aggressive in the home—shoving and pushing Jennifer and the children, obsessively cataloguing methods of killing people for the edification of their kids. Jennifer reports that Phillips's verdict was: "'Mark is an angry man, and that is wicked; but you, Jen, you are very wicked, you are rebellious, and you are a Jezebel.'"

The Epsteins' marital troubles weren't the only points of contention between Jennifer and Phillips. In the fall of 2004, Jennifer told a female volunteer at Vision Forum (a distinction from employees, Jennifer suggests, that exists to maintain a purist position on women working only in the home) that Phillips was not fulfilling his duty to "protect women and children" since he had not protected her and her family from her husband's wrath. This was an accusation that undermined not just Phillips's frequent and lofty appeals for chivalry and honor but also the ideal of his "Titanic Society," a father and son association dedicated to the ideal of "women and children first." When the charge reached Phillips, he ordered Jennifer to a series of counseling sessions with Beall and another church wife, Reba Short, who had long argued to Jennifer that her marriage problems were her fault.

In the counseling sessions, Jennifer was given a list of fourteen principles of submission that she was to follow in order to "make [her] husband successful," "demonstrate a submissive heart," and "bless" Mark. She could take them or leave them, Beall read in a prepared statement, but if she wanted to remain at BCA, she was "bound to live by [her] covenant. This means being under authority, and resisting the temptation to bring a false witness against other brothers, or seek to build a private case to justify such behavior." Jennifer was to show Mark a log of three days' worth of household activities so that he could prioritize her days; to ask Mark to tell her five things she should change about herself and focus on changing them; to never say anything negative to or about Mark but to praise him privately, in front of the family, and in public; to demonstrate physical affection of her own initiative; to greet him at the door with the children; to not provoke or manipulate him but to search herself for her blame in a dispute; to check with Mark before making any "unilateral" decisions, no matter how small; and to refrain from teaching or having theological discussions with any other men.

Jennifer told Beall and Reba she didn't "have the conviction" that women mustn't speak of theology to men, but she argued that she was already living out the other thirteen points. Beall responded that it was Mark who had complained about Jennifer's teaching and debating. (Mark later denied this.) Jennifer also disagreed with Beall's declaration that Jennifer, like herself, must be sinning constantly in her marriage as a result of her fallen nature, the "total depravity" of mankind as upheld by Reformed theology. Jennifer's response was to bring "several hundred verses" to her next counseling session that she felt supported her position on the mediating factor of grace. Beall cut her off. That was heresy, she said, a doctrine of "sinless perfection"; it was an argument that would later be used against Jennifer in her church discipline.

The counseling sessions ended without resolution in late October, when Jennifer again provoked Doug Phillips by challenging an essay he had posted on his Vision Forum blog, which argued by analogy that true Christians should vote neither Democratic nor Republican but instead for the candidate of his father's Constitution Party. Jennifer, a sharp critic who says Phillips once told her, derisively, that she should have been a lawyer, e-mailed Phillips a response essay arguing why voting for Bush was a biblical option. This prompted an immediate rebuke from Beall, reminding Jennifer that she'd been instructed not to teach men. It's hard to imagine that Jennifer, who always set herself diligently to learning a system of codes and laws, and who had been attracted to BCA precisely for its ornate, high-stakes rules, didn't understand she was being unsubmissive according to the norms of the church she had chosen, repeatedly making herself a gadfly in a congregation that prized obedience to authority, especially among its women. But it's no easier to understand why a woman with Jennifer's need for intellectual discourse and debate would put herself in a place where those qualities were not just unappreciated but vilified.

The next day at church, Jennifer made a partial peace attempt, apologizing to Phillips for an old grievance—her "gossiping" about his not protecting her family—but refused to apologize for the e-mail challenging his voting philosophy, a challenge Phillips told her would have been fine coming from Mark.

"He told me that I would 'pay for this,'" claims Jennifer, and to prove it, he proceeded to devote his two-hour sermon to reading and rebutting Jennifer's argument from the pulpit and preaching on the unlawfulness of a woman chastising her pastor.

In mid-December, Jennifer believes, she was the subject of a second sermon. She was home sick from church, but Natasha was present to hear Phillips preach about an "unsubmissive" woman in the congregation whose husband was repentant for his sins. Natasha left in mid-service, but when Jennifer asked Phillips if she had been the topic of the service, he brusquely referred her to Corinthians 14:35, the verse used to enforce women's silence in church: "The Bible says that if any woman has a question about the preaching of the Word she is to ask her husband at home."

A month later Phillips read his charges for the Epsteins' church discipline—their ongoing marital battles and Jennifer's old affair—aloud to the entire congregation: a body that formed the only extended family the Epsteins felt they had and from which, within two weeks, they were cut off forever.

Following the announcement of church discipline, one woman called Jennifer to comfort her, saying that the same thing had happened to her: she'd gone to church authorities for marriage counseling and was barred from communion for a year; she was threatened with excommunication if she told anyone else about her marriage difficulties. "She was silent, everyone was silent," says Jennifer. "But you could look around and see people unhappy."

Jennifer, not one to be silent, mailed her "defense" first to the five couples (including the Phillipses) who voted on the Epsteins' punishment and then to the entire congregation. "Frankly, I think you expect the Epsteins to leave and not submit to church discipline," she wrote, "however, we are people under authority." After the mailing to the congregation, the Epsteins were excommunicated in short order, left only with the advice that they fear for the state of their souls, repent, and flee to Christ that they might someday confess to the congregation all the sins they were charged with, and be welcomed home. "Until that time," the excommunication order read, "no true believer is to treat you as a Christian."

"Looking back on it now," Jennifer summed up her charge later in writing, "I can plainly see that we made a major mistake in ever sharing our hearts with Phillips. What we didn't understand at the time is that Phillips has a certain image, a 'vision' of what BCA must be. BCA isn't a church for the wounded and hurting. BCA is a church for those who already have their act together, and if they don't have their act together, they'd better keep their problems to themselves. They'd better just do their best to act like the vision. Disclosing family problems is a threat to Doug's vision."

. . .

To dull what Natasha calls the "incomprehensible" shock of abruptly losing their family of five years, the Epsteins immediately began attending one of BCA's sister churches, Living Water Fellowship, run by "Little Bear" Wheeler, a sort of evangelical Davy Crockett figure who sells Wild West–inspired Christian historical media and toys through Vision Forum's catalogue and his own Mantle Ministries. At first, Jennifer says, Little Bear took them into his protection, comparing Jennifer's treatment to the Salem witch trials. He offered the Epsteins a six-month shelter at his church while he tried to effect reconciliation.

In the outside world, when Jennifer or her family would run into people from Vision Forum or BCA, they were mocked or treated as pariahs; BCA members would cross the street when the Epsteins approached or refuse to look them in the eye. When she attended a homeschool forum to sell a math curriculum, Jennifer's booth was placed near Vision Forum's. All day, she recounts, the young men of Vision Forum made comments about heathens, and the young women of BCA would break into a run when they passed Jennifer's stand. When Natasha Epstein attempted to call her former best friend at BCA, Lourdes, a nanny for the Phillipses, she was told, "I can't talk to you anymore."

But the Epsteins didn't walk away from the conflict either. Increasingly, Jennifer took opportunities to rankle Phillips and his BCA faithful. She decided to donate clothing for homeschooling families affected by Hurricane Katrina via Vision Forum headquarters, prompting a clarification letter that she was barred from Vision Forum grounds as well as BCA property. She also sent several notices to homeschooling leaders associated with Vision Forum, explaining her side of the saga. Mark Epstein continued a writing campaign to Phillips, demanding a specific list of sins for which he and the family had been excommunicated. Unsatisfied with the response, Mark threatened Phillips, writing, "It only takes the touch of a button to find yourself in a similarly embarrassing situation as R. C. Sproul, Jr."

The evocation of Sproul, Phillips's friend as well as a prominent homeschooling leader, was a significant threat. Sproul was deposed from his office by the Reformed Presbyterian Church General Assembly in 2006 for abuse of authority against several congregant families in his Bristol, Virginia, agrarian Christian community. In fact, it was from the online testimony of one of the families who dissented from Sproul's teachings, the Austins, that the Epsteins drew inspiration for their own public offensive.

"Ask your IT folks how easy it is to reduce the BCA writings and subsequent USPS and electronic correspondence between us to Adobe files," Mark wrote, "and then ask yourself if you want Jennifer's letter of May 2005 seen side-by-side with your response, the tone of which embodies an almost palpable hatred."

This time the response came not from BCA elders but from Phillips's attorney, Don Hart, who accused them of blackmailing Phillips and threatened action against the family for slander and libel as well. Hart estimated that the damages the Phillipses could be awarded were substantial. Were it to come to that, wrote Hart, Phillips, as well as witnesses from BCA, would of course be compelled to testify as to the character of the Epsteins and the particulars of Jennifer's adultery.

"The best thing she could have done then was walk away," says Dustin Curlee, a church elder at Bridgeway Bible Church, where Jennifer attended services throughout 2007. Bridgeway is a local San Antonio church not part of the BCA community but still conservative enough to attract a sizable number of Vision Forum employees as congregants. For two years after their excommunication, the Epsteins tried to negotiate reconciliation with BCA with the help of both Living Water Fellowship and Faith Presbyterian, the second sister church in the BCA community. But both churches became embattled with BCA over the dispute, and both eventually posted documents online declaring allegiance to BCA on a new BCA Web site created solely to host testimonies related to the Epstein case—something that became necessary after the Epsteins publicized their story through a number of different blogs.

In the fall of 2006, the Epsteins pseudonymously began to tell the public about Doug Phillips's failings through a ministry watchdog site, Ministry Watchman, that had written extensively on the downfall of R. C. Sproul, Jr.

Soon, Jennifer created Jen's Gems, which received remarkably high traffic and attention among homeschoolers and launched several sympathetic blogs dedicated to scrutinizing Phillips and Vision Forum. It also inspired a backlash of blogs attacking and debunking the Epsteins' claims, two of which were created and run by Phillips's old friend Matt Chancey.

The controversy quickly reached across the corners of the conservative homeschooling world. The Epsteins amplified their offensive against Phillips by mailing copies of their testimony to the homeschool associations and leaders found in the directory of the Home School Legal Defense Association (HSLDA) and, later, by distributing copies of a critical article at a homeschooling convention. Phillips and BCA responded through surrogates, the blogs and commentary of Vision Forum allies and graduated interns, or more obliquely, through obscure references on his own blog: items posted with little or no comment, but signifying much to those aware of the controversy. There were news items about churches and ministries suing bloggers or regarding a Texas court ruling that recognized the authority of a local church to discipline and excommunicate a member. The court also ruled, Phillips took care to point out, that there is no legal ground for "pastoral confidence," and pastors therefore are not held from informing congregations of members' sins.

After the Epsteins' mailing to HSLDA members, Chris Ortiz, the public face of the Chalcedon Foundation, long connected to the Phillips family through both Howard Phillips and Vision Forum, posted a long essay, "In Defense of Doug Phillips," on the Chalcedon Web site. He discussed the Epsteins by name, focusing on Jennifer's adultery at length, and sympathized with Mark's failure to forgive her, calling such forgiveness "a tall order."

One blog called Little Geneva suggested that Jennifer "could only show true repentance by committing suicide." This blog sparked a subsidiary spat between the Epstein and Phillips camps that sheds light on the evolving face and etiquette of the Christian right in America. Both sides lobbed a potent accusation against the other, charging that their opponents had ties to "kinists." Kinism, as numerous readers in the blogosphere newly learned through the debate, is a movement of anti-immigrant, "Southern heritage" separatists who splintered off from Christian Reconstructionism to advocate that God's intended order is "loving one's own kind" by separating people along "tribal and ethnic" lines to live in large, extended-family groups. Little Geneva apparently housed a few such kinist sympathizers but was hacked—mysteriously, and shortly after Phillips supporters confronted one of its writers—and now only bears a black screen with a ghoulish face and menacing nonsense words. Phillips defender Matt Chancey wrote at length about how the Epsteins had worked together with kinists at Little Geneva as a strategy to discredit Phillips; Epstein supporters noted the attack-blogs' condemnation of Jennifer as a "race mixer" and also pointed to Phillips's eulogizing Confederate chaplain Robert Dabney as the "defender of the South." Both sides rushed to deny any such ties. Even among a group divided over their approach to a basic agreement—the inequality of the sexes, if not in the sight of God then at least here on His earth—nobody wanted to be called a racist.

And then, several months later, in January 2007, the Epsteins' activism ceased, and they removed all the critical blog posts about Phillips from Jennifer's blog. Faith Presbyterian was attempting to broker reconciliation as Living Water Fellowship had done. Phillips refused. Both churches wrote statements for the BCA Web site affirming its disciplinary decisions. The Epsteins were no longer welcome at the community churches. Jennifer's blog reappeared with renewed fire.

She moved beyond her story to personal accusations about the women in Phillips's life: his mother, Peggy Phillips, a recent Eagle Forum "Homemaker of the Year" who Phillips praised for bearing children that the world "needs," and Phillips's wife, Beall, whom Jennifer variously described as a beleaguered victim and as the real man of the house. Jennifer's blog commenters speculated about rumors of a planned marriage between the Phillips and Sproul children.

In the spring, an Illinois-based watchdog ministry specializing in publishing exposes of cultish or "spiritually abusive" groups, Midwest Christian Outreach, Inc. (MCOI), published an independent evaluation of Vision Forum. Jennifer had contacted them suggesting a report, but MCOI president Don Veinot told her one was already underway due to reports he'd received from churches that had fought, and even split, over Vision Forum's patriarchy and family-integration teachings. Veinot, who with his wife Joy had started their watchdog career by investigating Bill Gothard, leader of the Basic Life Principles Christian movement, focused on Phillips's connection with the underrecognized Gothard; Phillips had spoken at Gothard's conferences, praised Gothard's anti–birth control activism on the Vision Forum blog, and attributed the growth and fecundity of homeschoolers in America to Gothard's influence.

MCOI didn't find that Vision Forum was a cult—a potentially ministry-wrecking charge—but condemned Vision Forum's overemphasis on extrabiblical, or even "pagan" principles, such as patriarchy. Vision Forum risked sullying its otherwise good name, the Veinots determined, by promoting these "pagan" authoritarian ideas over servanthood as Jesus Christ practiced it.

The conclusion was similar to Jennifer's take on BCA: it was a movement begun in earnest, with the right Christian ideals—love and service demonstrated through following the biblical plan for marriage—that had hardened into something power-obsessed and "legalistic." But the rather fangless MCOI report itself, and particularly its association with an "anticult" ministry, still caused some damage. Jennifer distributed photocopies of the report outside an Arlington, Texas, homeschooling conference. She was kicked out, but Vision Forum began to attract unfavorable attention online, both from non-Christians and, more importantly, from critics within the church.

Meanwhile, the Epsteins' consuming interest in telling their story, and in keeping up with the reactions and attacks from supporters and critics, at first brought them together against a common enemy. But soon it became another source of conflict in their marriage. Having begun telling their story through third parties at the Ministry Watchman site, with whom they continued to plan further articles, storylines, and investigations, Jennifer spent hours talking on the phone with her male coauthors. Mark became jealous and began acting out online: dropping cryptic hints on his own blog that a new bombshell was brewing or mentioning facts out of order, causing confusion among Jennifer's growing readership.

"The others and I decided we couldn't trust Mark anymore with what was going on strategy-wise," Jennifer told me. They shut him out of plans about how to further unfold the story. Mark and Jennifer's marriage continued to deteriorate even as they wrote online about the havoc Phillips had wreaked on their family with his badly executed version of headship. This begins to get at the larger effect BCA's teachings had on Jennifer. An autodidact who taught herself theology in order to better understand the "whys" of the rules she loved, she had carved a narrow role for her own vindication. She saw herself as a "person under authority" as she'd protested in her pre-excommunication letter to BCA, but one who'd been misfortunate to fall under the wrong authority. Phillips acted as the lawyer he'd been trained to be for the Home School Legal Defense Association, and he turned his church into a courthouse, trying Jennifer with briefs and witnesses testifying to the state of her unrepentant heart. Jennifer responded in equally litigious fashion, charging that Phillips didn't follow proper methods of biblical conflict resolution as detailed in Matthew 18 and that the structure of BCA didn't follow Presbyterian guidelines and so couldn't constitute a fair court. In a way, Jennifer thrived in her crusade against Phillips, reveling in the feverish state of Internet celebrity, working long hours to craft new theological arguments against Phillips. It's not surprising; the rush of ideas and debate was what she'd wanted all along.

In June of 2007, half a year after they'd begun writing about the Phillipses, Jennifer began a Bible study with a retired pastor, "Mike," who regularly commented on her site and accused her of being "legalistic" in her own right, of being too preoccupied with the ways in which Phillips had broken various rules of church governance, and of being not concerned enough with God's grace. It was a lesson in Mike's own belief system, New Covenant Theology, which argues that Christians, saved under God's grace, are no longer bound by Moses's covenant with God and the Old Testament laws that go with it, but are only under the laws of the New Testament: to love God and love others. Jennifer broadcast her revelation: she wasn't an outlaw, an "antinomian" as Phillips had branded her, but a "supernomian," following a higher law.

Lest this sound like conventional, mainline Protestant theology, New Covenant Theology is a reaction within the conservative spectrum of Christianity against other conservative believers. Simplistically, it's a midpoint between Reformed, Calvinistic thought (or "Covenant Theology") and Dispensationalist beliefs about the imminent end times. But in practice, it is vastly closer to Reformed thought, and in fact, it seems to look much the same.

Jennifer explained the difference as she saw it. "I'd become a Pharisee. Just as with patriarchy, I'd start out with something biblical, and then added rules and became more detailed about those rules. You start out with the conviction to dress modestly so as not to cause your brother to stumble; then it becomes very particular: your dresses have to be this wide, then the buttons have to match the color of the cloth, then you have to wear a double covering. Instead of being a heart issue to dress with others' purity in mind, it becomes an overwhelming set of rules." The difference between her following those old Covenant rules of BCA and her new approach, Jennifer says, is that now she will still strive to dress modestly "not because I follow a long list of rules but because I love others, I obey those in proper authority over me, and I obey God. I do follow some of these ways to love others, such as submission and headship; that's God's way to show love to your husband. It might be the exact thing that you were [already] doing, but you're doing it now for a different set of reasons."

Jennifer denies that this is just a complicated way of restating her basic argument, that Doug Phillips's ideas were right, but he was doing it wrong, or that BCA began practicing patriarchy with good intentions that later soured. Following her Bible study with Mike in 2007, she felt that she understood, and was experiencing, grace for the first time in her life. She set about finding a new church that shared her convictions, and she found a local body practicing the tenets she'd newly adopted in Bridgeway Bible Church, where she would meet Dustin Curlee and his pastor, Kerry Kinchen.

At first, Bridgeway turned Jennifer down flatly, aware of her reputation in the local homeschooling community and fearing that she would sow division there as had occurred at all of the Epsteins' former congregations. It was a particular concern for Kinchen and Curlee considering the number of Vision Forum families that attended Bridgeway—a fact that seems to further underscore how similar a "New Covenant" church can appear to an "Old Covenant" church. In time, through theological discussions online, the Bridgeway elders found that Jennifer shared many of their views, and they warily began discussing terms for accepting her at the church. Foremost among those terms was reconciling with Phillips and BCA in such a way that both parties could move on with their lives.

And so, in December 2007, when I contacted Jennifer to check in after several months, it was Dustin Curlee, a San Antonio real estate broker and Bridgeway elder, who responded, afraid of publications that might jeopardize Bridgeway's reconciliation efforts. Jennifer, Curlee explained, had "had a miracle occur in her life by the sovereign work of the Holy Spirit" and now had an unprecedented understanding of grace in her life. It was almost a salvation experience and enough of a change of heart to freshly tackle the years of "miscommunications" between herself and Phillips. There would be no tallying of wrongs, Curlee said.

In the next several days, he said, there would be large changes on Jennifer's blog. "I'm convinced that Jen showing greater grace than they did can heal this. What she's done to this day has not been causing a cycle of growth, and what Vision Forum has done has torn the body down. These conflicts in the church at large are bound to continue, but what if we find a better way to resolve them? This started with Adam and Eve—they were the church at one point, and they did split—but what could have been if they hadn't? Jen can show real biblical grace to BCA and Doug Phillips. She can be the bigger man by humbling herself to them. If she considers them more worthy than herself, then Scripture says the Lord will exalt her."

It's an argument that seemed familiar by now, governed by the same verses that dictate peace between husband and wife—a soft answer turns away wrath; winning without a word—as well as the ones that promise delayed reward for those who suffer for God's sake: the meek shall inherit the earth. But seeing it in such terms—power struggles rather than love—is a secular blind-spot, Curlee tells me. As in marriage, submission is a fruit of salvation, and to understand the former, you have to have the latter—meaning a lost soul can't understand the heavenly bargain.

"It is a wrong premise to say one or the other has the sweeter deal. God being glorified is the sweetest deal, because He is worthy of all the honor and glorification. But from an experiential perspective, no one has a sweeter deal. The deals are equal in sweetness. If a woman is submissive to her husband, regardless of whether or not he is as he should be, then there is a satisfaction that comes with this that is unexplainable, that cannot be explained to someone who does not understand salvation," he says.

Three days later, Jennifer removed all of the posts on her blog that were critical of Doug Phillips, BCA, or Vision Forum, leaving up only her theological writings and an explanation for why she was finally "closing the book." She enumerated her missteps in telling her story, and she asked Phillips's forgiveness. Mark did not remove his posts. She hoped that she would be allowed to read a letter of repentance, and a request for forgiveness, to the entire BCA congregation that Sunday. If she was denied, she would send it as a Christmas letter to the Phillips family and the rest of the BCA congregation. She spoke of her love and pity for Phillips—the bondage of "living without grace," of "judging everyone you come into contact with"—and said that she'd love to see Vision Forum teaching headship and submission in a grace-inspired way, as she now understood it. A week later, Jennifer closed her blog and stopped responding to e-mails. The implications seemed clear, that Jennifer and her family had appealed for reconciliation and the price was her silence. Her readers, even many of her fiercest fellow fighters, expressed relief at the close of the saga. They bid the Epsteins to find peace quickly and move on.

But then, without warning, the blog posts reappeared once again. Bridgeway Bible Church, which had assured Jennifer (and, in my conversations with Curlee, me) that they would never give up their attempts at healing this "rift in Christ's body," had called Jennifer in late December with a concise message: we quit. One of the elders claimed that his wife was crying over the amount of time the church was dedicating to the cause of the Epstein-Phillips reconciliation.

Jennifer doubted this and suggested legal threats had been issued instead. With the fresh hurt of Bridgeway bowing out, and taking with them the summary prohibition they'd placed on Jennifer's blog, she reappeared with a new entry, suggesting new and outlandish behavior on Vision Forum's part: sums of money demanded for restitution and lawsuit threats levied against bloggers or churches supportive of the Epsteins. The new accusations, which Jennifer later tempered or withdrew, seemed as hyperbolic as had been Vision Forum's reaction to her blog when they called it a great conspiracy to assassinate Phillips's character. But Jennifer's story, provocative though it was, hadn't been ammunition enough against the sheer durability of Vision Forum's business and publicity machine. Fewer readers greeted her return, and a number of them told her in less gentle terms that it was time to move on.

When I asked her about the alleged "restitution fee," she told me the charge had come from Mark, and she couldn't get more information as they had filed for divorce in December, after a separation of several months. The communications that passed between them regarding "the story," as she'd come to call it, were tied up in other acrimonies as well.

Mark was writing erratically on his own blog, vacillating between reconciliatory praise for Phillips and threatening that 2008 would make 2007 look like a picnic. He reinvented his online persona with a photograph displaying two full sleeves of new tattoos. ("That was the first time I saw them," Jennifer said with a little laugh.) And he posted several photographs of a new girlfriend, a voluptuous, pretty brunette sitting astride a motorcycle, or posing in a soft-lit department-store portrait. Natasha, who at twenty was living a lifestyle her mother considered heavy sin, and who had pled with her parents for years to finally divorce, was suddenly struck with the prospect of losing her family, and she berated her father for posting the photos. He took them down a week later.

"It's been a long twenty years," said Jennifer stoically, growing emotional only when she turned to the topic of finding a new life. She began to cry while explaining that, likely, she wouldn't be able to stay at home with her youngest, developmentally disabled daughter, Alicia, anymore, but would have to return to work for the first time in fifteen years, as "Texas isn't an alimony state." Further, Mark had sued for custody of their son, Joshua (though not Alicia).

She didn't know if she'd try to return to a church, as the churches that would have her—"megachurches where I hate the music and the sermon is unbiblical," she said ruefully—aren't her idea of what church is supposed to be about.

And this finally seemed like it might be the sad center of what Doug Phillips's associates and employees had called a great "Internet conspiracy" of defamation: a life lived in a perpetual state of stumbling and repentance, writ large for the world to see. It was the Christian infatuation with the salvation story played out publicly, but with lives so messy that they could never fit easily into the idyllic male-headship family that Vision Forum promises is the solution to modern marriage woes. Instead, it might be simply the story of Jennifer, a sharp and intelligent woman who felt a need to make a mark for herself in the world she had chosen. She led her family in a search for distinctive holiness and took them into the arms of the patriarchy movement. There, she found that her husband's anger, violence, and jealousy were vindicated and that she was no longer allowed to lead, speak, debate, or distinguish herself in any way other than submissiveness. When she balked at those rules for holiness, she found herself in spiritual limbo: too holy for the churches that accept her as a broken sister and as a sharp, capable woman, and too tarnished and unsubmissive for the churches that meet her standards. Jennifer hopes still for a "perfect" church that can deliver the standard of righteousness patriarchs claim as their own, but in which female members play a role more substantial than that of "completer," or at least one where she can rise as an exception to the ranks of helpmeets. Sadly, it's not a combination she's likely to find where she's looking.

When I spoke to Jennifer last, she had just fired her divorce attorney for failing to abide by Jennifer's wishes in filing various motions for the divorce. She had recently undertaken to represent herself, spending long days watching her children and learning the law, preparing for her eventual day in court.

PART TWO

·

MOTHERS

CHAPTER ELEVEN

Be Fruitful and Multiply

When the Gospel Community Church in Coxsackie, New York, breaks midservice to excuse children for Sunday school, nearly half of the 225-strong congregation patters toward the back of the worship hall, including the five youngest children of Pastor Stan Slager's eight, Assistant Pastor Bartly Heneghan's eleven, and the Dufkin family's thirteen. The Missionettes, a team of young girls who perform ribbon dances during the praise music, put down their "glory hoops" to join their classmates; the pews empty out. It's the sort of unignorable difference between the families at Gospel Community and those in the rest of the town that's led some Coxsackie residents to wonder if the church isn't a cult that forces its disciples to keep pushing out children.

But after the kids leave, Pastor Stan doesn't exhort his congregation to bear children. Slager, a kindly Bronx-born blue-collar pastor in his sixties who labored for twenty years as a clam digger in Long Island before moving north, explains that "we're just a body of believers that loves children, that's very supportive of children, so that sets a certain atmosphere." But in addition to the atmosphere, there is a message for those that can hear: Slager reminds his congregants to present their bodies as living sacrifices to the Lord, and he preaches to them about Acts 5:20, instructing them to go tell "all the words of this life." In Pastor Stan's subtly guiding translation, this means to lead lives that make outsiders think, "Christianity is real," lives that "demand an explanation."

Lives such as these: Janet Wolfson is a forty-three-year-old mother of eight in Canton, Georgia. Tracey Moore, a thirty-nine-year-old midwife who lives in southern Kentucky, is mother to fourteen. Wendy Dufkin in

Coxsackie has her thirteen. And while Joanna Stoors, a twenty-six-year-old Illinois mom, only has four children so far, she jokes that she and her husband plan on bearing enough to populate "two teams." All four mothers are devoted to a lifestyle that the conservative columnist David Brooks praises as a new spiritual movement that's growing fast among exurban and Sunbelt families. Brooks calls these parents "natalists" and describes their progeny as a new wave of "red-diaper babies"—as in "red state."

But Wolfson, Moore, and thousands of mothers like them call themselves and their belief system "Quiverfull." They take their name from Psalm 127: "Like arrows in the hands of a warrior are sons born in one's youth. Blessed is the man whose quiver is full of them. They will not be put to shame when they contend with their enemies in the gate." Quiverfull mothers think of their children as no mere movement but as an army they're building for God.

Quiverfull parents try to have upwards of six children; many have more. They homeschool their families, attend fundamentalist churches, and follow biblical guidelines of male headship—"father knows best"—and female submissiveness. They refuse any attempt to regulate pregnancy. Quiverfull, as a contemporary movement, began with the publication of Rick and Jan Hess's 1989 book, *A Full Quiver: Family Planning and the Lordship of Christ,* in which the Hesses, a Nebraska couple encouraged to write by Mary Pride, argue that God, as the "Great Physician" and sole "Birth Controller," is in charge of opening and closing the womb on a case-by-case basis. Women's attempts to control their own bodies—the Lord's temple—are a seizure of divine power.

Though there are no exact figures for the size of the movement, the number of families that identify as Quiverfull is likely in the low tens of thousands (though many more families follow the same convictions without claiming the movement name). Its word-of-mouth growth can be traced back to conservative Protestant critiques of contraception —they consider all birth control, even natural family planning (the rhythm method), to be the province of prostitutes—and the growing belief among evangelicals that the decision of mainstream Protestant churches in the 1950s to approve contraception for married couples led directly to the sexual revolution and then to *Roe v. Wade.*

"Our bodies are meant to be a living sacrifice," write the Hesses. God may have given man dominion over the earth, but not over his own body, which must be dedicated to His ends. Or, as Mary Pride wrote in *The Way Home: Beyond Feminism, Back to Reality*, a foundational text for Quiverfull adherents as well as followers of submissive wifehood: "My body is not my own." This obvious rebuttal of the feminist health text *Our Bodies, Ourselves* is deliberate. Quiverfull women are more than mothers. They're domestic warriors in the battle against what they see as forty years of destruction wrought by women's liberation: contraception, women's careers, abortion, divorce, homosexuality, and child abuse, in that order.

Following Pride's insistence that feminism is a religion in its own right, incompatible with Christianity, she argues that accepting any aspect of women's liberation paves the way for gay rights and abortion. In this way, regulating one's fertility is a slippery slope: "Family planning," she writes, "is the mother of abortion. A generation had to be indoctrinated in the ideal of planning children around personal convenience before abortion could be popular."

"Abortion," writes Pride, "is first of all a heart attitude: 'Me first.' 'My career first.' 'My reputation first.' 'My convenience first.' 'My financial plans first.' And these same choices are what family planning, which the churches have endorsed for three decades, is all about." In this equation, family planning enabled women's careers, with abortion as a safety clause against an unintended pregnancy interrupting those careers. This led to women's decreased dependence on men, which enabled more women to divorce. Finally, this led to homosexuality—as permitting the separation of sex and procreation leads to confusion about the purpose of sex, making it harder to condemn homosexuality—"abortion on demand," and child abuse.

Women's roles, Pride writes, whether biological, economic, sexual, marital, or in the church, are all connected. By challenging any of them, feminism assaults them all. "Childbearing sums up all our special biological and domestic functions," she writes. That, and unending service. "God intended women to spend their lives serving other people. Young women serve their children, their mothers, their husbands, and the community at large. Older women train and assist the younger women, and in some cases become church helpers.... We are responsible for keeping society healthy and human. And for this, we get respect."

In their sexual lives, Pride argues that God's intention for marriage is paramount: a tool for subduing the earth and producing fruit, children, who will further His cause. For Pride, this means that nonprocreative sexual activities are forbidden, which is of particular note to women because, as Pride writes, "The Bible shows women leading the way into perversion." Rather, Pride argues, "For fruitfulness it is absolutely necessary that coupling be marital, heterosexual, and genital-to-genital, and nothing else."

This level of orthodoxy is largely limited to Pride as a Quiverfull pioneer and purist. Most other Quiverfull and biblical womanhood leaders are adamant about the sexual duties wives have to their husbands. The demand for wives' constant sexual availability, however, doesn't preclude the insistence of the Quiverfull movement—that sex be centered around and open to procreation.

It's also goal-oriented. Instead of picketing clinics, Pride writes that Christians should fight abortion by demonstrating to the world that children are "unqualified blessings" by having as many as God gives them. As long as churches don't insist that children are unqualified blessings, she writes, it will be hard to stop abortion. And the only way that the world will see children as unqualified blessings is for Christian families to be willing to have large families.

Only a determination among Christian women to take up their motherly roles with a "military air" and become "maternal missionaries" will lead the Christian army to victory, writes Pride. She explains how Quiverfull completes her whole-cloth alternative to women's liberation: it adds a natalist mission to the submissive sensibility and, by populating the world with right-thinking Christians, turns back the tide on a society gone wrong.

As for women with medical reasons for not getting pregnant, the common rejoinder is summarized by the Hesses, who write, "If you're too sick to have babies, you're too sick to have sex," and imply that most women balking at the Quiverfull lifestyle with medical excuses are fabricating their illnesses. On the other hand, if a woman knows she is too ill to bear children, or worse, knows she doesn't want any, she must inform any potential husband of the fact and should likely plan on remaining single. "If you know that you are not healthy enough to have children, you may want to consider being married only to Christ.... If you simply do not want to have children intruding into your life, please plan to remain single. That is a far better choice than getting married and still trying to live like a single."

· · ·

The gentle manner of Deirdre Welch, another Coxsackie mom to four boys, who meets me at Gospel Community Church in a flowing orange dress, crimped brown hair, and an engaging smile, seems at odds with Quiverfull's militaristic language, which describes children as weapons of spiritual war, as arrows shot out by their parents. But Welch is no stranger to culture war; she leads a local chapter of Teen Mania, the adolescent ministry cousin to the culture-warring teen group Battle Cry, the spiritual-warfare training program of Texas pastor Ron Luce. And Welch describes the movement toward larger families in the same way: "God is bringing revelation on the world. He wants to raise up His army. He wants His children to be."

Angel Mays, a thirty-one-year-old mother of three in West Virginia, spoke with me just before she was to have her tubal ligation reversed in order that she could make her body "God's home" again. Mays, who came to recognize and articulate her Quiverfull beliefs after reading Nancy Campbell and Doug Phillips, suspects a divine purpose to her change of heart, and she believes Quiverfull and the homeschooling movements are signs of a revival. "It seems the Lord is preparing for something, and I'm wondering if He's doing something big. There's so much selfishness with people thinking they need to make their lives easier. But we're to seek the Kingdom of God first. The further the nation gets away from God, the starker the Christian contrast grows. The darker the world gets, the more we stand out," she says.

In his column for the *New York Times,* David Brooks concluded in 2004 that mothers like Welch and Mays are too busy parenting to wage culture war. Cathi Warren, a homeschooling mother of nine, responded briskly to Brooks's misunderstanding of the movement's aims in a letter republished on Quiverfull Digest.com (an online forum in which twenty-six hundred families participate). Raising a large family, she replied, was itself her "battle station," as deliberately political an act as canvassing for conservative candidates, not to mention part of a long-term plan to win the culture war demographically.

Warren, who lives in San Antonio, clarified her letter further: what Brooks missed in his praise for the faithful parents of the heartland was the recognition that "this is the war to me." Though Warren is not a

Quiverfull Digest member, she is among the many families, perhaps the majority, living "Quiverfull" lifestyles without claiming the title—most of whom agree completely in spirit but see the movement as broader than one label can capture. And she does want to train her children for "culture war." "The Bible calls us 'salt and light,'" she tells me. "I understand the arrows metaphor, and raising my children is my battle station. Home is where I want to work and make an impact. My major task in life is to impact the nine people who will leave my home. Reviving that battle station is very important to me."

Wendy Dufkin, a petite, stylish woman with a smart, sharp appraisal of outsiders, looking more like a cosmopolitan businesswoman than a mother to thirteen, expresses Quiverfull believers' sense of themselves as holding a rampart against a sinful culture. "Many are the persecutions of those who choose not to use birth control," she tells me. But where national denominations and ministries may lag in providing leadership or encouragement, she finds growing acceptance in local churches and homeschooling ministries nationwide. She says her only regret is not having had more children, and it seems deliberately provocative: the new, countercultural clothes of what was, for centuries, the unchallenged status quo.

One of Dufkin's pastors at Gospel Community Church, Bartly Heneghan, agrees that large families face a sense of persecution, observing that they are subject to the charge that they're adding to overpopulation and poverty. "Some people think that what I'm doing, having eleven children, is wrong," he says. "I don't really get into that much. The Bible says, 'Be fruitful and multiply'; that's my belief system. They don't believe in God, so they think we have to conserve what we have. But in my belief system, He's going to give us a new earth." But theological explanations such as these, taken largely from Genesis and Revelation, go unrecognized in mainstream representations of the movement.

Increasingly, the presence of such large, ideologically driven families is being documented through the medium of the age: reality TV shows and lifestyle cable channel specials, all of which campily depict Quiverfull life as like regular motherhood, but amplified—more kids, more laundry, more merriment. The most famous of these families, Michelle Duggar and her husband, Jim Bob, a former Arkansas state representative, has been featured on a series of Discovery Channel specials. Their fame sprouts primarily from their novelty: in 2008 Michelle Duggar was pregnant with her eighteenth child *so far*. "So far" is a ubiquitous phrase in the movement, a minor jab at outsiders that cutely restates a Quiverfull family's continuing trust in God's control of the womb. But such theological underpinnings are glossed over to make room for the novel details of large family life.

As Jennifer Jones, a thirty-two-year-old Washington mother of six-so-far details, that means seventeen loads of laundry per week, constant bulk food shopping at stores like Costco, a limited range of vehicle options, from minivans to fifteen-seaters, and extra headaches when trying to secure a hotel or campsite that will allow a party of their size.

There are other commonalities, traded among Quiverfull comrades as badges of honor: the frequency with which they're stopped in line at the grocery store by someone asking if "they're feeding an army," if they know "what causes that," if they know "there's a pill for that"? Are they Catholic? Are they Mormon? Do they know God gave us brains to use them? They're also frequently met with a host of assumptions about their beliefs, economic status, ethnicity, and possible welfare reliance. (The last is particularly untrue. Many Quiverfull families have strong beliefs against government assistance and personal debt—often going to extreme measures of subsistence-level living, and the attendant hardships on dependent women and children that brings, in order to live debt-free. Moreover, among many conservative Christians, it's accepted that local church charity is the proper form of aid to the needy and that this should replace government assistance programs altogether.) Another Quiverfull truism, one given extended play by the Hesses, is a Quiverfull version of "he's one of ours": selectively appropriating historical figures who were the later-born children of their families to create a canon of the Western world's sixth-, seventh-, or eighth-born geniuses and greats. The moral is that the "contraceptive mentality" would have precluded the births of Washington, Mozart, Beethoven, and, by implication, possibly a savior.

Potential like this, and more broadly the conviction that God has a hand in every life from before conception, can outweigh any reasons women have to discontinue having children. Joanna Stoors, who authored a blog titled Living the 127th Psalm, explains that after she had two children in quick succession upon getting married at twenty-one, she suffered severe postpartum depression and was "very frustrated" when she became pregnant a third time. She'd been opposed to the birth control pill since college, when a friend told her that they caused abortions, but she and her husband discussed barrier methods of contraception and the possibility of a vasectomy. When her husband, Jacob, had a vasectomy appointment set up, Joanna had a change of heart. "I felt I'd overstepped my bounds as a wife, not looking at it as a family and asking Jacob what he wanted. I felt a kind of peace. With any repentance comes peace. It was calm and still, not a supernatural moment." Soon after, she found out she was pregnant again, and she accepted it with "much more" peace.

. . .

As a movement, Quiverfull has grown in a grassroots style. There's little top-down instruction or organization from church leaders. Instead it spreads person-to-person through community Bible studies, homeschooling forums, prolife activist circles, or small ministries such as Titus 2 groups. Quiverfull supporter Allan Carlson, an economist who heads the Howard Center for Family, Religion, and Society and advises conservative congressmen such as Senator Sam Brownback (R-Kans.) and Rep. Lee Terry (R-Neb.), sees Quiverfull's most significant roots in the homeschooling movement. Quiverfull is a populist movement with "a wonderful anarchy to it," as the early days of homeschooling had had. And indeed, homeschoolers, and the devout in general, tend to have more children than average American families.

But while homeschoolers may be more receptive to the idea of unplanned families, most prospective Quiverfull parents actually learn about the Quiverfull conviction through the movement's literature, such as Pride's and the Hesses' books, Nancy Campbell's *Be Fruitful and Multiply,* Rachel Scott's *Birthing God's Mighty Warriors,* or Sam and Bethany Torode's *Open Embrace.* And most of these people find these books after hearing the theory, as Stoors had, that birth control pills are an abortifacient. That is, that hormonal contraception such as the pill can cause the "chemical abortion" of accidentally fertilized eggs. This is one of the strongest ties between the Quiverfull conviction and the larger Christian right, connecting a radically expanded prolife agenda that has broadened its political interests from abortion to birth control and sexual abstinence to international pronatalist movements.

As the political power of the antiabortion movement has grown, emboldened activists have moved toward a purer ideological line, making birth control the next target of the prolife movement. Employing the same "chipping away" political strategy they successfully used to diminish abortion rights, anticontraception activists have moved from defending individual "conscientiously objecting" pharmacists seeking to refuse contraceptives on moral grounds, to extending the same "right of refusal" to corporate entities such as insurers, to an out-and-out offensive against birth control as the murder-through-prevention of three thousand lives a day and the future undoing of Western civilization.

The latter two points were made in Illinois in September 2006 by British demographer Andrew Pollard, a speaker at the "Contraception Is Not the Answer" conference. Calling contraception "societal suicide," Pollard calculated the reduced number of births due to contraception equivalent to a "9/11 every day for thirty-five years." Pollard argued that "this year, about 1.6 million will be lost because of contraception and sterilization in [the United States]…. [F]or every child lost through abortion, another is lost through contraception and sterilization. Countries cannot survive in the long run if they kill, or restrict, so many of their young shoots."

The conference followed an August 2006 cover story on "The Case for Kids" in the evangelical flagship magazine *Christianity Today,* as well as intermittent hand-wringing from pundits warning of a coming "demographic divide," wherein fertile red-staters will far outnumber barren blue-state liberals. It was organized by the Pro-Life Action League, a Chicago-area antiabortion group, which gathered two hundred and fifty activists to organize strategies against birth control. Attendees included Allan Carlson, representatives from the Catholic antiabortion group Human Life International, Catholic think-tank scholars, and natural family planning advocates.

The heavily Catholic representation among anticontraception activists is unsurprising. For several generations, opposition to birth control has been the province of the Pope and the Catholic Church: a historical stance reinforced by Pope John Paul II's insistence on the sinfulness of using contraception and given a symbolic boost in 2005 by John Paul's heir, Benedict XVI, who canonized an Italian farmer's wife for bearing twelve children in the late 1800s. The Protestant anticontraception revolution afoot is the adoption of the same arguments by a growing percentage of evangelicaldom.

Austin Ruse, head of the Catholic Family and Human Rights Institute, an ultraconservative group that lobbies the UN for profamily resolutions, as well as organizer of the influential Washington, D.C., National

Catholic Prayer Breakfast, speculates that "evangelicals have found that the best arguments for the things they believe in come from the Catholic Church." And indeed, the echoes resound, from what one Pope John Paul II eulogist termed the pontiff's lifelong crusade against a "liberty that enslaves" to the growing evangelical argument that modern women must choose between being slaves to righteousness and duty and being slaves to sin, selfish desires, and another man's time clock.

"They're responding to natural law," says Ruse, "a slow realization that there's something wrong here." Furthermore, Ruse, a convert to Catholicism with a zeal for purity that more liberal, cradle Catholics find suspect, thinks that evangelicals' changed convictions might reignite the issue among Catholics, many of whom practice birth control in spite of papal pronouncements. "I personally think that evangelicals will cast off contraception en masse and lead us Catholics back. I think they will teach us."

Such interfaith goodwill swells, at least publicly, over this issue, giving rise to a number of anticontraception organizations supported across denominational lines, including the Christian Medical and Dental Association, the Catholic Medical Association, Pharmacists for Life, the American Association of Pro-Life Obstetricians and Gynecologists, and the National Institute of Life Advocates. Groups like these popularize the scientifically unsupported argument that the birth control pill acts as an abortifacient and trade in controversial claims about a list of ailments they link to contraception. They also encourage OB-GYNs and other doctors to turn their practices into ministries for evangelism and spread a Christian family ethics and worldview. The effect of this can be seen in recent national policy crusades to codify a pharmacist's right to deny birth control prescriptions on religious or "conscience" grounds as an expansion of the traditional exemptions for doctors who don't want to perform abortions, or in the 2008 effort by the Department of Health and Human Services to label numerous forms of contraception, including birth control pills, emergency contraception, and IUDs, "abortion." And both abroad and at home, the anticontraception groups advocating such moves are at the head of efforts to restrict birth control availability.

One example of this is the work of former Bush administration FDA-appointee Dr. David Hager to prevent emergency contraception from gaining over-the-counter status. Hager, an antiabortion Christian Medical and Dental Association activist and evangelical OB-GYN, with a history of prescribing prayer and religious study for women's reproductive and menstrual difficulties, was appointed to the FDA's Reproductive Health Drugs Advisory Committee by President Bush in the fall of 2002. The appointment came just months after Hager petitioned the FDA to reverse its approval of mifepristone, which can be used either for early-term abortions or, in low doses, for immediate emergency contraception before pregnancy occurs. Once on the committee, in 2003, Hager almost single-handedly managed to obstruct the approval of "Plan B" emergency contraception for over-the-counter status by filing an opinion dissenting from the overwhelming approval of his fellow FDA colleagues. In a nearly unprecedented move (it had occurred only once before in the last fifty years), it was his minority opinion, representing four dissenters against twenty-three other committee members, that was picked up by the FDA, denying the OTC status.

Hager, incidentally, was brought to disgrace when his ex-wife, Linda Carruth Davis, went public with a description of his own family practice at home, where he interpreted the notion of Christian male headship as granting him unfettered sexual access to his wife's body. Hager's holy public persona, which earned him praise in Christian circles for doing righteous battle on behalf of the unborn, was supplemented, in a 2005 *Nation* article by Ayelish McGarvey, by the revelation that he had coerced his wife into undesired sex for years, culminating in a series of sexual assaults in which Hager raped and sodomized his unconscious wife, who suffered from narcolepsy.

Though Hager fell from any position of influence after the scandal, other advocates of advancing Christian and pronatalist theology through women's medicine abound. One such fellow-traveler is Byron Calhoun, a West Virginia neonatal specialist and the national medical advisor of the National Institute of Life Advocates, who argues that pregnant women should carry to term even fatally flawed pregnancies, certain to result in stillbirths, as a "God-honoring" way to demonstrate care and respect for the fetus. Calhoun is also president of the American Association of Pro-Life Obstetricians and Gynecologists (AAPLOG), a group that advances theories about links between abortion and breast cancer and psychological side-effects, such as depression or other symptoms of the controversial antiabortion diagnosis "postabortion syndrome." Through his work at the AAPLOG, Calhoun worked with Hager and others on a 1998 report about whether hormonal contraceptives are abortifacients.

AAPLOG also has named Dr. Bernard Nathanson, the culture-warring producer of the notorious antiabortion video *Silent Scream,* as an emeritus director of the organization.

Calhoun's own contributions to the movement are substantial. At a 2007 international meeting of the World Congress of Families organized by a coalition of U.S. religious right groups led by Allan Carlson, he described his own vision of life "beyond the contraceptive mentality" in his "Fruitful Family Manifesto." Calhoun's Manifesto reads like a description of the Quiverfull conviction: children are a blessing and the first end of marriage; the fruitful family is an autonomous unit and the government's main concern should be protecting it; family rights should trump individual rights; and public policy should encourage this hierarchy, reversing the influence of unfruitful "radical feminism" on society. Among his policy suggestions, Calhoun argues that schools should train children to be fruitful; no-fault divorce should be repealed; state programs of contraception and population control should be eradicated along with abortion, stem cell research, and in-vitro fertilization; tax breaks should be given to large families and childless citizens taxed higher; and the "state promotion of androgyny" through equal pay regulations for men and women should be replaced with laws encouraging employers to recognize men's and women's differing monetary needs by paying men—that is, fathers or prospective fathers—a "living wage."

In private practice, anticontraception doctors regularly turn away women looking for birth control. One of Calhoun's colleagues at the conference estimated that she has twelve conversations each day convincing patients that birth control use will lead to breast cancer. The other doctors and natural family planning advocates nodded in agreement, comparing their rates of refusal for birth control as well. Several speakers, including Dr. Dorota Czudowska and family counselor Jacek Pulikowski, both from Poland, argued that the use of contraceptives during sex had created a widespread distorted sexuality and an epidemic of frigid, headache-prone women: the experience of "relations with no future, incapable of giving life," they claimed, had instilled a deep fear of children into women, who were now too preoccupied with preventing pregnancy to enjoy sex. That the reverse has in fact been more women's experience—the inability to reliably control conception through Natural Family Planning negatively affecting their sexual lives—was not discussed by the panelists.

Profamily arguments like Calhoun's are informed by nearly a decade of interfaith activism, including growing Protestant political activism in the past several years as well as Mormon policy and academic work. The latter is exemplified by an influential study by Salt Lake City doctor Joseph B. Stanford, published in 2000 in the *Archives of Family Medicine,* a now-defunct American Medical Association journal. Stanford, a Mormon and the father of seven boys, based his argument for birth control's "postfertilization effect" of preventing an egg from implanting itself in the uterus on a new definition of pregnancy; he asserted that pregnancy occurs at fertilization rather than the medically recognized definition as beginning with implantation. Stanford also published his arguments in the conservative Catholic magazine *First Things,* an intellectual publishing platform that has dedicated itself to the pronatalist message, regularly featuring articles by advocates of large families and opponents of contraception.

But outside of such medical subtleties, a quieter opposition to birth control, and one with less use for discussion over uterine lining, preceded the political debut at the "Contraception Is Not the Answer" conference by years.

CHAPTER TWELVE

The Bible and Birth Control

Among the first contemporary Protestants advancing the theory that contraception is anathema to Scripture was Charles Provan, an independent Pennsylvania printer, lay theologian, and father to ten until his death in 2007. In 1989, Provan, whom both Pride and the Hesses name as an inspiration, published *The Bible and Birth Control,* which has been called the authoritative source for Protestants seeking scriptural guidance on contraception. In it, Provan traced Protestant opposition to birth control to three main scriptural bases: Psalm 127; the Genesis command to "be fruitful and multiply"; and the biblical story of Onan, slain by God for spilling his seed on the ground. This story is seen by Provan and the Protestant forefathers—Martin Luther, John Calvin, and John Wesley—whose commentaries he drew on, as a form of birth control. (Castigating the "contraceptive mentality" among the elites of his own day, Luther called birth control an "inhuman attitude, which is worse than barbarous," and lamented, "How many girls there are who prevent conception and kill and expel tender fetuses, although procreation is the work of God!") Provan argued that God punished Onan for his deliberate infertility, rather than for his disobedience to God, through a comparison study he made of sexual sins detailed in the Bible. Though all of the sins are condemned, only five are punished with death: male homosexuality, bestiality committed by either a man or a woman, intercourse with menstruating women, and Onan's withdrawal: capital offenses, Provan says, because all are intentionally sterile forms of sex, wasting the sperm of man or animal. Female homosexuality, conversely, is not punished by death because, though wicked, it doesn't spill semen.

"Birth control does the very same thing," writes Provan, "and so is likewise under the curse of God."

Provan, who lived most of his life in Monangahela, Pennsylvania, a picturesque village planted among the rolling hills southwest of Pittsburgh, was a heavy, slightly unkempt man who ran a printing press, Zimmer Printing, in the middle of town. When I met him in the fall of 2006, he wore a blue shirt with a pocket full of pens and suspenders holding up large blue jeans that stopped at his ankle. He had arched eyebrows over frantic light brown eyes, blue, ink-rimmed fingernails, and a half-inch of grayish-white beard on his chin. Gregarious and seeking to please, Provan considered it the duty of those who hold controversial opinions to explain them to skeptics; he had many to explain.

Amid the cascading mess in his office—printing supplies, half-repaired machines, and boxes of filled orders: raffle tickets, wholesale seafood pricelists, and political flyers for local candidates ("He cooked you hot dogs in Vietnam! He'll cook your drug dealers in Charleroi!")—were stacks of Provan's own publications, some still in galleys. They included the results of another of Provan's self-styled investigations: his study of gas chambers at Auschwitz, a complicated entry in the annals of Holocaust denial and revisionist history. Provan, in addition to being one of the preeminent anticontraception figures of modern Protestantism, was also notably a Holocaust revisionist who later came to believe in the existence of the genocide.

His study, which caused a stir far surpassing its humble appearance, was targeted at a favored revisionist theory for denying the mass murder in the Polish death camps: the gas chambers at Auschwitz hadn't had the proper holes for disseminating poison gas. Provan did indeed find holes at Auschwitz, but he'd begun to suspect that the Holocaust might have been real even before his trip to Poland's concentration camps. ("The best vacation I ever took," he told me, displaying a chronic tin ear for the socially unacceptable.) He'd become convinced after conducting an experiment in his home with several of his ten children. Provan, a large man, had long doubted reports of the number of people crammed into gas chambers for extermination: seven hundred to eight hundred people, half children, pushed into a 256-square-foot room. But one night, while rereading the eyewitness account of Kurt Gerstein, an SS officer who testified in 1945 to the atrocities in the camps before committing suicide, Provan was struck again by the makeup of the dead: half children. He gathered his own brood around him, had them strip to their underwear, and arranged them inside a scaled-down model chamber composed of cabinets and dresser drawers, explaining to his wife, "I'm gonna see how many kids can fit in a gas chamber!" When he saw that they fit, he started to cry.

Over the next several years, he became a gadfly among Holocaust revisionists, publishing essays on the existence of gas chambers in revisionist Christian newspapers and disrupting a revisionist conference with a speech that countered the denier's slogan, "No Holes, No Holocaust." Since the "holes" of the Holocaust gas chambers were real, Provan explained, it was time to take witness testimony at face value. His former allies in the revisionist movement promptly turned on Provan, dismissing his findings as the ramblings of a "fringe hillbilly."

Provan's internal contradictions didn't end there, though. A blue-collar contrarian fundamentalist as well as the former local Democratic Party committeeman, Provan's fierce ideology was delivered in person with a steady punctuation of nervous banter: "Does that make sense?" "You know what I mean?"

Provan grew up in Rust Belt Pennsylvania and, for a large portion of his boyhood, in a heavily Jewish Pittsburgh suburb where, Provan says without explanation for his later betrayal, most of his friends were Jewish. He was the son of fundamentalist John Bircher parents, a doctor father and a stay-at-home mother, who sent him to work for a family acquaintance at Zimmer Printing when he was sixteen years old. Later, they sent him to Bob Jones University in Greenville, South Carolina, the academy of old-school fundamentalism founded by a Bob Jones, Sr., a friend to populist preacher William Jennings Bryan, of Scopes trial fame, to quell his mother's fears that he would become a drug addict. (Provan, whose experience of the sixties was psychedelic in music if in nothing else—calling me one early morning to tell me the name of a favorite forgotten band, Strawberry Alarm Clock—laughed at the memory of his mother's concern: he'd never even drunk a beer in his life.)

There, Provan, ever an antiauthoritarian, became involved with what Bob Jones, Jr., then university president, castigated as a group of campus renegades he called the "flower people." The flower people weren't hippies, but Calvinists following the principles of TULIP (total depravity, unconditional election, limited atonement, irresistible grace, and perseverance of the saints): harbingers of the Reformed movement that has since swept Protestantism. In a story that even Provan realized sounds like a joke, he set about to find this underground movement of Calvinists bucking the "BoJo" fundamentalist norm, and he befriended the student leader of the movement, Scott Greene. Greene, a revolutionary in Provan's eyes, took him for car rides to explain the five points of Calvinism and lent him the neo-Puritan text *Today's Gospel: Authentic or Synthetic* by Walter J. Chantry. Provan, already twice-baptized, was finally saved. At Greene's prompting, he began an exhaustive study of the question: Is it right for people to not want to have a kid that God wants them to have?

Provan looked to Calvin, the father of his new faith, for answers. But in Calvin's commentaries, Provan found puzzling holes, as many versions of Protestant commentaries published in the late 1800s and early 1900s had excised the sexual doctrines laid out by the fathers of the Reformation. The Onan passage on spilled semen that Provan would come to rely on was marked by an asterisk, explaining that text had been omitted. Similarly, other passages on sexual matters were missing, including explanation of what proof of virginity a bride could offer her husband. ("Do you want me to tell you what it means?" Provan asked, with a mischievousness more naïve than leering.) In the end, to satisfy his curiosity, Provan went to the libraries of Pittsburgh synagogues and looked up the unexplained passages in Jewish commentaries.

Through this study, and Provan's transfer from Bob Jones to the University of Pittsburgh, he came to notice others moving in the same, strange theological circles as himself, including Herman Otten, the publisher of the liberal-bashing Missouri newspaper *Christian News* and a member of the archconservative Lutheran Church–Missouri Synod. Otten also had seven children, and Provan decided to call Otten up one day to find out, with his typical gee-whiz bluntness, "Pastor Otten, how come you got so many kids?"

Provan himself had since become married—proposing to his wife, Carol, a student in his Baptist adult Sunday school, on their first date—and had started his own large family. When he'd told his parents he didn't believe in birth control anymore, his father, a doctor who prescribed contraception but later came to oppose it, told him the only wife he'd find would be a "stupid Polish Catholic girl." Instead, Provan laughed, he married a Hungarian, and through his wife's appeal, turned to homeschooling. In 2003, the Provan's oldest son, Matthias, drowned in a creek north of Pittsburgh, a fact that Provan handled with the same ease as he described the deadly sins of Scripture. ("How long ago did Matthias drop?" Provan called across the shop to his third-youngest son, Tobias, brushing aside condolences with a fatalistic decree: "I'm not in charge of that, and neither are you.")

So when Otten shot back at Provan, "What do you mean, how come I got so many kids?" Provan assured him he had the same convictions and wanted to know if Otten's reasoning corresponded with his. The two became friends. Otten published Provan's first anti–birth control article, and Provan grew sympathetic to both Otten's firebrand conservatism and the *Christian News'* supplemental focus on Holocaust denial.

Unwinding, or even identifying, the strands that connect the anti–birth control movement and the ideology that informs racist thinking such as Holocaust revisionism is dizzying. Partly this has to do with the widespread history of manipulating population as a means of cultural domination, whether through limiting one group's freedom or ability to reproduce or mandating higher fertility from another group.

Population is a preoccupation for many Quiverfull believers who, like China watchers, trade statistics on the falling white birthrate in European countries such as Germany and France. Every ethnic conflict becomes evidence for their worldview: Muslim riots in France, Latino immigration in California, Sharia law in Canada. The motivations aren't always racist, but the subtext of "race suicide" is often there. It's little surprise that this focus can lend itself to other, more explicit forms of racial thinking.

Another of Provan's self-published books, *The Church Is Israel Now,* an argument for Christian "replacement theology," holds that the Christian Church has replaced Jews as God's chosen people—His Israel—after God grew angry with sinful Jews. Christian reviewers condemned the book for promoting a form of theological anti-Semitism that could further alienate Jews from would-be Christian allies. At the same time, Provan, even as he was a vocal Holocaust "doubter," offered a modernized antiabortion argument, one being put to great use by globally minded anticontraception activists: that birth control is a eugenicist movement intended to slow or extinguish minority births in favor of more white babies. "The greatest people on earth," Provan sneered, in sarcastic imitation of some conceived aristocratic racists. That this is a paper tiger argument seems well supported by the absurdity of a Holocaust revisionist arguing against birth control on antiracist grounds, but Provan's counterintuitive adoption of a liberal issue seems as prescient of contemporary Christian right politics as his early promotion of Quiverfull theology.

Provan's former revisionist colleagues inhabit a fringe world, but such, until recently, was the world of anticontraception activists. Provan, though an early father of the movement, wasn't up to date on its growing success. "The book I wrote is kind of known for being a hardcore punch in the face," he told me happily. "The Hess book is known for being more user-friendly. But mine is more, 'Here's a reason...,' 'here's a reason...,' 'here's another reason....'" He was pleased to hear that the Hesses and Pride admire him ("I like that. Oh!") and pleased to hear anecdotes of young Christian women demanding anticontraception doctors when they marry and embark on sexual lives.

Provan, as a lay theologian, took up the anti–birth control cause early, while prominent conservative theologians and fundamentalist leaders avoided the topic. Modern pronatalist leaders such as Allan Carlson have suggested that a number of the most prominent Christian leaders may have remained silent because they have themselves limited their family size. Many of the old guard could not lead by example, but that's changing now; a number of leading Christians have families of five, eight, and ten children. Now they are arguing what Provan said early on: all roads lead back to contraception. "Most any subject ties into it one way or another. Someone in church the other day was saying there's hardly any kids in church anymore. Well, that's all over the place. I'm mostly concerned about birth control within the church, but it does apply to everyone. I think Europe is dying because of it."

Non-Christians might not understand this duty, Provan allowed, seeing non-Christian sexuality as "a root animal reaction" between people who don't understand the holy cause and purpose of sex; Christian women, however, should know better, he said. They should know that Paul promised they were saved through childbirth. It's a verse of some scriptural controversy for Protestants, who balk at the "Catholic" notion that anyone can earn their salvation through good works, including childbirth. But Provan's side step around this issue is familiar.

"If a woman is truly saved, she will prove her faith and her salvation by pursuing good works which are (according to Jesus) inevitable for a true Christian. The pathway of teaching doctrine to husbands or ordering them around is not open to women. The pathway of obedience, which leads to eternal salvation, is (for married women) accompanied by childbearing if possible.... Those who reject childbearing reject the good works which Paul says accompany salvation." In other words, if women don't accept their full quiver of children, they might not really be saved. And even if they are, Provan quoted Martin Luther's qualification of their salvation: they are not saved for freedom or license, but for bearing children. Provan further explained the distinction to me:

"If you are a follower of Christ, then not only do you believe in this guy named Jesus, but [you also believe] that it produces fruits in your life. The works are necessary, not as a grounds of your salvation, but as its fruit. So I can't go to heaven by saying I printed raffle tickets for everyone and never cheated anyone. The answer is that I belong in heaven because I had faith in Christ that produced works in accordance with that faith. So there is no such thing as a Christian that has true faith but does not produce good works. Some Christians might be weak Christians. But the unifying factor is that the faith in your heart produces action. So the woman who is saved by childbirth is not saved because she had sex with her husband and everything is normal. She is saved because, out of faith in Christ, she is doing what is her duty."

CHAPTER THIRTEEN

Trust and Obey

No Protestant denomination accepted birth control until 1930, when the Anglican Church endorsed contraceptive use among married couples. Conservative Protestants at the time dissented, with the Missouri Synod branch of the Lutheran Church (LCMS)—which had long accused the Birth Control Federation of America of covering "the country with slime" and had called Margaret Sanger a "she-devil"—recalling the declaration of St. Augustine, that "contraception makes a prostitute out of the wife and an adulterer out of the husband." Over several decades, though, many members of conservative churches took up contraceptive use, and eventually, their denominations approved the practice (as the LCMS eventually did in 1981). Quiverfull author Rachel Scott sees the moment of first approval, at the Anglican Church's 1930 Lambeth contraception decision, as the beginning of a biblically prophesied era of "seventy years in Babylon." In this case, it was a spiritual Babylon that declared children to be a "choice," and which ended (rather inexactly) with 9/11, seventy-one years later.

The fall of the twin towers is a popular turning point to Quiverfull believers. Becca Campos, a thirty-four-year-old Nebraska mother of five who works as an administrator for a sterilization reversal ministry, Blessed Arrows, explains: "The Bible says that if a nation humbles itself and prays together, God will turn the hearts of the fathers back to the children. After 9/11, people started looking inward." Campos sees the schedule change of her 2001 tubal ligation reversal in Mexico, from September tenth to the eighth, as God's provision that she shouldn't be stuck south of the border during her recovery, unable to board a plane home. Myopia aside, though, the references aren't so much Falwellian bombast—9/11 as God's judgment on a sinful country—as the magical thinking that goes along with a faith strong enough to convince poor families struggling to make ends meet as it is that God will provide for them unequivocally.

"Lean not on your own understanding," Quiverfull mom Tracey Moore tells me, describing the scriptural foundation she discovered for Quiverfull after following the advice of formerly Amish families in Kentucky. They'd held on to their family beliefs and told her to check a concordance and read what the Bible says about children: they're a blessing, a reward, an inheritance. Don't worry about money—the Moores have never had much of it, and they've mowed lawns and been jacks-of-all-trades when husband David was out of work—because God will provide for his flock.

Nancy Campbell similarly warns her readers not to overthink the Quiverfull decision. One's own understanding will buckle under the pressure of living faithful lives. Reason-based analysis can't support the acts of faith that God requires, whether a man leaving a secure job to follow God into a new Christian ministry or mission, or a woman seeking another child when she's prone, as many Quiverfull women are, to pregnancies that require strict bed rest, or when logic would dictate that she's giving birth to another mouth that she cannot feed. In other words, don't trust your instincts, but follow—trust, lean on—the directives of God, and through your faithfulness, you will be rewarded.

"When we lean to our own understanding, we lean to what suits us and our particular circumstances," writes Campbell. "We lean toward selfishness.... Although we may feel that 'our way' is best for us now, it is not always the best in the long run. Obedience to God's ways, even when we feel they don't suit us and it is contrary to everything we want to do, will always lead us to the ultimate blessing.

"The bottom line is that we will know the truth if we walk in obedience. If we don't, we can be led into deception. Disobedience leads to deception. Obedience leads to truth! Obedience is always related to blessing.... The truth of the old hymn still stands: Trust and obey, for there's no other way / To be happy in Jesus, but to trust and obey." There's something bleak in this reference, taken from a Presbyterian hymn of the late 1800s that commands obedience to God through all of life's trials, small and large, and trust that God is managing all areas of your life for the best. In part, it's a neat summation of women's role in the conservative, patriarchal church: obedient to their authorities and compelled to trust that the men they are subordinate to do in fact know best. But it's also a grim picture of the believer's relationship with Christ, the coupling on which Christian marriage is supposed to be modeled: even with their Savior, the love of Christian women's lives, the only path to peace, the only way to "be happy in Jesus," is through submission and unquestioning trust.

To many literalist Christians, though, this is believing: trusting that God is invested in every detail of their lives and that He takes care of His own. And in its most innocuous self-explanations, this is what Quiverfull is about: faith, pure and simple. Faith that God won't give a woman more children than she can handle, and faith that by opening themselves up to receive multiple "blessings," they will bring God's favor upon them in other areas of life as well: their husbands will get better jobs; God will send a neighbor with a sack of used children's clothes just when the soles on Johnny's shoes fall out. God hands out provision according to the size of their faith, and the latter can be estimated by how many children they trust God to give them. God deals with their hearts about birth control, and if they submit, they are cared for.

The Hesses agree: "Remember what faith actually is: the assurance of things hoped for, the conviction of things not seen." In light of Abraham's sacrifice, "why then should it be so difficult for us to believe, entirely by faith alone, that if we sacrifice on the altar our own plans about what size family we want, God will work His plan for our good and His glory?" Or, in starker terms, the Hesses say their argument really boils down to whether or not a believer accepts that God is sovereign, and therefore in charge of their entire lives, including their reproductive lives: Lord of all or not Lord at all.

Rachel Scott likewise writes that after she and her husband became open to the idea of more children, God began blessing them financially; He doubled her husband's salary with the birth of another child, a gift of providence that they never would have experienced had they followed their own judgment and stopped having children. The key, Scott says, is making the leap of faith first, not waiting for God to line up the ideal circumstances: "God never brings the increase until after the child is born." The undercurrent to all these claims about the rewards for faith, literal and spiritual rewards, is a pivotal and pervasive message to women: the constantly reinforced idea that they are never in authority to know what they can handle and that God, or those God has placed over them, knows best.

Though Scott brings a peculiarly literal timeline to the equation, the general principle—submit and be cared for—is a fitting summary of the non–faith-based rationales for the Quiverfull lifestyle as well. While many Quiverfull families are solidly working class, with lower incomes, even those in the middle-income brackets struggle with the financial challenges of caring for a ten-person family. But for many Quiverfull mothers, this struggle is still preferable to the alternatives they see society offering to women of their class, alternatives they see as the fruit of secular feminism. For poorer women, the feminist fight for job equality won them no career path but the right to pink-collar labor, as a housekeeper, a waitress, a clerk. The sexual revolution brought them not self-exploration and fulfillment, but rather loosened the social restraints that bound men to the household as husbands and fathers. Even for women who stayed in the home, the incidence of women in the workplace led employers to stop offering a "family wage" that could sustain both parents and children.

Mary Pride puts it in biblical terms—feminism made wage-slaves out of women who had once been slaves to God; it made "unpaid prostitutes" out of women who should have been godly mothers and wives—but the economic undercurrent is the same. As social scientist Phillip Longman says, "The trade-offs of feminism weren't what they thought they were. For most women, and men, work is not particularly fulfilling. They don't want to drop off their kids at some sub-standard day care to rush over on the bus to clean someone else's house."

As sociologists or feminist theorists would summarize, many housewives and stay-at-home mothers have instead opted for an older bargain. Angus McLaren, author of *A History of Contraception: From Antiquity to the Present Day,* argues that point regarding the leagues of women filling the antiabortion movement. "There is a logic in such women's thinking. Their family structure is based on a bargain between a husband who provides financial support and a wife who in return provides sex and child care. Easily accessible abortion and contraception, they fear, undercut the argument that a woman can only risk providing sexual favors if guaranteed the protection of a traditional marriage."

But there's something deeper here than standard antifeminist back-lash. While economic and cultural complaints may attract believers to Quiverfull, conviction, and the momentum of a growing movement, are what sustain them.

Pronatalism and anti–birth control "encouragement" is where Nancy Campbell's Above Rubies ministry really comes into its own. *Be Fruitful and Multiply*, a Vision Forum publication with an introduction written by Doug Phillips, argues that, "an evil world is the very reason for having children. We train them to be the 'light' and the 'salt' in this dark world. We train and sharpen them to be 'arrows' for God's army." It was Satan's successful plan, Phillips argues in the introduction, to destroy Christian life in the womb and to limit God's army by limiting the godly seed that Christians could have produced. "If the Christian Church had not listened to the humanistic lies of the enemy and limited their families, the army of God would be more powerful in this hour. The enemy's camp would be trembling. Instead they are laughing."

Carmon Friedrich, whose writing on Buried Treasures encourages large families as well as submissive wives, is one of the numerous women living Quiverfull lifestyles who does not use the term but who otherwise affirms the aims and motivations of the movement. Strongly influenced by Mary Pride, she agrees that Christians taking dominion of the nation through the raising of a large family is indeed the primary role God has planned for women and men. However, she protests, the military meta-phors employed by Quiverfull followers that outside observers pick up on are singled out from the sea of metaphors that God offers in the Bible to describe the dominion role for his believers. It's a conveniently fright-ening focus, she politely chastises me, for an observer frightened about "Christian breeders."

> The military metaphor is only one of many metaphors God uses to communicate His truth to us mere mortals. Yes, there is a real battle of competing ideas about reality, but there's also a relationship with our Creator, which He says is akin to a marriage, with the Church as the Bride and Christ as the Groom. There are agrarian analogies, banking scenarios, pictures painted with food, athletic references to running races and winning a prize, philosophical references, and a zillion other wonderful and rich ideas we are given to convey who God is and what He requires of us.... If you have any acquaintance with classical litera-

ture and history, you will realize that a military story is about good guys and bad guys.... Christians just happen to understand that there are battles which have eternal importance, and that one doesn't really get to choose whether or not to participate.

Despite Friedrich's description of the wealth of other analogies on hand for Quiverfull activists, it is war that they most choose as their recurring theme. Nancy Campbell lists in detail the weapons of war Christian parents need to craft out of their children, "sharpening" their offspring for battle: arrows that are polished, piercing, scattering, sticking fast, sharp, bright, light giving, going abroad, destroying, hitting the mark, shooting, on fire, delivering. If that alone does not extinguish the placid image of Christian broods as peacefully rising bread, Campbell removes all doubt: "What were they trained for? For war! We cannot live with our head in the sand. We are in a war. Our children must be trained for battle. They must be trained to stand and fight against the enemy of their souls. They must be trained to be warriors for God."

Rachel Scott further clarifies the metaphor: "Children are our ammunition in the spiritual realm to whip the enemy! Scripture says that one of God's people can chase one thousand enemies, and two can put ten thousand to flight," she writes. "These special arrows were handcrafted by the warrior himself and were carefully fashioned to achieve the purpose of annihilating the enemy."

"Oh what a vision," Campbell writes, "to invade the earth with mighty sons and daughters who have been trained and prepared for God's divine purposes."

It's a vision she espouses through her magazine, retreats, speaking engagements, and books on the subject, including *A Change of Heart,* a collection of sterilization-reversal testimonials, *God's Vision for Families,* and *The Power of Motherhood,* which describes at length woman's "distinguishing identity" in her womb and the need to protect the womb from attack by abortion, birth control, sterilization, unnecessary hysterectomies, and curses, such as past sins, which include complaining about one's reproductive organs or menstrual cycles.

There's a point where the emphasis on the womb's sacred potential, and the promise of destiny tied up in childbirth, approaches mystical proportions.

Scott, an Orlando-area mother to seven who was raised Catholic and converted to evangelical Christianity, describes herself as a "one-woman Quiverfull activist." She explains the night she was brought to the Quiverfull conviction, after the birth of her fourth child, her third "oops" baby due to birth control failures. The prospect of tuition for four consumed her husband, Christopher, and their pastor was urging vasectomy. But that night, Christopher saw a warrior angel in a dream, a "large, worrying, warrior angel" with a flaming sword that he pointed at Christopher's genitals, telling him, "Do not change God's plan." In Scott's book, *Birthing God's Mighty Warriors,* the angel is even more specific, telling Christopher, "Do not abort God's plan." Scott's husband awoke her, gray and shaking, "the color of death," unable to speak but to repeat: "The angel, the sword. The angel, the sword."

While Scott pays tribute to the groundwork of the Quiverfull movement built by Pride's books and the homeschooling movement, she distinguishes herself from the "hard line" of Quiverfull believers, whom she sees as holding each other to purity tests. And at times, she says, she doesn't even care for the Quiverfull label, calling it an old-fashioned term that could turn people off. She prefers a cross-denominational approach—she herself works with the ultraconservative Catholic group Regnum Christi (a politically influential organization that includes among its members Cathy Cleaver Ruse, wife of Catholic Family and Human Rights Institute's Austin Ruse)—and a broad focus on the coming family revival.

"Like all good buildings, the foundation needs to be strong. But the Bible says, 'All men come.' The foundation's been laid and now God's starting to change people's minds, both inside and outside of the church. Before the end times, the Bible says the family will be restored, whether they're in church or out of church." But though Scott tells me that she's interested in promoting large families across religious lines, even to Buddhists, pagans, or nonbelievers such as myself, and that she's only interested in educating people about God's plan for their happiness—through children—this is belied by her writing.

Along the range of Quiverfull sensibilities that reflects the various concerns and styles of Christians—from charismatic to evangelical to fundamentalist to Reformed—*Birthing God's Mighty Warriors* treads in dark and fearful theological waters. Scott considers herself a "very prophetic person" and delves deep into the idea of spiritual battle against

Satan's dark forces when rallying the would-be parents of God's warriors. She expresses a vision of a coming generation of "anointed" children who will sweep the earth with a great revival, "march[ing] in unison," caring nothing for the world but "consumed with the things of the Lord."

"The children we are birthing right now," she writes, "are the beginnings of this end-time army of worshippers who will prepare the way of the Lord."

Seeing the current era as the end times, Scott sees the revival of the family that will preface Christ's return as the paramount issue in the church today. To that end, she reinterprets the Ten Commandments solely through a Quiverfull lens that focuses on turning family planning over to God—a matter of trust and obedience foundational to understanding His other commands. As such, the worship of idols becomes minding any other considerations for family planning besides God's wishes; adultery becomes the increased temptation facing couples who are defiling their marriage with contraception; and murder becomes all forms of preventing conception or pregnancy, ranging from a bad attitude about one's menstrual cycle to contraception, abortion, and sterilization, which Scott surprisingly considers the ultimate sin—worse than abortion, for its potential to prevent not one birth but many.

Sterilization, Scott writes, is also dangerous ground because it "takes us very close to the realms of witchcraft, divination, idolatry, and fortune-telling.... The reasoning involved to justify the sterilization decision mimics the process that psychics use to get their information. Both must speculate upon a future that God says is His.... God's word calls predicting the future witchcraft and divination." It's also like witchcraft, Scott argues, for rebelling against God's design by altering the functioning of the reproductive system He built.

Women who get their tubes tied or whose husbands get vasectomies are lining up not just for holy judgment, but a range of earthly consequences as well, including a generational curse of miscarriage on the land and on their descendents; a painful and difficult menopause (which Scott claims was, in the past, a peaceful time of transition after a job well done for women who hadn't controlled their fertility); depression, as sterilized women "no longer feel that they have any use"; and the collapse of their marriages, as husbands don't find their infertile wives worth having sex with, since they can no longer be "conquered" through pregnancy.

There is some hope though, and Scott includes at the end of each chapter a series of prayers to be used for specific afflictions, such as the plague of miscarriages Scott sees around her, caused by women's various reproductive sins. In the case of miscarriage, those sins could be becoming too worldly and adopting society's ways by seeing secular doctors and taking secular contraceptives; a woman using the pill and thus opening herself up to the devil; past abortions or premarital sex; the generational curse of relatives, such as grandparents who'd used birth control and who will need to repent of their own witchcraft; personal fears about one's health and insufficient faith; feelings of rejection toward children; or mocking Christian leaders and televangelists. Each miscarriage-inducing sin comes with a prayer of repentance from ungodly activity and an affirmation: "I place the future back in Your hands, and I repent for desiring to ever control [my life and future] in this way. I do not desire to be close to the witchcraft realm." Scott suggests further that churches begin to look into specific fertility-related services, such as Bible studies looking into the sin-causes of congregants' miscarriages and hysterectomies, or, as her own church does every Mother's Day, surrounding infertile couples to pray for the restoration of their fertility or regeneration of the wives' wombs.

When this mentality, that infertile women have no remaining purpose in life, bleeds into the church consciousness, a despair for lack of babies becomes the norm, not the acceptance of God's will that Quiverfull believers are supposed to represent. One Quiverfull mother told me that the attitude of, "If we were really spiritual, we'd have a lot of kids," has led to women's meetings where she's seen mothers to a paltry quiver of three or four children weep and plead to God to give them more. On Quiverfull and biblical womanhood discussion boards, screen names such as Praying for More are commonplace.

The charges of witchcraft that Scott raises against unsubmissive, unmotherly women go farther still in the words of Michael Woroniecki, the itinerant preacher who mentored and was in authority over a sadly famous Quiverfull couple, Andrea and Rusty Yates. All five of the Yates children were killed in 2001 when Andrea, suffering from severe postpartum depression as well as mental illness likely exacerbated by the teachings she was receiving from Woroniecki, drowned her children to save their souls. Woroniecki, raised as a charismatic Catholic but rejected from Catholic seminaries for excessive zeal and what seminary professors took to be a harsh judgment of his fellow students, is an independent fundamentalist preacher who evangelizes from the bus he lives in with his wife and six children. Woroniecki believes that only he and his family are saved among all the world's Christians and non-Christians alike, and he's traveled the country, surfacing in places such as the conservative campus of Utah's Brigham Young University, to hurl abuse at "hypocritical" conservative Christian students not living as true believers.

After a falling out between Woroniecki and Rusty Yates, Woroniecki reinforced his particularly vicious misogynistic theology in a series of pamphlets he sent to Andrea Yates, condemning her as a character he called Modern Mother Worldly, whose children ran amok and who was cast into hell for her failures as a wife and mother. In another pamphlet sent to Yates, titled *The Witch and the Whimp* [sic], he railed against women's innate "witch" natures. The pamphlet was illustrated with a crude drawing of a witch in a pointed hat dangling a naked, puppet-strung man from the end of her broom: an inherently rebellious Jezebel ruling over modern, passive wimps of men. The pamphlet read,

> The word of God is very sobering when it warns, "For rebellion is as the sin of witchcraft, and stubbornness is iniquity and adultery." Although rebellion is common to all, the word of God continually emphasizes the particularly destructive power latent in "the contentious woman." Witchcraft, as seen in the nature of Eve, is the underlying AT-TITUDE of contention or insistence to HAVE YOUR WAY. Witchcraft is cooperating with Satanic motivation to manipulate, control and rule.... This is the way of the adulterous woman. She eats and wipes her mouth and says, "I have done no wrong." (Pr. 30:20). God says, "I find more bitter than death the woman WHOSE HEART IS SNARES AND NETS AND HER HANDS ARE CHAINS. Whoever is pleasing to God shall escape from her." ... You may be married or single, brazen or reserved, striking or simple, a pagan or a Christian, but as a daughter of Eve you are born with the nature of a witch. No matter how blatant or subtle, "God is not mocked."

A further tract sent to Yates shortly before she killed her children emphasized women's helper role as something more than mere wifehood. "It means a servant, single or married. If a girl does not know how to be a servant then she is learning how to be a ruler. It's called witchcraft."

Though the Woroniecki's theology castigated even the most fundamentalist of fellow Christians as insufficiently faithful—not renouncing housing and employment to live as street preachers, as did the Woronieckis—they share substantial common ground with Quiverfull families in terms of desiring as many children as God or nature allows, their emphasis on patriarchy and rigid gender divisions, and in their sense of being a remnant of God's holy few and elect. It's a similar impulse, carried to a far extreme, as that which leads many Quiverfull families to break off from churches to form home churches more devoted to righteousness and doctrine than their lax denominations.

Likewise, the teachings of Carol Balizet, head of the obscure, Tampa, Florida–based Home in Zion Ministries and author of a number of books on Christian home life, motherhood, and home birthing, represents another fringe Quiverfull submovement. Balizet condemns many conventional institutions, including banks, public schools, "statist" government, and denominational churches, but she saves her harshest judgment for institutional medicine: a bastion of pagan religion, where doctors serve as "high priests." These priests, Balizet argues, make pagan sacrifices through their surgical incisions, so that through cesarean-section births, the newborn is delivered, as it were, directly to Satan.

Balizet further believes that medical ailments from blindness to warts are brought on by spiritual missteps including idol worship and witchcraft. Adultery will cause menstrual disorders, and a woman rejecting her pregnancy is the real cause of morning sickness. Balizet urges Christian mothers to deliver their babies at home, a movement she advocated through her book *Born in Zion,* which gained access to a wide audience when Nancy Campbell's Above Rubies ministry endorsed the book.

Such teachings, though not representative of Quiverfull, do point to the antiestablishment, separatist, or agrarian off-the-grid ethos of many believers. And homebirthing isn't just the relic of extremists like Balizet, but a submovement within Quiverfull for families hoping to make the birthing experience a part of the productive, independent home as well. For the later of Tracey Moore's fourteen childbirths, husband David learned how to "catch the babies" at home. The Moores had gone from conventional hospital births to midwife-assisted births at home to the small but growing movement of unattended home births. This represents the arc of yet another logical extreme of the movement, which has a naturalistic bent that overlaps with back-to-the-land hippie counterculture in some ways. It's a deliciously amusing irony to some Quiverfull moms, who stake out their territory of natural pregnancy in the odd company of feminist doulas and naturopaths opposed, as they are, to high rates of hospital cesarean sections.

Above Rubies does not make the same claims as Balizet regarding the medical establishment, but as critics at the Australian cult-watch organization Concerned Christian Growth Ministries, Inc., have argued, "The Above Rubies emphasis on the importance of wombs, breasts, motherhood, and fertility, the judgmental comments against all forms of contraception ... provide a ready groundwork for the acceptance of the more extreme and bizarre claims of Carol Balizet." And indeed, Above Rubies, which is very active in Campbell's former countries of New Zealand and Australia as well, sold the book at camps and retreats and listed *Born in Zion* on its Web site's "Resource Materials" section with the plug, "A book about home birth that will inspire your faith. Even if you are not interested in home birth, this book is a great faith builder."

The endorsement didn't last. In 2001, Balizet's antipathy to medicine brought her name and work into a tragic scandal when a thirty-one-year-old Australian mother of five died following Balizet's proscription of hospitals during an unassisted, unattended "Zion home birth." The mother suffered severe hemorrhaging and swelling during the birth, but received no medical attention. After several weeks of extreme pain, she died. Balizet's teachings were subsequently publicized and derided as cultish and irresponsible, and Above Rubies' Australian director, Val Stares, author of books including *Accepting Our Husband's Authority,* appeared on national news to give a tepid defense of the book, arguing that the mother's death was not necessarily a "failure" of Balizet's philosophy but rather showed the mother had been "seeking truth and walking in faith." Above Rubies in Australia and the United States later declared they would no longer carry Balizet's book.

Though arguments such as Scott's and Balizet's are particularly supernatural, they're not anomalous. F. Carolyn Graglia, author of *Domestic Tranquility: A Brief Against Feminism,* sounds similar notes about women who choose individual goals over motherhood. Graglia, wife to judge Lino Graglia, a conservative Catholic whose controversial comments regarding race and affirmative action cost him a federal judgeship under the Reagan administration, holds a couple of impressive degrees herself and worked as a lawyer before quitting to raise her children. But she describes a fear as primal as Christopher Scott's castration fears, and one far more prevalent in Quiverfull literature: the fear of drying up, withering away, becoming an empty skin—fates, incidentally, that both the Prides and the Hesses list as side effects of birth control, leaving women wrinkled and haggard. Graglia writes:

> When I first began reading feminists' scornful denunciation of my own life and their exhortation that I return to market production—in [Betty] Friedan's words, that I juggle pregnancies and turn my children and home over to nannies and housekeepers—my stomach would turn and I would be suffused with a chilling dread. Seeking the source of my fear, I realized it came from my perception that what the woman's movement was asking me to become seemed, to me at least, something like the witch figure described by Margaret Mead. This figure, said Mead, is "a statement of human fear of what can be done to mankind by the woman who denies or is forced to deny childbearing, child cherishing. She is seen as able to withhold herself from men's desire, and so to veil the nexus with life itself. 'She may ride away leaving her empty skin by her husband's side.'"
>
> A woman like me believes that if she conscientiously fulfills the demands of market production, she will leave a much-desiccated, if not wholly empty, skin by her husband's side....I saw feminism as a force beckoning me to ride away from husband and children—not on a broomstick, but on a briefcase.

CHAPTER FOURTEEN

Blessed Arrows

For women who've started down the path to such unnatural and witchy barrenness by getting a sterilization for either themselves or their husband, there is hope—if not of conceiving again successfully, at least of making amends to God for taking your fertility into your own hands.

Dawn Irons started Blessed Arrows in 1997 as an offshoot of the Quiverfull Digest when that Listserv had grown to five hundred people and a number of the families were discussing reversals for their vasectomies and tubal ligations. Irons, who'd had a tubal ligation during an economic dry spell in her marriage, when her husband had been laid off twice in one year, figured if everyone on the Digest chipped in eight dollars per month, they could fund twelve reversals annually. Though this goal wasn't realized, twenty-three families pulled away from the Digest to form Blessed Arrows, and today the membership ranges between eighty and three hundred families, a membership that is culled twice a year to remove families that haven't contributed to the common pot in six months. Fund drives to pay for reversal surgeries last nowadays between one and six months, topping out at a particularly sluggish eleven-month fund drive for one woman's tubal ligation reversal in 2006.

Deirdre Welch came to Blessed Arrows on the personal recommendation of Nancy Campbell, to whom she had written requesting advice for her husband's vasectomy reversal. After a speedy fund drive enabled her husband to get a reversal in just four months, Welch committed herself to becoming Blessed Arrows' ambassador, distributing flyers for the group to friends, in church pews, and in gynecologists' offices.

More than just raising funds, the community serves as a clearinghouse for information on Christian doctors providing reversals at discounted prices nationwide as part of a medical ministry to help restore Christian fertility. It also provides a support network for families undertaking the reversal journey—quite literally in some cases, as when Irons traveled from Texas to North Carolina for her reversal and stayed with three Blessed Arrows families en route—the kind of community support Irons feels when she meets the "reversal children" of members who've conceived, and delivered, after reversal.

Irons herself has not. "Disease wreaked havoc on my fertility," she says, and her current infertility—she had seven miscarriages after her reversal and is now on a prohibitively high dose of medication for Lyme disease that keeps her from conceiving at all—has made her sensitive to the judgmental drift that she sees in Quiverfull circles. Even in her own Blessed Arrows group, a leadership change was necessary two years ago when the directors of the ministry were tending toward an exclusionary approach with the reversal funding applications, demanding to know whether the applicants drank or smoked and how many miscarriages they'd had.

As is, the Blessed Arrows application has its share of spiritual qualifications. Applicants must be married and active church members who are applying with their pastor's knowledge and consent. Both husband and wife must supply their testimonies of salvation and detail their repentance from sterilization and their current attitudes toward birth control. The husband must sign a statement confirming that he, as head of the household and spiritual leader of the family, approves the Quiverfull conviction of allowing God to plan their family. And both spouses must answer a spate of doctrinal questions that seem to enforce a pure Protestant line: How does salvation occur? Are you one hundred percent sure you are going to Heaven? Do good works influence getting into Heaven? How do you feel about tithing? Would you ever use birth control again?

But within these specifications, the "postfertile" Irons feels stung by the assertions of "movement Quiverfullers," whom she feels view the number of children one has as a gauge of holiness or spirituality. "If you follow the discussions on the Quiverfull Digest right now, you can see what happens when a 'movement' mentality sets in. Someone just asked the question today if a person can really be considered Quiverfull if they're past the age of childbearing...as if being able to birth a baby is all that makes one Quiverfull. It's a heart change."

Becca Campos agrees. She says that Quiverfull shouldn't be thought of as a movement but as a return to an old ideal. Current speculation on the Quiverfull Digest as to whether larger families are becoming "a fad" grows from some people "making an idol of it." Of course, the nature of mass movements is a blunting of subtleties and a winnowing down of theology to the most easily understood denominator. In this case: babies, lots of them, for God.

In the spring of 2005, I visited Janet and Ted Wolfson at their paintball farm in Canton, Georgia—a Cherokee County town growing as fast as the kudzu that swallowed the Georgia highways, increasing by nearly ten thousand people in five years to become the fifth-fastest-growing city in the country—for a planned Quiverfull picnic. Of the number of families that had intended to come and fellowship, only Lindsay and Keith Morrison, a young Alabama couple with three small children, had been able to make it in the end; the party had been curtailed by bad weather and Rachel Scott's cardinal rule that, "With eight children, plans are always subject to change."

Ted, a sharp-eyed, athletic man, was in charge of the green expanse of field where Atlanta's affluent youth were thrown paintball birthday parties (in one memorable occasion, arriving from the city some forty-five miles south in a helicopter). His wife Janet, a quiet, pretty woman in shorts and a T-shirt and bobbed brown hair—one of many Quiverfull women who bucks the gingham and denim jumper stereotypes—was shy and self-conscious about the missing guests. But even with only the Wolfson family and the Morrisons, they still made a party of fifteen: four adults and two broods of distinctly polite and respectful children, the eldest of whom automatically rose from the picnic table to look after the younger children, responding without a word to pick up a fallen, wailing toddler outside while their parents relaxed in their chairs.

This was, in action, what Quiverfull families think of as their evangelism by example: proving through their own children that large families do not have to be unruly or misbehaved, but that well-behaved children can serve as inspiration to couples on the fence, who compare mature, dutiful offspring like the Wolfsons' with the misbehaving brats they encounter in the street. Then they'll ask, how did you raise kids like that?

In part, through Michael Pearl's controversial manual, *To Train Up a Child,* says Lindsay Morrison in a soothing Deep South drawl. Morrison, a willowy woman in a floor-length dress and long hair—a closer approximation of the homeschooling mom uniform—rocked her three-week-old baby on her chest with a palpable sense of calm. At her side, her husband Keith, a mustached redhead in gray Carhartt work clothes who's active in Howard Phillips's Constitution Party, recounted a shameful story about an ill-behaved boy at a Chattanooga train museum. The shame wasn't in the bad son but his worse father, who laughed when his son refused to heed him. The Wolfsons shook their heads: this kind of misbehavior they see as indicative of a rampant culture of immaturity that hurts children in the long run.

The two couples discussed the reasons for sticking with Quiverfull through the difficult times. An anonymous mother had written in to the Quiverfull Digest full of despair, talking about suicide. Her husband was older and unhelpful around the house, and she feared he would die and leave her to raise their six children alone and destitute. She wanted someone on the forum to give her a reason—*besides* the Bible—why one should be Quiverfull. The answers were quick and pointed: apart from Scripture, there's really no reason why one should be Quiverfull, but why would a Christian woman need more reason anyway?

"If you don't invoke God's word, then there's really no reason," the Wolfsons explained. "Kids are great and all that, but in reality, it's all about the Bible."

But of course, the Bible is not the only reason. Just as the mystical math that allows Rachel Scott to see 9/11 as the end of the Babylonian era has its secular side—as Scott suggests herself, 9/11 led people to seek comfort in family ties—so too does the Quiverfull mandate to be fruitful and multiply have a nonscriptural rationale. Namely, as Rick and Jan Hess argue in *Full Quiver,* to provide "arrows for the war."

After arguing Scripture, the Hesses point to a number of more worldly effects that a Christian embrace of Quiverfull could bring. "If the body of Christ had been reproducing as we were designed to do, we would not be in the mess we are today."

Imagine what they could accomplish with full quivers of children—not five or six children, the Hesses add, but more like twelve to fifteen. "When at the height of the Reagan Revolution," they write, "the conservative faction in Washington was enforced [*sic*] with squads of new conservative congressmen, legislators often found themselves handcuffed by lack of like-minded staff. There simply weren't enough conservatives trained to serve in Washington in the lower and middle capacities." But if just eight million American Christians began supplying more "arrows for the war" by having even six children each, they propose that the Christian right ranks could rise to 550 million within a century ("assuming Christ doesn't return before then"). They like to ponder the spiritual victory that such numbers could bring: both houses of Congress and the majority of state governors' mansions filled by Christians, universities that embrace creationism, sinful cities reclaimed for the faithful, and the swift blows dealt to companies that offend Christian sensibilities.

"God also says there is power in numbers!" rallies Rachel Scott in *Birthing God's Mighty Warriors*. "When God's people are plentiful, we can come up against society going in the wrong direction, against wicked political systems, against immoral laws and antifamily legislation, and make them back down!"

The Hesses continue:

> With the nation's low birthrate, the high divorce rate, an un-marrying and antichild viewpoint, and a debauched nation perhaps unable to slow down the spread of AIDS, we can begin to see what happens politically. A half-billion person boycott of a company that violates God's standards could be very effective.... Through God's blessing, we would be part of a replay of Exodus 1:7: "But the sons of Israel were fruitful and increased greatly, and multiplied, and became exceedingly mighty, so that the land was filled with them."... Brethren, it's time for a comeback.

CHAPTER FIFTEEN

The Natural Family

The fact that, in 2008, the Hesses' predictions about the growing power in numbers of the Christian right read less like *Left Behind* fantasies than a slight exaggeration of the past few years' religious news is testament to what's changed since they published their book twenty years ago.

Quiverfull is not yet a large movement. The number of families who have committed themselves wholly to the Quiverfull path doesn't represent any pollster's idea of a key demographic. But the movement is nonetheless significant for representing an ideal family structure that many conservatives reference as a counterexample when they condemn modern society. Not every family has to be "Quiverfull" in the sense of having eight children for the movement to make an impact. Mothers who have four kids instead of three can also reinforce the Quiverfull goal of a return to the traditional, patriarchal family as the basic economic unit of society.

Even as the movement seeks to mellow its image to mainstream its message, the birthrate revival dreams the Hesses had in the '90s have become conventional talking points in their own right through the work of social scientists like Phillip Longman, a demographer at the centrist New America Institute and the author of *The Empty Cradle: How Falling Birth Rates Threaten World Prosperity and What To Do About It,* and the man he describes as his "dark shadow," Allan Carlson. Though Carlson comes at natalism from the right, and Longman, putatively the secular vanguard of the movement, is working on the issue from the middle, their positions are sufficiently similar for Longman to have endorsed Carlson's controversial pro-Quiverfull treatise *The Natural Family: A Manifesto.*

Carlson is fond of recalling early opponents to birth control, such as Theodore Roosevelt and, several decades later, the New Deal–era "maternalists" who pushed through the traditionalist strictures written into the first Social Security Act. This legislation defined beneficiary families as composed of breadwinning fathers and homemaking mothers, and it bestowed no benefits on "female jobs" such as teaching, nursing, or charity work; instead it provided for women based on whether or not they had borne children, through a limited number of women's provisions tied specifically to natal and infant care. Thirty years before his cousin Franklin Delano launched the surprisingly conservative New Deal, Teddy Roosevelt associated birth control with "race suicide" and the shameful need to "import our babies from abroad" due to the selfishness of white women failing their duty to bear children for the nation: "If you do not believe in your own stock enough to wish to see the stock kept up," wrote Roosevelt, "then you are not good Americans, you are not patriots. I, for one, would not mourn your extinction."

The nation's survival, Roosevelt argued, was dependent on women being "good wives, housekeepers, and mothers of enough healthy children to keep the nation going forward." Efforts at economic parity between the sexes created an untenable independence of women that led to friction between the sexes, and Roosevelt fought this with family-friendly, or rather, patriarchy-friendly taxation schemes that encouraged women to stay at home, penalized unmarried men, gave tax breaks for each child, and paid childless workers less than fathers with dependents: legal wage discrimination that created one of the biggest incentives for women to stay home instead of work.

Among the strongest supporters of this maternalist ideology were traditional German families in the Midwest who opposed women's suffrage and the growing American ethos of individualism, praising instead the intermediary institutions between the individual and the state: the family, the church, and the local community. While these German families, at one point a separatist community that aspired to Germanize their New World, had to rapidly Americanize when the two world wars made their German-speaking communitarian enclaves in the Midwest targets of wartime xenophobia, Carlson argues that their fertility accomplished over generations what their deliberate cultural influence could not. The German-American notion of the family good over individual rights and their romantic ideal of doting motherhood became the American norm. What's now taken as a quintessentially American attitude toward hearth and home was not always the standard, and other paths were possible. Other immigrant populations had different traditions of childrearing and had long seen mothers working outside the home. But the ascendancy of the sentimental German approach to motherhood, Carlson argues, was in fact the slow and unnoticed triumph of the Germanic sense of the good life: a patriarchal idea that gained its place in time through the steady accumulation of numbers. To prove it, he says that, as of 1990, more Americans claimed German heritage than any other "ethnic stock."

Like Teddy Roosevelt and the later New Deal maternalists, Carlson, a former Reagan appointee to the National Commission on Children, wants to construct a secular social policy case for natalism. Carlson's case is based on the importance of large families to sustaining a Social Security system crippled by childless "free riders"—citizens deemed "deadbeats" in the social welfare system, not for failure to pay taxes but for failure to add additional children to the labor and taxation pool. Carlson and his colleagues, including Steve Mosher, founder of the Catholic anticontraception lobbyist group Population Research Institute, which was a strong influence in pushing the George W. Bush administration to cut funding for the United Nations Population Fund, suggest that parents who contribute abundant "human capital" to society in the form of many children should be spared from paying taxes themselves. The burden should be shifted instead to singles and childless couples, who are seen as an affluent class of leisure-seekers, buying boats and summer homes by the millions rather than raising more kids. Carlson has written or consulted for conservative politicians on somewhat progressive, "family-friendly" tax policies, which reward large families with hefty tax cuts for each child. "Pronatalism is the subtheme of all I do," he says. "While many profamily groups are more indirect about it, perhaps because they only have a few children themselves, I preach it all the time."

As much is shown in his numerous books that touch on the subject: *Fractured Generations: Crafting a Family Policy for Twenty-first Century America, Family Questions: Reflections on the American Social Crisis, The American Way: Family and Community in the Shaping of the American Identity,* and *The New Agrarian Mind: The Movement Toward Decentralist Thought in Twentieth-century America.* The last is a book that struck Carmon Friedrich, who frequently brings ideological and theological analysis to her biblical womanhood blog. While Carlson has specific praise for agrarian movements in Texas—for their separatist creation of alternative, orthodox communities and distinct, independent households—Friedrich sees Carlson's agrarianism as something broader. It offers a frame of mind that steps back from the onslaught of modern life—media, infotainment, the glut of material available to be digested—and says, "We've gotten away from God's things."

Agrarianism means getting back to the important things, "the permanent things." That can mean getting back, literally, to the land, but it's also the guiding philosophy behind decentralized Christian movements like homeschooling, home businesses, and home-based churches. The goal, Friedrich says, is "taking control of this area," the home, as thoroughly as possible. Carlson says simply that he aims to make the home "a productive place" once again.

This is the ideal that Allan Carlson, a former official of the Lutheran Council in the United States of America, envisioned when he, along with his Mormon colleague Paul Mero of the Utah think tank the Sutherland Institute, coauthored *The Natural Family: A Manifesto.* The authors present a correction to Marx and echo the call to arms of the ecumenical Christian profamily movement that is attempting to politicize and spread the theology of patriarchy and Quiverfull conviction across denominations, where fathers lead and women honor their highest domestic calling by becoming prolific mothers. Because families are seen as the fundamental unit of society, individual rights are valued only insofar as they correspond with pronatalist, profamily goals. Thus Carlson and Mero qualify their wholehearted support of women's rights: "Above all, we believe in rights that recognize women's unique gifts of pregnancy, childbirth, and breastfeeding."

According to Doris Buss and Didi Herman, law professors and coauthors of *Globalizing Family Values: The Christian Right in International Politics,* documents like the *Manifesto,* embodying "a mixture of divinity and data," Scripture and conservative social science, serve to codify a new family theology and orthodox doctrine for a coalition working across denominational lines and traditions. The result, they see, is "an ever-increasing convergence in ideology among the different sectors of the Christian right," wherein conservative members of different faiths have more in common with each other than with the liberal members of their own churches.

Carlson frequently writes for the conservative Catholic magazine *First Things* and constantly seeks to make common cause with orthodox believers across Christianity and, to some extent, orthodox Judaism and Islam as well. The common cause is the recognition that "children are the first end or purpose of marriage" and that couples are called to "fill the earth" with them. This fixed goal partly explains why, in contrast to Carlson's reactionary social policies, his economics have an almost socialist tint: capitalist or communist, what matters most to Carlson is patriarchy and pronatalism.

Carlson cut his teeth studying family and fertility in Sweden: the egalitarian, sexually liberal social democracy that he sees as "the root of most of the bad ideas in Europe," encouraging the state to subvert the "natural complementarity between men and women." The upset of these given sex roles due to individualism, Carlson writes, has plagued society since the industrial revolution, and he gleefully cites Friedrich Engels's lament about out-of-work men, emasculated beside their working wives, as proof of the durability of gender norms across the political spectrum and throughout the ages. In this selective march through history, Carlson sees patriarchal family-wage regimes as the steadfast upholders of democracy against totalitarianism.

Carlson hopes to involve the state in a profamily welfare system, soothing the country's industrial alienation not with communist revolution but a preindustrial revival of family order and centrality. "The ideal government, in this sense, is local," he and Mero write, and again quote Teddy Roosevelt: "A nation is nothing but the aggregate of the families within its borders." Carlson and Mero continue, "States exist to protect families and to encourage family growth and integrity."

This is to be done through taxation, of course, but also by keeping government out of other family affairs: removing "witch-hunting" child-abuse laws restricting parental discipline; eliminating social engineering through pensions for individual workers instead of heads of households and their dependents; and replacing the marriage-delaying and fertility-disrupting machine of post-secondary education with correspondence universities and apprenticeship programs for young men to learn trades.

In the church, Carlson suggests that all liberalizing measures, such as female ordination, have had the same negative effect on the natural family, particularly in displacing the important role of the pastor's wife as exemplar to the rest of a congregation's women: "By upending and confusing sexual differences and by granting to women the religious functions long held exclusively by men, the ordination of women marginalized the special works and responsibilities of clerical wives, including their task of being model mothers with full quivers of children."

The tenets of *The Natural Family: A Manifesto* are finding local political support. In 2006, the manifesto, with its directive that parents open themselves up to receiving a "full quiver" of children, was adopted by the town council of Kanab, Utah. Liberal protests followed, including a campaign of feminist protest buttons reading "Quiver-less!" that tickles Carlson to this day. In Idaho, State Representative Steven Thayne, a homeschooling father of eight, ran for office in 2006 on a "natural family" platform. He followed through on his campaign in 2007 by joining a task force aimed at keeping mothers in the home by ending no-fault divorce and cracking down on day care centers, pre-kindergarten, and Head Start as "free babysitting services" that make it too easy for mothers to leave the home. These are early, local steps toward the realization of Carlson's natural family goal, which includes public school campaigns teaching children that "the calling of each girl is to become wife and mother"; an increase in homeschooling; the end of easy divorces; the rise of "covenant marriages" that are more difficult to dissolve; tax penalties for unmarried cohabitation; incentives for larger families and more babies; a final scrubbing of school sex-ed and reproductive health education; and an explicit return to sex-segregated job listings and family wages that "reinforce natural family bonds."

But faith, Carlson says, is the necessary yeast to make any secular movement rise, and religion has always been the driving force behind the family movement, with fertility rising in tandem with all of America's periodic Great Awakenings. In the same way that Carlson recalls the "strand of garrison life" that the Cold War fight against communism brought to American society, in the conservative Christian world that sees Europe as the measure of mankind's fall, a besieged, wartime mentality is a given. In Carlson's writings, as well as in the work of Mary Pride and the Hesses, this is reflected in the military rankings they assign to spouses following patriarchal, biblical gender roles (commanding officers and privates) or similar hierarchical terminology (the husband described as company

CEO, the wife as plant manager, and the children as workers). These Protestant couples, Carlson says, "are going to become the salt of the church." And their kids? Presumably ammunition, arrows, weapons for the war.

CHAPTER SIXTEEN

Return to Patriarchy

How well are Quiverfull's arguments promoting large, traditional families filtering out into the larger society? There are some signs of denominations and churches picking up the Quiverfull conviction, not least of which is Southern Baptist Theological Seminary president Al Mohler's statement in 2005 that deliberate childlessness among Christian couples is "an absolute revolt against God's design."

"The Scripture does not even envision married couples who choose not to have children," he writes. "The church must help this society regain its sanity on the gift of children. Willful barrenness and chosen childlessness must be named as moral rebellion. To demand that marriage means sex—but not children—is to defraud the creator of His joy and pleasure in seeing the saints raising His children."

Likewise, Pastor Mark Driscoll of Mars Hill Church has preached a pronatalist message from his Seattle pulpit, praying for high fertility in the pews and telling congregants, "We are in a city with less children per capita than any city but San Francisco, and we consider it our personal mission to turn that around." One woman in the church, reports Lauren Sandler in *Righteous: Dispatches from the Evangelical Youth Movement,* interpreted this as a directive to "repopulate the city with Christians." And apparently, it's a directive being followed by Driscoll's fundamentalist hipster flock, which, he says, is birthing hundreds of babies every year.

Allan Carlson also points to the resurgence of Calvinism as well as a new movement among lay Missouri Synod Lutherans to reclaim Luther's teachings against contraception as indications of natalism's growing influence. Other examples are beginning to accumulate: Pat Robertson declared in 2007 that "only those with strong religious faith" are having children. Steve Schlissel, a converted Jew who pastors the Brooklyn Reformed church Messiah's Covenant Community (and a friend of Doug Phillips), exhorted his followers to accept five, ten, fifteen, or twenty children from God, as "the very employment of birth control is a statement against the gifts of God…the very foundation of choice against love." Philip "Flip" Benham, director of the vigilante antiabortion group Operation Save America, declared that large, godly families are the hated enemy of the devil, who aims to raise children instead in broken, Muslim, or atheist homes. And David Bentley Hart, an Eastern Orthodox theologian who writes frequently for *First Things,* argues that, in cultural battle, "probably the most subversive and effective strategy we might undertake would be one of militant fecundity: abundant, relentless, exuberant, and defiant childbearing. Given the reluctance of modern men and women to be fruitful and multiply, it would not be difficult, surely, for the devout to accomplish—in no more than a generation or two—a demographic revolution."

A new generation of Christian leaders in the homeschooling movement is able to point to their own large families as an example to follow. Among that new guard is Michael Farris, father of ten as well as founder of the Home School Legal Defense Association and the homeschooling college, Patrick Henry College, that supplies a steady stream of young conservative graduates to work for conservative politicians in Washington. Farris, as his wife Vickie details in her Titus 2 book of encouragement to homeschooling mothers, *A Mom Just Like You* (cowritten with her daughter Jayme), came to his Quiverfull beliefs through the ministry of Bill Gothard.

Through the 1980s and '90s, Gothard spread his pronatalist message that God is the authority of family size to many thousands of Southern Baptists and other conservative Christians. One of Gothard's early converts was Farris, who was already primed for the message of letting God control Vickie's fertility by early anticontraception literature and his immersion, in the late '70s, in a conservative Christian movement in Washington State. The homeschooling movement was thriving with youth groups and churches that emphasized themes about "God's sovereign hand in our lives," the hymn "Trust and Obey," and verses like Proverbs 3:5–6: "Trust in the Lord with all thine heart; and lean not unto thine own understanding. In all ways acknowledge him, and he shall direct thy paths." Into the Farrises' faith, readied to honor authority with obedience and trust, Bill Gothard planted the seed that men should "have as many children as their faith could handle."

Vickie Farris kept up with her husband's changing convictions by reading Mary Pride, and she was struck by Pride's blunt challenge: "Family planning is the mother of abortion." She began to feel that her own attitudes toward children and birth control and her desire to exert control over the spacing of her children even through such a natural, God-given means as breastfeeding were helping foster the "abortion environment" of selfish individualism. "If we do choose to become bondservants to our Lord (and we do have a choice), then our bodies are no longer our own," writes Farris in a neat encapsulation of the lessons Pride taught over twenty years earlier.

Today Farris, mother to ten, is among the most prominent homeschooling mothers in the movement. She is doing her part to pass on the message to her daughter's generation that "our sphere of influence and our ability to 'do battle' for the Kingdom of God is dramatically increased when our quiver is full of these little 'arrows.' ... Like those old Russian grandmothers," she continues, describing underground Christians who kept the faith inside the Soviet empire, "we homeschooling moms are building a counterculture beneath the rotting structure of today's American society. Our faithfulness is creating a sound structure that, by the grace of God, will last even after the rotting outer shell of our culture has crumbled away. We are not 'abandoning ship': we are building a lifeboat."

Whether that lifeboat can bear mothers like Vickie Farris herself, once they've past their childbearing prime, is another question. As her fertility began to wane in her forties, Farris writes, and she suffered more miscarriages and difficulties in conceiving, she began to feel like an "old, dried-out, dead tree," suffering an identity crisis for lack of a new baby to care for. But these feelings, she told herself, were more of the same selfish individualism that led women into family planning in the first place: insufficient trust that God had her where she was meant to be.

. . .

If this is the growing language and ideology of the right, shepherded by pastors across denominational lines and introduced into government by conservative think-tank scholars like Carlson, centrist Democrats like Phillip Longman hardly offer a left-wing counterpoint. Instead Longman has searched—at the request of the Democratic Leadership Council, which published his findings in its *Blueprint* policy organ—for a way to appeal to the same voters Carlson is organizing: a typically "radical middle" quest to figure out how Democrats can make nice with Kansas.

"Who are these evangelicals?" asks Longman. "Is there anything about them that makes them inherently pro-war and for tax cuts for the rich?" No, he concludes. "What's irreducible about these religious voters is that they're for the family." Asked whether the absolutist position Quiverfull takes on birth control, let alone abortion, might interfere with his strategy, Longman admits that abortion rights would have to take a back seat to profamily policies that promote large, traditionalist families, but that, in politics, "nobody ever gets everything they need."

But aside from the centrist tax proposals Longman is crafting to rival Carlson's, he urges a return to patriarchy—properly understood, he assures, as not just male domination but also increased male responsibility as husbands and fathers—on more universal grounds. Taking a long view as unsettling in its way as Pastor Bartly's rapture talk, Longman says that no society can survive to reproduce itself without following patriarchy. "As secular and libertarian elements in society fail to reproduce, people adhering to more traditional, patriarchal values inherit society by default," Longman argues, pointing to cyclical demographic upheavals from ancient Greece and Rome to the present day, where falling birthrates have consistently augured conservative, even reactionary, comebacks, marked by increased nationalism, religious fundamentalism, and deep societal conservatism. Presenting a thinly veiled ultimatum to moderates and liberals, Longman cites the political sea change in the Netherlands in recent years, where, he charges, a population dearth led to a vacuum that "Muslim extremists came in to fill." Though individual non-patriarchal elements of a society may die out, he says, societies as a whole will survive and "through a process of cultural evolution, a set of values and norms that can roughly be described as patriarchy reemerge."

That's how Quiverfull mother Wendy Dufkin sees it, give or take a few mentions of the Lord's name: God is leading Quiverfull families at the head of a "return to patriarchy, to father-led families. 'Patriarchy' may be a loaded word for some, but it's not for me. There are so many woman-led families, whether single mothers or families where the father is just absent. I think it's gone to such an extreme with those families for a while that now we're returning to another extreme, patriarchy."

She recounts the seven stages of decline of the Roman empire as illustration: from men failing to lead their families to God, through adultery, divorce, homosexuality, barrenness, atheism, and then, in the end, an invasion of barbarians from abroad.

The invasion, the war, is to be understood on both planes: the worldly war that a good patriot like Dufkin likely supports and the spiritual war of the church, which will continue indefinitely. Where the two meet—in the frequently low-income households of believers who feel a conviction to supply their children, their arrows for God—you might expect a clash of consciences, such as when Deirdre Welch explains what she sees as a "media attitude" about bearing many children, "This idea of, why bring children into this world, a world of violence, just to get drafted?" The example seems poignant—her oldest son had just left for Iraq when I spoke with her in 2006—but Welch remains optimistic, bearing in mind what she sees as a biblical promise, that "God can use your Quiverfull to bring up his army of belief." As a believer and a loving mother, perhaps she sees this path—worldwide redemption through spiritual and actual warfare—as the one that will lead to the end of wars, even if that path means the wars will be fought with arrows such as her son.

CHAPTER SEVENTEEN

Godly Seeds

Mixed with a fearful take on international news, the sense of a coming clash of civilizations in the realm of demography quickly lends itself to practical applications when comparing family sizes in the United States to those in countries overseas. Nancy Campbell is far more explicit in speculating about the implications of the natalist theology she teaches.

> When godly people stop having children, we are wasting the godly seed. So today, we are facing a very, very serious threat: the threat of Islam. They are outnumbering us seven to one. And there's eight million Islamics here in America. When you think of Osama bin Laden, he is one of fifty-three children. He has twenty-seven himself. So between him and his father, they've fathered eighty children. What about his other fifty-two brothers and sisters? How many have they fathered? Say they've only fathered or mothered twenty each—less than him—but in the thousands when you think of their grandchildren, who would now be having children today.
>
> When I talk to parents today and ask how many grandchildren they have, they tell me, "Oh, we have two! Isn't it wonderful?" "Two?" Is that going to impact the world? Two? When you get someone like, say, Osama bin Laden, for example, he's just representative of so many Islamics, well, you see how they're populating.

Campbell, grandmother to thirty-two and counting, pauses before delivering an unintentional punch line: "I'm not racist by any means." So much so, she says, that she and her husband had adopted "three

183

183

black children we hope will be here by Christmas." One of Campbell's three daughters adopted six more. "But I am concerned because I don't like this sort of Islam—I don't dislike the people," she says, but she is worried "since they want to kill all Jews and all Christians and wipe us off the face of the earth, and they want world domination and nothing less."

Campbell gives a little laugh, thinking of her pantry, stocked with the Middle Eastern foods she loves from a Muslim-run shop in Nashville. "So, help, here I am advocating for them because we buy from them, because we love their food. We buy from them, and they're like friends, and they're not radicals. But I know, when radical Islam begins to take over, they will have to get in line or look out, they'll be wiped out like we will be.

"So you see what happens when the Christian church refuses to have children. *That* starts filling the earth, instead of what we're meant to be filling the earth with: a godly seed."

Andrew Pollard, a British demographer and anticontraception activist, makes a similar point, lambasting liberals who argue that immigration can supplement workforces in low-fertility countries. "Up to now, for Britain alone, they've been taking them [immigrants] from Pakistan, India, and Bangladesh. And the problem is, we've been growing our own bombers."

The enemy, of course, includes secularists as well as Muslims; gays and abortionists are another nasty side effect of Christians using birth control, says Campbell. And that's not just Scripture talking, she says, but common sense.

> See, it's an eternal war. You are fruitful and multiply, you will take dominion. It's those who multiply who will take dominion. So if we're not prepared to multiply, we, who are the greatest nation on earth at this time, what if our future generations will continue to have their 1.8 children, as opposed to 7.1, isn't it logical that those who do what the Bible says and be fruitful, multiply, replenish the earth, will take dominion? It's a matter of course. It's what happens as you multiply. It is God's eternal law, but it's logical. It can't be any other way. You can't be the greatest nation on earth if you're going to become smaller and smaller. It won't happen tomorrow, but I'm thinking of future generations.

Campbell's not the only one. In 2006, the growing movement among ultra-Orthodox Jews in Israel to have families numbering up to eighteen children or more was covered in the newspaper *Haaretz,* when Ahuva Klachkin, a forty-four-year-old mother of eighteen, died and was given funeral and eulogy honors equivalent to those given prominent citizens or rabbis, transforming the mother into a near-saint. Klachkin, explains *Haaretz* reporter Tamar Rotem, was just one mother among many who are raising not merely traditionally large families but families that eclipse even Hassidic tradition in size: well over twelve children and continuing to bear into their late forties in what one midwife called "a social obsession to get pregnant." Such mothers are highly honored in the ultra-Orthodox community, with some families, descendants of Holocaust survivors, claiming every baby born as a "blow to Hitler." But other families are motivated by a more contemporary threat—the fear that Muslim women within and without Israel's borders are having more children than are Jewish Israelis.

"The womb is seen as a weapon of demographic warfare," says a doctor I'll refer to by the pseudonym Dr. Singer. Singer, who works in a women's clinic in Israel that serves mostly religious women, wished to remain anonymous for the security of her clinic in a deeply Orthodox community that vehemently disapproves of dissent. Yasir Arafat's bombastic declaration that "the womb of the Arab woman is my best weapon" is widely quoted in Dr. Singer's community as a reminder of the necessity of large families, though she sees it also as part of a domestic power struggle on the part of the ultraconservative Orthodox community. "There's a self-interest as well. To be fruitful and multiply may lead to political power in Israeli government and as a religious and nationalistic movement."

Below such grand schemes, though, the effects on the health of these mothers and on their families, often living in poverty, can be tragic—lives of quiet scarcity and unceasing labor, housework, and births. Elder daughters are required to pick up a great deal of household responsibilities early on in life while their mothers recover from pregnancies or, in the case of Klachkin, die early. "They're workhorses," says Dr. Singer. "Their lives, looking from the outside, look like a form of slavery, never-ending. Sometimes I'm incredibly admiring of their stamina, what they're able to do day after day, after so many children."

The women Dr. Singer describes live in a particular community, with distinct religious traditions and norms, but the stresses and social pressures they face are similar to those women confront in any community where extremely patriarchal, pronatalist theology becomes the norm. The women Dr. Singer treats are Haredi, or ultra-Orthodox women of various religious sects, and are considered to be the most extremely devout women in Israel. They often give birth to large families, ranging regularly between five and fourteen children. While the women's husbands study in yeshiva all day long, the mothers stay at home, "doing everything—laundry, housework, kids." Women marry into this lifestyle very young, often having two or three children by the time they are twenty-two, and they subsequently become grandparents while they're still in the thick of child-raising themselves. There's a joke about various denominations in Israel, Dr. Singer tells me: at Reformed weddings (Reformed Judaism being the most liberal branch of the faith), the rabbi is pregnant; at Conservative weddings, the bride is pregnant; and at Orthodox weddings, the mother-in-law is pregnant. It's a light-hearted take at what, from the inside, is often a crushing life of toil, as with one of Dr. Singer's patients, a woman in her fifties with nine children of her own and twenty-five grandchildren she is expected to help raise.

Part of the upsurge in large families is economic. Arab-Israelis and the ultra-Orthodox are among the poorest groups in Israel. When ultra-Orthodox husbands go to yeshiva to study, the government, which seeks to encourage the preservation of Torah learning, gives a stipend to the family for each child that they have, with the stipend increasing after a family has four children. The stipends do cause grumbling in outer society, with non-Orthodox Israelis considering the stipends "a reward for being poor," but they've led to a booming Orthodox population in cities such as Jerusalem.

"There's a tremendous pressure to have lots and lots of babies," says Dr. Singer. While the total Israeli fertility rate hasn't changed much over the years, when it's broken down by subpopulation, it's clear that ultra-Orthodox families have increased dramatically. This is largely because they've continued having children later into life.

But the level of what Dr. Singer calls near-slave labor is striking, with the women working nonstop from dawn till bedtime. As a result, she sees a high rate of depression among overwhelmed women and epidemic self-neglect resulting from women's unquestioning allegiance to their rabbis, some of whom insert themselves into women's medical lives in destructive ways. For example, a sixty-three-year-old patient of Dr. Singer's with breast cancer refused treatment after her rabbi told her she didn't need a mammogram or any further treatment. A more common problem is the Orthodox ban on contraception, which proscribes men "spilling their seed" and views barrier contraceptives such as condoms as an impediment to intimacy between husband and wife. In order to use contraception in compliance with their religious laws, ultra-Orthodox women must obtain a dispensation, or approval, from their rabbi. Whether or not they will be granted the dispensation depends in greatest part on the beliefs of their rabbi.

Rabbis who take an extremist stance on the ultra-Orthodox ban on contraception and on children as unconditional blessings sometimes take it upon themselves to dispense fertility drugs to couples hoping to conceive: an outrage in Singer's eyes for its potential to dramatically increase the risk of multiple births, pregnancies of twins and triplets, which have much higher rates of complications for the mother's health. "If you don't have a baby within your first year of marriage," Dr. Singer says, "people start to talk. Women get so very pressured that they will often approach a physician at the age of twenty-one if they're not pregnant within six months of marriage."

That many women don't become pregnant immediately upon marriage is predictable, says Dr. Singer, as almost all ultra-Orthodox women do take birth control pills regularly at one point in their lives: during the three months before their weddings, in order to regulate their periods and make sure that they aren't menstruating on their wedding night, and thus ritually unclean and forbidden from contact with their new husbands. That the pressure on them to be pregnant begins before their hormones have readjusted after ceasing birth control use—on the night they are married—is an indication of how harshly women who do not conceive will be judged. Dr. Singer treated a twenty-two-year-old woman in such a situation; she hadn't gotten pregnant within the first three months of her marriage and so went to her rabbi to receive a blessing to get ovulation-inducing drugs. She shortly conceived twins.

"It's a good example of the abuse of the ignorance of young women, who have no clue, who have no means of giving informed consent," Dr. Singer explains. When she sees young teenage women to prescribe birth control pills in the months before their marriage—eighteen-year-old women who will go from never having kissed a boy to having sex on their wedding night—Dr. Singer must also use the appointment as a preconception checkup on the assumption that, by the patient's next appointment, she'll likely be pregnant.

In a very real sense, in these communities, women are always seen as "pre-pregnant" or potentially pregnant, to borrow a phrase from conservative policy-writers at the U.S. Centers for Disease Control and Prevention, which counseled in 2006 that all women of childbearing age should be treated as though they might soon become pregnant. Among the ultra-Orthodox in Israel, these value suppositions are the norm, with *kala* bridal classes teaching girls how to be good wives and keep to the purity laws, but only able to teach them about sex and pregnancy to the degree that the instructor herself understands them. "It's pretty depressing to see women get trapped in the circular tasks of housework and childcare like this. They become very much de-selfed," says Dr. Singer. And, she continues, the glorification of mothers of many children and the community's belief that women, while pregnant, are fulfilling their roles, leads to women scarcely able to articulate that they wish to stop having children.

"They won't even let themselves say the words, 'I don't want any more children,' but will rather say, 'I'll bear as many children as God gives me,'" even as they tell Dr. Singer that they're exhausted. Some couples, hoping to build a case to cease having children with their rabbi's blessing—rabbis who often tell couples they need to "keep going" as long as their fertility allows—come to Dr. Singer with hypothetical arguments they can pass on to their rabbi. "'Isn't it true,' they ask, 'that pregnancy could worsen this condition?'" Dr. Singer will nod. "I always say yes. 'Absolutely, pregnancy will make this worse.' Sometimes you can just tell the way they look at you, they want you to say, 'You need to stop having children.' There are times they feel out of control, and that's the hardest part, that you have to go against the whole culture."

CHAPTER EIGHTEEN

Demographic Winter

In the United States, far away from ultra-Orthodox communities in Israel, with their pressures and sad resonances of replacing the dead, profamily advocates posture as countercultural rebels striking out against a tyranny of contraception and childlessness.

So it was in sunny Front Royal, Virginia, where Steve Mosher told me about wolves returning to the streets of European towns. Not as part of some Vermont-model wildlife-recovery scenario but as emblems of a harsh comeuppance mankind is due—wolves stalking out of the forests like an ancient judgment, coming to claim mankind's ceded land. Sitting in a Main Street café in a beautifying ex-industrial town in the Shenandoah Valley that, at the far edge of D.C.'s suburban sprawl, is lately home to a surprising number of conservative Christian ministries, Mosher described his grim vision of Europe's future: fields will lie fallow and economies will wither. A great depression will sink over the continent as it undergoes "a decline that Europe hasn't experienced since the Black Death." The comeuppance has a name, one being fervently hawked among a group of Christian-right profamily activists hoping to spark a movement in secular Europe. It's called the "demographic winter," a more austere brand of apocalypse than doomsayers normally trade in, evoking not a nuclear inferno but a quiet and cold blanket of snow in which, they charge, Western civilization is laying itself down to die.

How so? It's the argument Quiverfull advocates have been making amongst themselves for years, that Europe is failing to produce enough babies—the right babies—to replace its old and dying. It's "the baby bust," "the birth dearth," "the graying of the continent": modern euphemisms for old-fashioned race panic as low fertility among white couples coincides with an increasingly visible immigrant population across Europe. The real root of racial tensions in the Netherlands and France, America's culture warriors tell anxious Europeans, isn't ineffective methods of assimilating new citizens but, rather, decades of antifamily permissiveness—contraception, abortion, divorce, population control, women's liberation and careers, "selfish" secularism, and gay rights—enabling "decadent" couples to neglect their reproductive duties. Defying the biblical command to "be fruitful and multiply," Europeans have failed to produce the magic number of 2.1 children per couple, the estimated replacement-level fertility rate for developed nations (and a figure repeated so frequently it becomes a near incantation). The West, meaning the white Christian West, in this telling, is in danger of forfeiting itself through sheer lack of numbers to an onslaught of Muslim immigrants and their purportedly numerous offspring. In other words, Mosher and his colleagues aren't really concerned about wolves.

Another profamily soldier banging the drum about demographic winter, Christine de Vollmer, head of the U.S.-funded Latin American Alliance for the Family, says that thanks to "obstinate antifamily policies, the end of European civilization can be calculated in years." Such predictions are winning the ear of top U.S. conservatives, with Mitt Romney taking time during his campaign exit speech in February 2008 to warn that "Europe is facing a demographic disaster" due to its modernized, secular culture, particularly its "weakened faith in the Creator, failed families, disrespect for human life, and eroded morality." With this, the American Christian right has hit on a potent formula: grafting falling Western birthrates onto old morality arguments to craft a tidy cause-and-effect model that its members hope will provide their ideology an entry into European politics.

The imminent demise of Europe is a popular prediction these days, with books such as Catholic scholar George Weigel's *The Cube and the Cathedral,* Melanie Phillips's *Londonistan,* Bruce Bawer's *While Europe Slept,* and Pat Buchanan's *Death of the West* all appearing since 2001. The 2006 film *Children of Men* sketched a sterile, dystopian world thrown into chaos for lack of babies (though with less blatant antiabortion implications than the Christian allegorical P. D. James novel on which it was based). The media increasingly sound the alarm as Eastern European countries register birthrates halved since the last generation. And in February 2008, the Family First Foundation, a profamily group in the same movement circles as Mosher and de Vollmer, released a documentary dedicated to the threat, *Demographic Winter: The Decline of the Human Family*.

What was a conservative drumbeat about Europe's death has become mainstream media shorthand, complementing ominous news items about Muslim riots, boycotts across the continent, and empty European churches transformed into mosques with calls to prayer replacing church bells. Evangelical luminary Chuck Colson, head of the vast Prison Fellowship ministry and a close ally of George W. Bush, espoused a conspiracy theory in which he construed an Islamic Council of Europe handbook for Muslims trying to keep the faith abroad, living as religious minorities in largely Christian or secular cultures, as a "soft terrorism" plot for takeover. The late Oriana Fallaci lambasted Europe's transformation into a Muslim colony she called "Eurabia." And as part of a 2007 political campaign in Switzerland, a poster depicted a flock of white sheep kicking a black sheep out of their pasture and featured the motto, "For Greater Security." The refrain is that the good-faith multicultural tolerance approach of the Netherlands has been tried and has failed, which is arguably a few polite steps from Mosher's summary of the problem: Muslim immigrants are simply "too many and too culturally different from their new countries' populations to assimilate quickly.... They are contributing to the cultural suicide of these nations as they commit demographic suicide." Or, as he declared while rallying a gathering of profamily activists in Poland in 2007, "I want to see more Poles!"

Or more Russians, or more Italians, as the case may be. The fever for more "European" babies is widespread. The last two popes have involved themselves in the debate, with John Paul II pronouncing a "crisis of births" in 2002 in an anomalous papal address to Italy's Parliament and Benedict XVI remarking on the "tragedy" of childless European couples and beatifying an Italian peasant woman for bearing and raising twelve children.

At the national level, in 2004, Italian Prime Minister Silvio Berlusconi offered a "baby bonus" of about a thousand dollars to parents who had a second child, and Russia, which has a history of pronatalist policies, including its 1980s-era "motherhood medals," sweetened the offer to its citizens with several birth initiatives for hesitant couples, including an $8,900 award to families who produce a second child and a stipend of

40 percent of salary to women who leave work to become stay-at-home moms. One Russian province made novelty news worldwide with its Day of Conception in September 2007, when residents of Ulyanovsk got time off work to "conceive a patriot" for the country. Prizes for successful delivery nine months later included refrigerators and cars. The theme is present enough in the popular consciousness that a Swedish underwear company cashed in on the anxiety with a provocative ad campaign featuring a cast of Nordic men wearing lapel pins that resembled the European Union flag commanding Swedes to "Fuck for the Future" and "Drop Your Pants or Drop Dead."

The nativist motivations for such campaigns move beyond the subliminal at times. Elizabeth Krause, an anthropologist and author of *A Crisis of Births: Population Politics and Family-Making in Italy*, tracked that country's population efforts over the past decade and found politicians demanding more babies "to keep away the armadas of immigrants from the southern shores of the Mediterranean" and priests calling for a "Christian dike against the Muslim invasion of Italy." The racial preferences behind Berlusconi's "baby bonus" came into embarrassing relief when immigrant parents were accidentally sent checks for their offspring and then asked to return the money: the Italian government hadn't meant to promote *those* births.

· · ·

The American Christian right, increasingly seeking influence abroad, has recognized that this anxiety over shifting national identities creates fertile terrain for spreading its ideology of traditional sexual morality as a quick fix for a postmodern age.

In the documentary *Demographic Winter*, the imagery of a frosty End of Days, accompanied by a foreboding, skeletal piano score, is played for full effect over somber interviews with conservative scholars, activists, and European politicians. "One of the most ominous events of modern history is quietly unfolding," the film promises. "We are headed toward a demographic winter, which threatens to have catastrophic social and economic consequences. The effects will be severe and long-lasting and are already becoming manifest in much of Europe."

In trailers for the film, but strangely missing from the film itself (the distribution of which was delayed several months, following early criticism, as producers reedited it), Allan Carlson discusses the "demographic winter of Western societies" as a blanket of snow covers the United States, then Europe, and finally the rest of the world. Catholic activist de Vollmer talks about the intergenerational collapse family planning will bring: an echo of her charge that contraception, by splitting sexuality from procreation and rejecting potential offspring, leads to generations of damaged, alienated children, "like Bucharest orphans," who will later refuse to care for their own aged parents. As she describes a dysfunctional global family where the elderly are too many to care for and the young too few to run the trains, the camera cuts to a lonely street shot of pastel European row houses framing a desolate walkway and a confused grandfather left untended and alone. As a Latvian legislator describes the devastating impact of demographic winter on countries with already-small populations, a child playing on a swing set disappears and snowflakes start to fly.

In fact, everywhere throughout the film there is a plague of disappearing bodies. Children vanish in a slow flurry from classrooms, walkways, dens, and teeter-totters in a seemingly gentle evocation of historical horrors—the disappearing bodies a muted rendition of nuclear flash incineration, the snow that replaces them evoking atomic and crematorium ashes as well as emblemizing the frostier demographic death the filmmakers envision. Either way, it signals massive dying, and in case the rhetorical stakes for the demographic winter theory weren't high enough, the filmmakers declared, in a banner at their Heritage Foundation premiere in mid-February, that the film's topic is "the single most powerful force directing the fate and future of society."

"No part of the world stays dominant forever," says Harry S. Dent, Jr., an economist who specializes in demographic-based economic forecasting, toward the close of the film. "Rome was great," says Dent, but Italy today "is nowhere near ruling the world." Another speaker, David Popenoe, of the National Marriage Project, summarizes the moral of the movie in its closing line, "Maybe the time of Western civilization has come and now we're going into a retreat," before the screen cuts abruptly to black.

In an interesting happenstance, Dent's father was the late Harry S. Dent, Sr., a top Nixon aide largely credited for developing the Republican Party's "Southern strategy," broadly criticized as a race-baiting ploy to tap white Southerners' racial fears for political gain. Without intending to visit the father's sins on the son, it is worth noting this poignant legacy for a film connected to a new global profamily movement that has taken marketing savvy to an entirely new level.

Phillip Longman appears as well, reprising his role as a deliberately counterintuitive face for demographic winter, warning that Europe is becoming a continent of the elderly, with death rates exceeding birthrates on the scale of nuclear war. Words for extended family members, he warns—uncle, aunt, even sibling—will disappear as shrinking families render them obsolete. In the rosiest endgame he allows, Longman predicts that the fertile faithful will inherit the earth and that "those who remain will be committed to God." In this light, Carlson says, "Secularism is a societal death wish." Or, as Longman puts it, delivering a mournful cosmic punch line to gratified Christian-right audiences, "Your children won't grow up to be secular humanists."

To those secular humanists—a "sterile" elite Longman sees as too self-absorbed to reproduce—he delivers an ominous ultimatum. Though it's tough for a generation educated to fear the population bomb and value women's rights, gay rights, and environmentalism to accept these trends, unless they temper their 1970s notions of individual fulfillment, they'll be among the "certain kinds of human beings" who "are on their way to extinction." Just what the putatively liberal Longman intends by these threats seems to depend on the rationale behind his allegiance to the profamily/demographic winter coalition. While ostensibly he's warning liberals to get in line with traditional family morality *or else,* his presence at the helm of the movement seems targeted toward the conservative choir, reminding them that they have two foes in this battle, two enemies within: a tangible human population expanding within their borders and a sexually liberal frame of mind endemic to modern society.

As Rick Stout and Barry McLerran, producers of *Demographic Winter,* argue, "Only if the political incorrectness of talking about the natural family within policy circles is overcome will solutions begin to be found. These solutions will necessarily result in policy changes, changes that will support and promote the natural, intact family." The rhetoric of the "natural family" is taken from Carlson and Mero's *The Natural Family: A Manifesto* and the strong cross-denominational profamily movement that inspired it. Stout, a Brigham Young University graduate, and McLerran, executive director of the Family First Foundation, a grant-making organization based in the aptly named Salt Lake City suburb of Bountiful, are among the hundreds of Mormon profamily activists who have made common cause with conservative Catholic and evangelical ideologues.

The interdenominational alliance of Mormon, Catholic, and evangelical profamily advocates, as well as the token link between this pan-

Christian front and a handful of Orthodox Jewish and Muslim representatives, is the hallmark of Carlson's work, whether with the Howard Center, the Family First Foundation—of which he is also a director—or as secretary and cofounder of the World Congress of Families (WCF), an international, interfaith, profamily conference.

The WCF is just one channel for Carlson's profamily goal. It's a locus for heavyweight U.S. conservative actors from the Heritage Foundation, the Family Research Council, Concerned Women for America, and James Dobson's Focus on the Family—a who's who of the American Christian right—to network with representatives from the Vatican, conservative Christians from developing nations, and a smattering of Muslim groups seeking allies to fight gay and women's rights at the United Nations. The result is the spread of U.S. culture-war tactics across the globe, from the Czech Republic to Qatar—where right-wing Mormon activist and WCF cofounder Richard Wilkins has found enough common cause with Muslim fundamentalists to build the Doha International Institute for Family Studies and Development.

Arguably, the greatest impact profamily efforts such as the WCF have is in helping conservative European leaders hone a common message about the "natural family" as a necessary counter to demographic anxieties.

The fourth conference of the WCF, held in Warsaw in May 2007, provided much of the commentary for the *Demographic Winter* film. And little wonder: besides Carlson, Family First Foundation's board of directors is composed entirely of WCF leaders and speakers, all of whom gathered in Warsaw's grand Palace of Culture and Science, the old Polish Communist Party headquarters, with more than three thousand other religious conservatives to hear predictions about Europe as a sinking ship, a *Titanic* nearly lost to the repercussions of the sexual revolution. But for the first time in a long time, the "natural family" has a white knight in Europe: brave Poland, the anti-Sweden. Following Pope John Paul II's philosophy that particular countries can change the course of Europe, Poland has been heralded in U.S. profamily literature as the likely salvation of the continent: a heavily Catholic bastion of conservatism amid the gay-friendly EU with a long history of Catholic-evangelical cooperation. (In fact, it was in Poland that this partnership began in the 1970s, with future Pope John Paul II helping Billy Graham to introduce Campus Crusade for Christ to the country and Graham guest-preaching from the pope's Krakow church on the day of John Paul's papal coronation.) Under the leadership of the Kaczynski brothers—Lech and Jaroslaw, extremist twins who held office as president and prime minister—the country shifted far to the right, embracing a social conservatism that aggressively targets gays, Jews, women's rights, and foreigners and that in 2006 went so far as to propose that Jesus be named honorary king of Poland.

To Carlson, this proves Poland is "an island of profamily values" amid the tides of "Christophobic" "population-control types" who dominate the rest of the continent. Poland, he says, could provide an important counterbalance to European modernity and become a launching point for a profamily resistance. It could thereby "save Europe again": a not-so-coded reference to the Battle of Vienna in 1683, where Polish King John III Sobieski led a "holy league" army of Christian soldiers against the Ottoman Empire, culminating in a decisive victory for Christendom over the invading Muslim troops. The profamily movement's bald reference to this ancient holy war informs new conservative foot soldiers who see today's immigration conflicts as a new phase of a very old war. And so the WCF chose Poland as the site of its 2007 massing of the troops, drawing thousands of leaders from across the spectrum of religious-right activism: from U.S. evangelical and Catholic nonprofits to Eastern European Catholic and Eastern Orthodox antiabortion and anti–gay rights groups to bureaucrats from national European governments as well as the EU and the United States—all taking policy notes to bring back home.

The architects of the WCF have persuaded traditionally isolationist American conservatives to care about the fate of secular, impious Europe with two main arguments: one, that Europe is a bulwark against a Muslim "invasion" of America—"If Europe is lost to demographic winter and radical secularism, much of the world will go with it," Carlson warns—and two, that global trends, such as the normalization of gay and women's rights through international court decisions, can impact life at home.

If Europe has a sickness of the soul, the WCF claims to have the cure. Specifically, that cure is a version of the practice of American women living Allan Carlson's "natural family" vision of having full quivers of children. But on the international stage, the vision was packaged for popular culture: encouraging families to become Great Families, with three to four children each, enough of an increase to stave off the winter.

"The new view is that in order to create and defend a profamily culture, we also have to have a friendly international environment," says Carlson. "So you see something fundamentally new: the social conservative movement going global."

Austin Ruse says the WCF is just one expression of an ever-growing conservative coalition. Its hatred of liberalism, feminism, and the sexual revolution outweighs theological differences, and it is branching out worldwide. His Catholic Family and Human Rights Institute (C-FAM) is opening offices in Brussels to lobby the EU directly.

Ruse's goals for EU activism are likely in line with his accomplishments at the UN, where he worked to establish a permanent bloc of antiabortion nations and gained notoriety for his incendiary rhetoric (comparing his lobby to a plague of locusts descending on women's rights) and political theater, which, even with few allies, effectively stalled progress on a number of women's rights initiatives. Christian-right watchers agree that the demographic winter appeals to struggling new EU countries in devout Eastern Europe could have serious results. Ruse himself, not given to understatement, imagines the global Christian profamily alliance is "unlike anything we've seen since the Reformation." A bloc like this, he boasts, is capable of mayhem: "Picture the documentaries about Africa: the hyenas going after the wildebeest. You're just surrounded. We are everywhere, doing everything."

Jennifer Butler, author of *Born Again: The Christian Right Globalized* and a witness to the havoc that Ruse brought to the UN during the 1990s, has tracked the rise of the international Christian right with apprehension since she first encountered the tactics of Ruse and his colleagues. C-FAM sent representatives dressed as monks to pray for the souls of feminist NGO workers at the UN and seated themselves in the formation of a cross. She has also seen the rise of pronatalist advocacy in the pages of the Catholic intellectual journal *First Things,* which she describes as at the forefront of conservative efforts to weave two strands of conservatism together: the social conservatives with a "racialized apocalyptic worldview" and neoconservatives aware of the traditional partnership between religion and empire. It's a movement of coalitions, and Butler recalls the chills she felt in 2000, when Austin Ruse "sent around a note asking the Abrahamic faiths to rise up together. From the standpoint of the Presbyterian Church," for which Butler was a UN representative, "I had seen conservative tactics rise in our own assemblies. I knew what they'd done to our denomination." But at the UN, Butler's colleagues were unfamiliar with the church-splitting conflicts conservatives had brought to mainline U.S. Protestant churches. "I felt that nobody else knew what they were up to. You can't underestimate what they can do."

What they are up to now is on full display for interested observers: a battle on many fronts against what they call "the autonomy revolution" of the 1960s—a worldview shift far broader than a mere sexual revolution. The multiple prongs and minutiae of the "natural family" revival they intend are being addressed by hundreds of conservative activists. Paige Patterson lamented to the World Congress of Families the high percentage of female university students as an impediment to stay-at-home motherhood. Carol Soelberg, president of the Mormon group United Families International and the mother of thirteen, exhorts women to realize their true mission in the home. Paul Mero encourages early marriage by declaring bachelors over thirty "a menace to society." Carlson continually seeks ways to turn tax law into a vehicle for rewarding fertility. And Mosher advocates cutting all funding for contraception to developing nations (to "err on the side of caution when it comes to identifying the beginning of life") and implementing pronatal policies in countries such as Poland and Armenia, where the birthrates are far below replacement levels.

· · ·

How far these activists can go with the natural family revival depends in part on how convincing their population threats—and solutions—seem to countries grappling with cultural growing pains, as well as how deftly the proponents of demographic winter navigate their own abundant internal contradictions.

Despite the lip service the profamily movement gives to uniting "all the children of Abraham" against common enemies, the sense of Muslim immigration as a more tangible foe bleeds through their cooperative rhetoric. Farooq Hassan, a Harvard law professor and one of the few Muslim representatives in this profamily movement, chastised his colleagues for their transparent appeals to nationalism: "The rest of the world doesn't have the same problems as Europe. The Western world wants more people in Europe, but you don't care if there are more families in the Third World. You want less families there."

As if to demonstrate Hassan's point, Mosher's Population Research

Institute (PRI) claims to fight population control on behalf of women in developing nations—lumping instances of real abuse, such as the history of coerced sterilizations performed on developing-world women, together with all efforts to expand family planning options, with the effect of stifling debate on contraception options in developing nations such as Peru. But Mosher reveals the limits of his professed concern for women's rights when he tells me that Israel relinquished Gaza because of Yasir Arafat's "best weapon," the "womb of the Arab woman"—an example of fertility that Mosher finds "very sobering if you're concerned about the future of Israel, as I am."

In the context of the competing narratives conservatives hope to bend to their purposes, Mosher's slightly off-message slip is understandable. Another instance of this took place when American antiabortion OB/GYN Byron Calhoun lectured against contraception at the WCF, telling the largely Polish audience that birth control was a continuation of an old evil, child sacrifice—a fraught evocation in post-Holocaust Poland, where anti-Semitic slurs against the nearly destroyed Jewish population, including the old blood libel charging Jews with ritual child murder, are far from forgotten. The inference isn't much of a stretch in a country where the government blames shadowy "webs of influence" for Poland's lagging economy; where sociologists describe a widespread conceptualized anti-Semitism that casts gays, feminists, and secularists as symbolic "Jews" in a country with few actual Jews left; and where Jews are blamed for Communism and abortion, both of which are widely reviled. (Such associations aren't limited to Poland's profamily movement: Fr. Paul Marx, the founder of both PRI and C-FAM's parent group, Human Life International, which has been active in organizing and training antiabortion groups across Central Europe since at least the 1990s, likewise charged that Jews control the abortion "industry," and have created "the greatest holocaust of all time, the war on unborn babies.")

These relics of demagogy—blurring the lines between the various enemies of Polish nationalism, whether Jewish, secular, or Muslim—have helped foster a climate in which Poland, which has among the lowest fertility rates in Europe, widely accepts the concept of demographic winter, and all it entails, as truth. Members of the right-wing ideological youth brigade All-Polish Youth, which was linked to neo-Nazi activities in 2008, refine their politics by reading Pat Buchanan's *The Death of the West,* in which he describes a generalized Western diaspora—including

Australia, Canada, the United States, and Russia—as a vanishing race. (The youth group's honorary chairman, Roman Giertych, Poland's former Minister of Education from the extremist League of Polish Families party, was a featured speaker of the WCF, where he promised the crowd that the world of heterosexual normality would triumph over Europe's antifamily philosophy.) Meanwhile, to reverse the winter, Poland is enshrining Catholic doctrine into law; it is relegating contraception and sex ed to private clinics and crafting laws to ban discussions on homosexuality from public schools and to prosecute abortion as murder.

Elzbieta Korolczuk, a scholar working on her Ph.D. at the Graduate School for Social Research at the Polish Academy of Sciences, has found that abortion debates in Poland since the end of Communism in the 1990s are centered around a nationalist question: "whether letting women decide to perform an abortion or not is in contradiction with the interests of the Polish family and nation, and if women who have abortions 'betray' Poland, since they do not want to reproduce it. Thus, women's bodies are treated as a 'national boundary' and women are subjected to the supervision of the state as family members, namely, actual and potential mothers."

Jon O'Brien, president of the liberal reproductive-rights group Catholics for Choice, tells me that Poland is "a classic example of what you can expect if the World Congress of Families' fantasy came true."

This is where O'Brien, generally skeptical of the profamily movement's international appeal, sees a dangerous opportunity for its extremist patriarchal ideas to bloom: in Eastern European countries new to democracy and more accustomed to totalitarian traditions and an ultranationalism born of fear, poverty, and porous borders. "When you have someone powerful like Putin talking to people in these circumstances about the necessity of Russian women giving birth, then you have to worry about it—how that could be turned into policy."

"There's been some talk about depopulation at the UN," says Adrienne Germain, president of the International Women's Health Coalition, "which speaks to the fact that most countries see it as an issue they need to address—in terms of social security, the labor force, but not as a matter of absolute numbers." But she sees the profamily movement's new demographic focus as a logical extreme for a Christian right savvy at crafting appeals to their audience. "To me, it was obvious that they'd reach this point. It just seems early," she says. The worrying thing is that whether countries push pro- or antinatalist policies, "the first thing down the drain is a woman's ability to control her body."

And this, of course, is the (largely unacknowledged) rub with the profamily movement's focus on procreation: it requires a world of women to dedicate their lives and wombs to demographic battle. "The shadow of Fascism still hovers over demographic science," the anthropologist Elizabeth Krause tells me, and lends a chilling factor to "moralizing" language that pathologizes the childless as sick or, in Italy, as anorexics refusing to eat. Indeed, when Pope John Paul II raised his demographic concerns to the Italian Parliament, it was unprecedented since the Fascist years and evoked a painful social memory of Mussolini's fertility project, which attacked bachelors, rewarded mothers of many children, criminalized abortion, and banned contraception. Women's pregnancies were described in terms of duty to the nation. "They were reproducing the state. There's nothing fertile about it."

Of course, such programs weren't limited to Italian Fascism. A similar trajectory occurred in wartime Germany, writes historian Claudia Koonz, author of *Mothers in the Fatherland,* where "in an atmosphere of heightened danger and conflict, women as well as men experienced freedom in obedience to a rebellious movement," and where there arose the idea of "emancipation from emancipation," which centered around its own family vision: "a dream of a strong man and a gentle woman, cooperating under the stern guidance of an orderly state." While other nations in Depression-era Europe grew concerned about falling birthrates, under Fascism's extreme gender divisions and the escalating sense of crisis pervading the country, early eugenic motherhood schools and rewards for fertile women morphed by war's end into the brutalizing demographic demands of the Lebensborn breeding program. What began as organizing housewives through affirmations of their traditionalist decisions—"the cradle and the ladle"—became a heavy-handed state program designed to mass-produce more Aryan soldiers and factory hands as part of the "motherhood crusade," and which castigated "selfish" women who weren't doing their part to guarantee the increase and preservation of the race.

The implication of current pronatalist arguments, that women are the source of population problems, may be less extreme, argues Krause, but it is still deeply troublesome. "To state that women's interests are at odds with those of babies is to stake out a moral ground on which women's primary role is as a biological reproducer for the nation—much as it was during the Fascist years." Furthermore, Krause says, calling for Italian women to begin having three or four children "erases the trauma of peasant women who've historically borne large families in crushing poverty" and labels women's decisions to limit their families a disease in need of a cure. But these things are quickly forgotten in the panic for more "European" babies.

As for the idea of cultural identity implicit in the notion of "European babies," Krause delivers a salient reminder that some multicultural liberal truisms hold and that what unifies a population is often a deliberate decision to welcome and integrate new elements into society rather than cling to ever-shifting notions of "true" European heritage and race. To wit, the very insults hurled at today's Muslim immigrants in Italy are themselves repurposed echoes of old slurs that northern Italians made against their southern countrymen up to a short decade ago, deriding them as too dark and too foreign to qualify as "authentically" Italian. The population that is being banded together against a new outsider was, until very recently, fractured within itself, still struggling after more than one hundred and fifty years to forge a common identity out of the many regional groups that make up the state. "One of the famous quotes from [newly unified] Italy in the 1860s," Krause recalls, "was, 'Now that we've made Italy, we need to make Italians.' Making Italians, Russians, Americans is a constant project."

But such slow-slogging and fragile projects of community-building are jeopardized by the hasty purity standards implied by the Great Family "cure" for demographic winter, in which belonging is defined by ethnicity alone and demographic winter itself begins to seem just a prelude for a new cold war, a "clash of civilizations" to be fought through women's bodies, with the maternity ward as battleground.

CHAPTER NINETEEN

Exiting the Movement

While the Quiverfull movement does not have the institutional and traditional grounding of the ultra-Orthodox pronatalist movement in Israel, within its own close-knit communities, the cultural force for women to toe the line can be as powerful. The story of Cheryl Lindsey Seelhoff, a fifty-five-year-old former Quiverfull woman turned radical feminist writer and blogger, as well as a successful litigant against a number of Christian right leaders, shows the lengths to which patriarchal communities will go to maintain the male-headship and submissive wife order of their theology.

Seelhoff, who today lives with her third husband and the youngest three of her eleven children on a farm near Tacoma, Washington, is an unlikely figure in the conservative homeschooling movement. Seelhoff was raised by liberal Democratic parents during the 1960s and was greatly influenced by the civil rights movement of the era, saying that Martin Luther King, Jr.'s assassination and the televised images of police violence against black demonstrators were formative experiences in her life. In 1969, when she entered the University of Washington, she studied political science and became an antiracism activist, traveling to Cincinnati during her freshman summer to work at an inner-city employment service for young black teens. Also at UW, she met her first husband, an African American man who'd worked with the Black Panthers in Seattle. The couple had two children and a tumultuous marriage that ended after a few years.

While waitressing in Seattle to support her two children, Seelhoff met her second husband, Claude Lindsey, also a black man and an employee of nearby IBM. After Seelhoff and Lindsey had had two more children, in 1978 Lindsey converted to evangelical, charismatic Christianity, and Seelhoff renewed her own religious beliefs. She'd been saved as a young girl in a Baptist church but had strayed from the faith during her teens. They joined an Assemblies of God church in Bellevue and, Seelhoff says, "we plunged, as a family, wholeheartedly into conservative Christianity." They became active in church life and eventually moved to the more radical Calvary Chapel in Tacoma—part of a nondenominational, semi-Calvinist evangelical and "Bible-believing" fellowship of churches that began in Costa Mesa, California, and that is today one of the largest Protestant church communities, with more than thirteen hundred affiliates worldwide and a wide-ranging radio presence. Calvary's emphasis on Bible study led Seelhoff and Lindsey along a common path for conservative Christians, from evangelicals happy to find spiritual community to devout believers and students of Scripture. Seelhoff recounts, "Our studies resulted, ironically—as is not unusual—in dissatisfaction with most twentieth-century evangelical/fundamentalist churches, including Calvary Chapel. We wanted to not only read and study the Word, but to live it, to 'do' it. We became Bible literalists, agreeing with the adage that, 'If the plain sense of Scripture makes common sense,' the believer should 'seek no other sense.'"

Tacoma's Calvary Chapel was pastored by a black man in an interracial marriage, as Seelhoff and Lindsey were, but where they opposed racism, they taught and preached inequality of the sexes as God's order. Seelhoff subsequently quit her job working as a court stenographer and had her fifth child in 1983, determined to be a stay-at-home mother who let God plan her family. In time, Seelhoff and Lindsey met a number of homeschooling families around Washington and began attending workshops and seminars with them, eventually forming a local support group for homeschooling families. In 1986 Seelhoff wrote a homeschooling resource book, *Homeschooling: A Mother's Guide and Resource Book,* and three years later she developed a newsletter on living simply called *Gentle Spirit,* which eventually caught the attention of James Dobson of Focus on the Family. With the endorsement of Dobson, Seelhoff's stapled-paper newsletter, which started with twenty-three subscribers, grew over five years to a glossy magazine with a circulation of seventeen thousand that brought her an annual gross income of approximately three hundred thousand dollars.

By this time homeschooling, which in its conception was not necessarily a religious movement, had been largely taken over by fundamentalist leadership that began enforcing doctrinal tests on members of homeschooling organizations, requiring them to sign statements of faith and encouraging them toward rigid fundamentalist parenting mores. Washington state, where Seelhoff was living, became one of the early centers of this newly Christian homeschooling movement, and Seelhoff, who was also speaking at conferences, was soon approached by Sue Welch, publisher of *The Teaching Home* magazine, to advertise herself and her work in Welch's publication. Welch was considered one of the four pillars of homeschooling that also included Michael Farris, of the Home School Legal Defense Association; Gregg Harris, a veteran organizer of Christian homeschooling conferences as well as father to celebrity Reformed pastor and courtship advocate Joshua Harris and his younger brothers at the Christian youth blog Rebelution; and Brian Ray, president of the HSLDA-affiliated National Home Education Research Institute.

Sue Welch began publicizing Seelhoff's conferences in her magazine, once complaining that Seelhoff was being deceitful by not disclosing to readers that she was in an interracial marriage. Seelhoff's *Gentle Spirit* enjoyed substantial success for five years, even attracting an offer from Mary Pride (who in addition to her books such as *The Way Home* was also publisher of several homeschooling periodicals, including *HELP for Growing Families*) that Seelhoff buy out Pride's struggling magazine. At the time, many magazines in the homeschooling community, including Seelhoff's, were publishing articles on what would come to be known as the Quiverfull lifestyle. Seelhoff sees the roots of the conviction as a combination of various strands of Christianity: pre–Vatican II Catholicism; the beliefs of agrarian, "plain people" communities such as the Amish and Mennonites; and the Reformed tradition and disciples of Francis and Edith Schaeffer, such as Mary Pride and Bill Gothard.

During the heady early days of the movement, Seelhoff tells me, "Pride's book, *The Way Home,* was a kind of manifesto, outlining what Pride envisioned as the lifestyle of the new renaissance woman: Bible-believing, devout, home-centered, homeschooling, operating a home business, gardening, showing hospitality. Pride's teachings pulled all of the various strands of home-centered life together and made them a sort of lifestyle choice for Christian women, with homeschooling very central." And within the homeschooling movement, Seelhoff remembers, many publications and organizations were putting their muscle behind supporting large families, encouraging "women [who] found support and respect in the Quiverfull movement that they could not find anywhere else in quite the same way," as well as a "certain type of man, who enjoyed being the 'priest of his home,' honored and revered by family and church community." She observes that "many otherwise ordinary men with ordinary jobs who didn't command high levels of respect, societally, found a way to obtain respect in the Quiverfull community by being the leader of a devout, large family—the husband of a submissive wife, raising sons who would be future leaders in the church and daughters who would bear large families and care for them at home, and so on. All under the aegis of being the 'faithful remnant,' God's chosen people, true believers, the 'New Testament church,' etc."

Missing from the glowing, folksy depictions of large, simple family life pictured in the homeschooling magazines is the reality of Quiverfull life as it is lived by the majority of women in the movement, says Seelhoff.

> The Quiverfull movement holds up as examples families like the Duggars, the Doug Phillips family, the Michael Farris family—all men of means. But for every family like this, there are ten or fifty or one hundred Quiverfull families living in what most would consider to be poverty. Quiverfull families are one-income families and believe the father should be the provider and breadwinner and the mother should be caring for hearth and home. They are usually attempting to get a home business of some kind off the ground, [reflecting] another goal of the Quiverfull movement, that families be self-supporting. There are children to homeschool, feed, care for, raise. Mothers are in a constant cycle, often, of pregnancy, breastfeeding, and the care of toddlers. Living simply is often practiced as a lifestyle choice, but it is also a necessity with this many children. I had a friend with six children who, for all the years that I knew her, was given twenty-five dollars per week for groceries and twenty-five dollars per month for clothing for her family.

Making this work, Seelhoff explains, means growing one's own vegetables, certainly, but also gleaning fields, eating little meat, and, in bad situations, even Dumpster-diving. Quiverfull life can get even harder, and more desperate, when fathers act on the popular Quiverfull aim of living debt-free and move families to dilapidated trailers, school buses, or tarp configurations on isolated parcels of land without water or other amenities. Seelhoff herself fed her family for years on two hundred dollars per month, cooking and freezing thirty dinners one day each month, a monthly miracle of physical labor that she transformed into a regular magazine feature: thirty-meal meal plans and recipes for bulk cooking and baking. Of course, she says, children, and particularly daughters, are enlisted in the process and thus learn early that their lot in life is to be submissive, faithful, chaste, and discreet. As proof of the wearying life with no end to obligation and duty, Seelhoff points to Beverly Murch, wife of Bruce Murch, the founder of the zealous antiabortion ministry Full Quiver Mission, whom Seelhoff describes as having fallen into a deep depression following a hysterectomy due to uterine cancer. Murch, the mother of nine, Seelhoff speculates, was likely depressed because she feared her surgery was an affront to God that He would punish with death even after she'd spent a lifetime caring for a family of eleven.

Women who attempt to opt out of this lifestyle are often left empty-handed, except for their dozens of children who they are now at a loss to support, with years of missing work on their résumés and no references forthcoming from the community they've broken with. Instead, many stay in what can be abusive or humiliating circumstances, following submission teachings that emphasize their role in sexually satisfying their husbands or else being subjected to church discipline procedures if their husbands complain that they aren't being submissive or affectionate wives. With children, Seelhoff notes, physical discipline such as Michael and Debi Pearl advocate is the norm, but this may extend in some circumstances to physical "discipline" of wives. Such discipline may include the quasi-religious and sexually fetishistic "domestic discipline" Internet groups dedicated to wife spanking (though it's important to note that this seems more a Christian-flavored version of sexual kinks than a vibrant branch of the patriarchy movement). The far more common practice of requiring daughters to sign "purity pledges" bears what Seelhoff calls "an incestuous quality," "communicating the view that daughters are the property of their fathers until such time as they become the property of their husbands."

This sense of female subordination is drummed in every day, subjecting women, both wives and daughters, to a Scripture-based train-

ing in self-hatred and hatred of other women. These Scriptures include:
1 Timothy 2:11, "Let the woman learn in silence"; Ephesians 5:22,
"Wives, submit yourselves unto your own husbands"; Jesus's words in
Revelation 2:20, "I have a few things against you, because you suffer
that woman Jezebel"; and Proverbs 5:3–5, "The lips of an adulteress drip
honey… but in the end she is bitter as gall… Her feet go down to death."
The last, Seelhoff says, is a verse sometimes read aloud each day a child is
growing up, training children of both sexes to despise the "wrong" sort of
woman. Seelhoff explains that Scripture is used to rear girls to

> believe themselves to be easily deceived, manipulative, likely to de-
> ceive, "unclean," in need of protection from men, and in great danger
> if they are out from under men's protection. Overwhelmed with the
> demands of their lives, possibly abused, possibly raped by their hus-
> bands or forced to have sex they do not want on a regular basis, and
> also doubting themselves on these very deep levels, believing them-
> selves to be deceived and deceivers—God himself said that they are in
> the Bible—it is completely understandable that a certain number of
> these women will break in various ways. It surprises me that we do not
> have more situations like the Andrea Yates situation.

Seelhoff's own break came in the early '90s when Claude Lindsey,
who she says had long been an authoritative, angry, and abusive husband,
went into early retirement and moved the family to the country. Lindsey
left the family in 1994 for New Orleans, claiming to seek biblical anger
counseling.

During this time, Seelhoff met the man who would become her third
husband, Rick Seelhoff, a Minnesota native and a member of a cult-watch
organization. The two became romantically involved, and Seelhoff went
to her pastor at Calvary Chapel, Joe Williams, and his wife, Irene, seeking confidential counsel about her disintegrating marriage and pleading
that they keep her confession secret. They did so until Lindsey returned
to Washington to accost Seelhoff's new partner and empty the family
bank accounts before leaving town again, whereupon Seelhoff filed for
divorce. This is when the gears of the homeschooling leadership began
to turn, organizing a number of influential men and women around the
country for the purpose of condemning their fallen sister.

Seelhoff, a popular homeschooling conference speaker who traveled across the United States to address female audiences, had a full slate of conference workshops and speeches in Columbus, Ohio, for Christian Home Educators of Ohio, scheduled for the week after she filed for divorce. But in that time, Lindsey had alerted Gregg Harris, who would also be speaking at the Ohio conference, to the couple's impending divorce and asked him to watch Seelhoff at the conference, in case Rick joined her. Harris took the initiative to call Seelhoff's pastor's wife, Irene, and ask her whether Seelhoff was having an affair and whether the Williamses intended to exercise church discipline on her. Sue Welch also called Irene with similar questions and information. After the conference, Seelhoff says, Harris called Rick Seelhoff pretending to be a hotel concierge from Columbus in order to trick him into disclosing that he'd been at the event.

On July 4, 1994, Seelhoff was called by the organizer of the Ohio conference at which she'd just spoken, Michael Boutot. Boutot chastised her for speaking at the conference while she was involved in "unrepentant adultery" and a divorce "without grounds." Lindsey and Pastor Williams, who was letting Lindsey stay at his house, had called Boutot and a number of national homeschooling organizations and publishers, including Michael Farris, Mary Pride, officials at Focus on the Family, as well as subscribers, advertisers, and writers for *Gentle Spirit*.

During her phone call with Boutot, Seelhoff was given a list of ultimatums, or "fruits of repentance," that she would be required to demonstrate in order to avoid a letter of censure and church discipline being read first to her congregation and then mailed to her extended community in the national homeschooling movement. Among the demands were that Seelhoff return her speaking honorarium; write letters of apology to Lindsey, Pastor Williams, and a number of homeschooling leaders; stop divorce proceedings and end her relationship with Rick; cease writing, publishing, and public speaking; turn over all private e-mail, postal communications, and bank records to Pastor Williams; agree to never go out alone; and report for two weeks of intensive biblical marriage counseling in the Midwest.

When Seelhoff didn't agree to the terms, the effort to shame her nationally began in earnest. At Calvary Chapel, Pastor Williams read aloud a letter of discipline excommunicating Seelhoff and turning her "over to Satan for the destruction of her flesh." The Williamses prepared to send their letter nationwide, and Sue Welch offered to prepare and print mailing labels for the letter, sent on July 7. Welch also contacted Michael Farris to ask about the legality of advising all *Gentle Spirit* advertisers and columnists to cease business dealings with Seelhoff, and she faxed the information about the divorce and adultery to Mary Pride. Pride promptly revised her Summer 1994 issue of *HELP for Growing Families* to include mention of the scandal and further set up two separate AOL discussion folders dedicated to disseminating information about the Cheryl Lindsey affair. Pride instructed her assistant David Ayers, a part-time employee who would later be a contributing author to John Piper and Wayne Grudem's *Recovering Biblical Manhood and Womanhood* (and who quit working for Pride within months of the scandal, faulting Pride's "authoritarian" and "micromanaging" personality), to formulate a plan to woo *Gentle Spirit* advertisers to Pride's *HELP for Growing Families*. Advertisers later testified that Ayers had called them and told them that *Gentle Spirit* was folding and that Seelhoff had had an adulterous affair they could read more about on AOL. Seelhoff says that Doug Phillips, who had been an attorney in HSLDA under Farris, renounced her at a homeschooling conference as a "Jezebel" and that Valerie Jill Barrett, the wife of Tim Barrett, a Reconstructionist attorney in the movement, e-mailed Seelhoff a shocking condemnation: "You are outrageous in your brazen apostasy. If this were a truly godly nation, you wouldn't only have been excommunicated. You would have been executed."

In the meantime, Seelhoff lost her entire source of income, and angry subscribers, egged on by the campaign against Seelhoff, wrote in demanding refunds she was unable to fulfill. Her house and land went into foreclosure and her car mysteriously burned to the ground. Unknown men appeared at her house to "pray" with her, and everyone she knew shunned her presence. She had nine children, and far from receiving any child support, she instead had to pay her ex-husband spousal maintenance fees due to his early retirement. Her two oldest sons turned against her, angered by her relationship with Rick, and Seelhoff began to suffer debilitating panic attacks and slid into a suicidal depression that, she says, "lasted for some time. It was a horrifying and dark time, and I still am not sure how I survived it."

In 1997, three years after the harassment began, Seelhoff filed a lawsuit against her antagonists, including her local church and the Williamses, Calvary Chapel's parent church in California, Sue Welch and her magazine, Gregg Harris, Michael Boutot, and Mary and Bill Pride, charging the lot with defamation, outrage, interference with commerce, and violation of the Sherman Antitrust Act by conspiring to restrain trade. "I sued when I realized I would not be allowed to move forward with my life," Seelhoff says, explaining that despite her remarriage to Rick Seelhoff, all of her efforts to reestablish her publishing business, or a Web site, triggered new waves of threats and attacks. Harris, the Prides, Boutot's Christian Home Educators of Ohio, and the California Calvary Chapel settled for confidential amounts, and the remaining suit against Welch and the Williamses was ruled in Seelhoff's favor, awarding her an initial judgment of $435,000, which, automatically tripled in antitrust cases, became an award in excess of $1.3 million (but which was later reduced on appeal and a mediated settlement). The harassment stopped and an uncomfortable silence held in the homeschooling community, which discouraged further discussion of the case. "The strangest phenomenon, in my opinion," Seelhoff told a more liberal homeschooling magazine, "is the silence that has followed the jury verdict and the final resolution of the case. In 1994, thousands of homeschooling families were made aware of the crisis in my private life within a few short weeks, yet the lawsuit which grew out of those events has remained, by and large, a secret."

"It is as though," she tells me, "so far as they are concerned, I am dead."

Seelhoff sees her experience of church discipline and shunning as not uncommon throughout the Quiverfull and patriarchy communities. Indeed, in 2008, the *Wall Street Journal* reported on an upswing in church disciplinary actions, shunnings, and excommunications among independent Protestant denominations, these churches cleaving to the Matthew 18 guidelines for churches' role as moral enforcers and hoping to counteract lax suburban megachurches that they see as focused more on self-affirmation than sin and salvation.

The movement toward churches with the authority to discipline their members for personal offenses could just as easily be viewed, though, as a series of graduated steps along the evangelical path, from seeker to purist, which so many of the Christian men and women I've spoken to have traversed—a walk that American Christendom as a body seems to be taking alongside its individual members, moving from church-building openness to ever-rigidifying doctrine. Approximately 15 percent of evangelical churches practice church discipline, frequently involving the public disclosure of congregants' confessions that were given under the assumption of privacy. As a result, hundreds of congregants in fundamentalist Baptist and other evangelical churches have been excommunicated or shunned for misdeeds ranging from drunkenness, adultery, refusal to honor church elders, gossiping, and sowing disharmony.

And women, who under patriarchy have a longer list of potential sins to commit and who remain a lifelong underclass in the ranks of spiritual warriors, are inherently under greater susceptibility to church discipline and its abuses than are their husbands and brothers in Christ. Seelhoff asserts:

> Women are taught that it is a sin to speak against church authority and their husbands' authority, or their husbands just in general, and so women ordinarily do not compare [their] circumstances, even apart from church discipline. If any woman dares to share her husband's abuse, she will be urged by other women to pray or to consider how she might be offending her husband or why what he is doing might be her fault. If she is disciplined she knows—because she has been taught—that it is sinful to "speak evil of dignities" and that if she does she will only bring more discipline down on her head for being a gossip or a heretic or for causing schism. Church members do not openly speak of this discipline because they know they will be subjected to public scrutiny, and they fear it. They know that [their churches] are authoritarian, and they know that what they do, allow, approve, or teach so far as discipline of women and children is considered abuse by the surrounding culture, but they believe it is God-ordained and God-ordered and biblical. They take a sort of martyr's stance that they should keep this private so as not to have to suffer for their faithfulness to church or Scripture. They believe that worldly people cannot possibly correctly understand or interpret what goes on in the church, including around church discipline.

If this psychological sketch sounds familiar, it should. Seelhoff, who now describes herself as a radical feminist and disciple of Andrea Dworkin, compares the religious right to an abusive husband, and urges comparable sympathy and care be extended to spiritually battered women leaving an abusive church as to those fleeing an abusive man. And though she's helped a number of her former Quiverfull sisters establish themselves outside the community after their marriages deteriorated, she realizes that the pull back into the community can be overwhelming. She comments with compassion about the push and pull Jennifer Epstein still feels for the BCA community that shuns her.

Apart from the logistical and practical hardships of setting oneself up in mainstream society after years on the fringe, there's a sense of spiritual demotion at work as well. Without membership in the elect club of elite believers, and what Seelhoff calls the "status/perks/benefits that come from her connection with the Vision Forum crowd"—or any other crowd of self-appointed remnants of the faithful, for that matter—exited women have to move on as ordinary women, leading ordinary lives: a loss that may eclipse whatever hardships women faced while in the "elect" groups. It can come down to a question of the evil that you know, and women in these communities, who have long been trained to doubt their own perceptions and consider themselves as malleable and easily deceived as Eve, look instead for their own sin and strain to repent in order to gain reentry into their worlds. "That looks better to her at the moment than being cut off from her entire community and having to start from scratch, this time with an excommunication in her history to explain to others," Seelhoff says.

A substantial settlement can likely ease the path a bit, and with her award, Cheryl and Rick Seelhoff bought the farm they currently live on. This is where Seelhoff writes her women-only blog, *Women's Space*, a radical corner of the feminist blogosphere, where one day last year, Seelhoff received a surprising comment to a blog post. It was a note from Jill Barrett, the woman who'd previously told Seelhoff her adultery and apostasy were worthy of death.

Barrett was divorced and, she wrote, living in the "lowest circle of legal hell" for it: fighting charges from her lawyer ex-husband that several favorable reviews she'd written on Amazon.com about domestic violence books constituted defamation of her ex's character. She didn't remember writing the execution e-mail to Seelhoff, she said, but she remembered showing it to her husband, "the Lord and Master," when he came home that night. "I'm sure I sent the e-mail," she wrote, "and I beg your forgiveness. I lashed out at anyone who attacked my brainwashed existence and false faith.... Some cults exist within a single house, or a trailer, or a bus." She closed her apology, "Here's to liberty, and to the new world.... Eyes wide open."

PART THREE

·

DAUGHTERS

CHAPTER TWENTY

Victory through Daughters

There were complications when Anna Sofia Botkin, the eldest daughter of Geoffrey Botkin, one of Vision Forum's leading voices and an elder-in-training for Doug Phillips's church, Boerne Christian Assembly, was born. Her mother, Victoria Botkin, might have died. While doctors attended to the post-labor mother, Geoffrey Botkin held his newborn daughter perfectly still in his cupped hands, and prayed to God for guidance: after having raised two older sons, how should he raise a daughter? As he prayed, he felt God move him to a specific prayer for the infant sleeping in his hands, a prayer for her body. He remembered baby girls are born with two ovaries and a finite number of eggs that will last them a lifetime. He placed his hand over his new daughter's abdomen and prayed for Anna Sofia to be the "future mother of tens of millions." He prayed that the Lord would order everything in his daughter's life: "What You will do with every single egg here. How many children will this young lady have? Who will be her husband? With what other legacy will these little eggs be joined to produce the next generation for the glory of God?" He explained to a room full of about six hundred fathers and daughters gathered for the annual Vision Forum Father and Daughter Retreat that he had prayed that his new daughter might marry young.

Today, Anna Sofia and her sister, Elizabeth, strikingly poised young women in their early twenties, are the preeminent Vision Forum brand for promoting biblical womanhood to the unmarried daughters of homeschooling families, girls largely raised in the patriarchal faith but susceptible to temptations from the outside world. In all their testimony to fellow young "maidens," the Botkin daughters, raised in both the American South and the Botkins' Seven Arrows Ranch in New Zealand, stress the dire importance of one of their father's favorite talking points: "multigenerational faithfulness." That is, the necessity of the sons and daughters of the movement—especially the daughters—cleaving to the ways of their parents and not abandoning the dominion project the older generation has begun.

Some children do rebel, as Natasha Epstein recalls. There were several runaway girls from Boerne Christian Assembly, she says, who ultimately succeeded in leaving the lifestyle after having been caught and brought back to the church by their fathers and other men in the church. Natasha herself ran away from home following the excommunication of her family, living with her grandparents in Oregon for a period before returning to Texas and taking up the modern young woman's lifestyle that her mother grieves. But the more common—and more dangerous—rebellion is the quieter assimilation of movement children into modern society, not running away but merely drifting into more lax expressions of the faith and away from patriarchal, Quiverfull adulthood.

A common nay-saying liberal reaction to the patriarchy and Quiverfull movements is to assume that the children of strict homeschooling families will rebel en masse—like the 1960s youth rebellions against a conservative status quo. However, the heads of the movement are already well aware of this threat, and they are taking all the precautions they can to cut off the possibility of such defection in the cradle.

As Jennie Chancey tells the Botkin sisters in their book, *So Much More: The Remarkable Influence of Visionary Daughters on the Kingdom of God,* children of the movement should have "little to no association with peers outside of family and relatives" as insulation from a corrupting society. Daughters shouldn't forgo education but should consider to what ends their education is intended and should place their efforts in "advanced homemaking" skills.

Concretely, Geoffrey Botkin explains, this means evaluating all materials and media that daughters receive from childhood on as it pertains to their future role. The Botkin sisters received no Barbie dolls—idols that inspire girls to lead selfish lives—but rather a "doll estate" that could help them learn to manage a household of assets, furniture, and servants in the aristocratic vision of Quiverfull life which Botkin paints for the families around the room. The toys the girls played with were "tools for dominion," such as kitchen utensils and other "tools for their laboratory": the kitchen.

R. C. Sproul, Jr., in a book of advice to homeschooling parents, *When You Rise Up,* describes the critical secret of God's covenants as the cornerstone of the homeschool movement: the imperative of covenants, he says, is to "pass it on to the next generation." He's done so himself, he relates, in what he calls the R. C. Sproul, Jr., School for Spiritual Warfare, in which he crafts "covenant children" with an "agrarian approach" and stresses that obedience is the good life in and of itself, "not a set of rules designed to frustrate us but a series of directions designed to liberate us." In that freedom, boys and girls are educated according to their future roles in life, and girls are taught that they will pursue spiritual warfare by being keepers in the home.

To gauge the amount of secular baggage his homeschooling readers are trailing, he tells the story of a family friend whose homeschooled nine-year-old daughter still cannot read. "Does that make you uncomfortable?" he asks.

> Are you thinking, "Mercy, what would the superintendent say if he knew?"...But my friend went on to explain, "She doesn't know how to read, but every morning she gets up and gets ready for the day. Then she takes care of her three youngest siblings. She takes them to potty, she cleans and dresses them, makes their breakfasts, brushes their teeth, clears their dishes, and makes their beds." Now I saw her rightly, as an overachiever. If she didn't know how to read but did know all the Looney Tunes characters, that would be a problem. But here is a young girl being trained to be a keeper at home. Do I want her to read? Of course I do....But this little girl was learning what God requires, to be a help in the family business, with a focus on tending the garden.

It's this kind of separatist, radical thinking, advocating both physical and mental withdrawal from the world of public schooling, that informs the mission of E. Ray Moore, a retired Army chaplain and head of the homeschool ministry Exodus Mandate. Michael McVicar, who studies Reconstructionism and has written about R. J. Rushdoony, sees Moore's homeschool ministry as one of the most direct embodiments of Rushdoony's ideas. Exodus Mandate, as its name hints, expresses an explicitly secessionist ethos that aims for ultimate removal of Christian families from state rule—leaving "Pharaoh's school system" for the Promised Land—but in the intermediate future, pushes Christians to remove their children from public schools as a ploy to collapse by attrition what they consider a wicked, humanist institution.

Moore has worked with Vision Forum as well as large denominations such as the Southern Baptist Convention (SBC) to spread his message. In 2008, when California passed legislation mandating that schools teach nondiscrimination on the grounds of sexuality and perceived gender—a demand that conservative Christians quickly identified as "indoctrination"—Exodus Mandate organized a California Exodus subgroup to work together with homeschooling movement veterans, conservative celebrity Phyllis Schlafly, and Christian leaders such as Dr. Voddie Baucham, a Southern Baptist preacher, to urge California Christians to leave the public school system in droves. Baucham, a Vision Forum associate himself, further charged the SBC to pass a resolution encouraging the California exodus.

When I met Moore in Jamestown, Virginia, he told me that the homeschooling movement was growing at such a rapid clip that, if Exodus Mandate could help double the percentage of students outside the state school system (an ambiguous number, as homeschoolers assert that their population is at least twice the one million students recognized by the U.S. Department of Education), it might collapse the U.S. public school system entirely.

Susan Wise Bauer, the homeschooling author and reluctant patriarchy critic, sees such strategies as ultimately unsustainable. "By forgoing college education and any meaningful interaction with culture, they become increasingly isolated communities from the mainstream. And isolated communities are ultimately doomed to fade."

The patriarchy community, however, is dedicated to building up its own, purist alternatives to the interaction mainstream society provides. Vision Forum gears its entire Beautiful Girlhood catalogue collection— replete with tea sets, white gloves, "modesty slips," and Victorian manners books—to the proper raising of daughters in the faith. Both Vision Forum and the Chalcedon Foundation sponsor girls' essay contests on subjects such as fulfilling one's vocation as a daughter and the enduring appeal of Elsie Dinsmore—a heroine in Martha Finley's Victorian-era children's book series, an obedient and priggishly pious daughter of the

Antebellum South who aspired to be a submissive daughter and wife. (Dinsmore, as one contest winner wrote, shows daughters how "to rise up by stepping down.")

Elaborate courtship mechanisms are being worked out by fathers hoping to make alliances through the marriages of their daughters to the sons of men in the fold. And home business projects, largely home-based sewing businesses that produce modest clothing or home decorations, are cropping up among young daughters of the movement to such an extent that in 2007 James and Stacy McDonald urged homeschooled daughters to consider signing up with a new young-woman's home business ministry, the Proverbs 31 Project. The project, evoking the many virtues of the storied Proverbs 31 woman, is a Mary Kay–like franchise that promises to help young daughters "build a business for herself around the use of therapeutic-grade essential oils," thereby helping her find a way to bring a home business into her marriage, making her a more attractive prospect to potential suitors.

"There's a generation of daughters in this room today that we have not seen for one hundred years of American history," exclaimed one of the speakers at the Vision Forum Father and Daughter Retreat, Scott Brown. He attributes the rise of this new breed of daughters to a "revival in the land." But it's also the fruit of twenty-five years of work, he says, when parents turned their hearts to their children and began doing "many culture-defying things," such as homeschooling their children, fighting feminism, and leading their daughters in the opposite direction of women's lib.

The education of the young Botkin women is the current key example that Vision Forum is offering to parents following its model, and the reasons are clear. The Botkin sisters in the past several years have released a polemical book, *So Much More,* as well as a companion documentary, *The Return of the Daughters: A Vision of Victory for the Single Women of the Twenty-first Century,* in which the daughters, staring regally, unblinkingly at the camera, appear in front of a fireplace in a vaulted room decorated in rustic country elegance. They further spread the message through their blog, Visionary Daughters, and they speak or play the harp frequently at events for women and daughters, including Vision Forum's annual Father and Daughter Retreat. Appearing on book jackets, on film, or on stage (their iconic public personas are captured in photographs with upswept hair and softly made-up, flushed faces turned toward the camera in three-quarter profile), they're an elegant pair possessed of the distinct, romantic beauty ideal biblical womanhood seeks to claim as its own.

"Heroine" is a key word here, and in all of their work—a mix of standard Vision Forum/biblical womanhood theology and encouraging portraits of other young movement daughters following the path—they seek to highlight "heroines of the faith," frequently a familiar mix of daughters from families associated with Vision Forum and its sister ministries.

At the 2007 retreat, at Calloway Gardens in Georgia, the Botkin sisters delivered one such address as part of a conference that cost upwards of five hundred dollars per father-daughter couple (and which was recorded and repackaged as a CD set for families unable to afford or to attend). In it, Anna Sofia and Elizabeth speak in a soft, flat Kansas accent, Dorothies in a perpetual Oz, with a deliberate diction suggestive of public-speaking lessons. They opened by setting the stakes: if Alexis de Toqueville, the French surveyor of the budding New World, once attributed America's prosperity and strength to its "superior" women, the Botkins see "the weakness and growing apostasy" of the country as the fault of modern women, who are selfish and petty.

Model daughters of the patriarchy movement, the Botkin girls express a hatred of feminism that is pure, and they hate it in a variety of flavors most feminists wouldn't recognize as their cause. To the Botkins, all bad women—from the seductress hoping to "subdue masculinity" with her womanly wiles and charms to vain pageant queens to career women to even conservative Christian wives who aren't fervent enough about spiritual war—are feministic, seeking to "weaken and dominate men."

On stage, the sisters explained to an audience of fathers and daughters, young women to very young girls, the ways in which daughters should go beyond a lukewarm acceptance of biblical femininity to a full-on embrace of a deliberately countercultural girlhood. They should be modest servants who don't cause their brothers in Christ to stumble with temptation. They should "learn to ignore [their] comfort zone" in the interest of a higher calling, as Elizabeth, a formerly terminally shy child, describes her father's insistence on her "godly boldness." They should teach their younger sisters in the Titus 2 spirit and should honor and defer to their brothers—older and younger—in recognition that even young boys need to be treated as wise leaders by their older sisters in order to gain the confidence to be leaders of their future families. They should wear feminine clothes to prove to their fathers that they are virtuous women worthy of protection. They should not learn career skills as emergency "backups" to support themselves, as "learning to 'survive' can teach girls attitudes of independence, hardness." They should understand that singleness is a very rare calling from God, and so they must prepare to marry and conduct war on "the home front": in other words, they must understand there is no opting out of this revolution without turning their backs on the faith. But most of all, the Botkins explain, a virtuous daughter should "turn her heart to her father" in the spirit of Malachi 4:6: "And he shall turn the heart of the fathers to the children, and the heart of the children to their fathers, lest I come and smite the earth with a curse."

The turning of daughters' hearts to their fathers is the driving theme of the retreat, which besides the Botkin girls, features the sermons and messages of Doug Phillips, Geoffrey Botkin, and Scott Brown, a board member of Vision Forum and a leader in Phillips's family-integrated church movement. All three men explain what is at stake to the girls and young women in the room: they are daughters of Zion, of Judah, of Jerusalem. They are future mothers of Israel. As such, they have no time to waste, or spirits to risk, by leaving home for college, work, or missions. They must instead make the revolutionary choice to "redeem the years" they have with their fathers and view their single lives as preparation for marriage: submitting themselves to their fathers and, to some extent, their brothers, as they will one day submit themselves to their husbands.

Living always under a man's authority like this, Phillips explains, is order, God's beautiful order, but also a safety precaution for naturally more gullible women. It gives daughters, and later wives, a "covering" that protects them in all ways from the dangers of the world: physically, emotionally, spiritually, and legally. The only biblical example of a woman out from under her father's authority, Phillips says, is that of Dinah. And what happened to Dinah, raped and defiled in her independence, is a lesson for all.

Citing a favored verse, Numbers 30, which holds that fathers can override vows, or contracts, that daughters make without paternal permission, Phillips explains the implications for such a law under the future theonomy he's fighting for: "If a daughter or wife has gotten off the reservation of authority," any "vows" she makes, meaning any legally binding decisions, are voided. Business arrangements can be undone, as they were commissioned by persons without legal agency. And eloped daughters can even be reclaimed, as the daughter had no right to give herself away in marriage. As a window into the society they would like to raise, Phillips offers the example of marital law in Calvin's Geneva, wherein a man who married a woman without her parents' consent was guilty of rape, as he'd obtained access to a woman who had no authority to say "yes."

"This puts the whole world on notice," Phillips announces, setting a standard for how his disciples should approach potential suitors and how they themselves should consider business dealings with women. "The buck stops with Dad. If I were a purchaser, engaging in business, or entering into an agreement with a daughter, I'd want to know, do we have your father's permission on this one? Is your husband backing you up on this?"

As husbands represent God's will for their wives under patriarchy, fathers "pattern" the role a husband will play to their daughters, that of "Lord." And in fact, as a number of speakers repeat, in tones of hushed revelation, fathers are "a conduit, a pipeline, a representative head to express His love to you." Daughters who don't understand that, who have been blinded by the devil to the true meaning of headship, will be unhappy and lost. And, in a familiar tweaking of the Protestant denial of salvation through works, Scott Brown tells the fathers present that if their daughters are angry or rebellious, they should assume that the girls are unsaved; the fruits of salvation would make a daughter eager to please and follow her father's guidance as diligently as do the model daughters trotted out on stage. This is a frightful accusation for girls living in a world where their virtue is judged by their perceived spirituality—an intangible faith that, with pronouncements like Brown's, becomes tied to following very particular rules.

Girls whose hearts are turned to their fathers will behave as do Phillips's daughters: anticipating his needs, offering encouragement through physical affection ("rubbing their fingers in Daddy's hair"), and rejecting "patricidal" friends who encourage them to ignore their parents' wishes or keep secrets from their fathers. The effect of such daughterly devotion Phillips describes in terms usually reserved for less paternal relations: "It puts fire in the heart of a man. It encourages him to stand up strong and be a missionary."

This wavering line and unsettling ambiguity between the responsibilities and effects of daughters and wives is a common thread in the literature of "virtuous daughterhood." In more mainstream evangelical adaptations, such as "purity ring" and "purity ball" ceremonies, a similar crossover is noted by many critics and writers: fathers taking their daughters to purity balls are on a very literal level acting out dating, wedding, and courtship scenarios with daughters ranging from elementary school age to their late teens. This outcropping of the abstinence movement sports equally militant language as that of their Reformed fundamentalist brethren, steeling fathers to "war" for their daughters' purity and leading the father-daughter couples under an archway of crossed swords. Following ceremonies of mock-prom pomp and dress, many of the balls include wedding cake desserts, girls donning purity rings or lockets that are to be worn until traded for wedding rings, and the signing of covenant agreements wherein daughters promise their virginity to their fathers until their fathers transfer that prize to their husbands. The fathers at these popular balls, which began in Colorado Springs and have since spread across the nation, repeat a covenantal agreement promising "before God to cover my daughter as her authority and protection in the area of purity."

How different in substance is this increasingly widespread ceremony from an essay written by Sarah Schlissel, daughter of Reformed Brooklyn pastor Steve Schlissel, another leading figure in patriarchy circles? In a piece entitled "Daddy's Girl: Courtship and a Father's Rights," published on the Web site of the Chalcedon Foundation, the keepers of R. J. Rushdoony's Reconstructionist legacy, Sarah Schlissel counsels daughters to remember the possessive tense of being "Daddy's girls": that daughters are literally the property of their fathers until they become the property of their husbands.

> Any man seeking to beg, borrow, or steal a daughter's hand without her father's endorsement is seeking to gain, in unlawful ways, "property" not his own....I am owned by my father. If someone is interested in me, he should see him....And no man can approach me as an independent agent because I am not my own, but belong, until my marriage, to my father. At the time of my marriage, my father gives me away to my husband and there is a lawful change of ownership....No-

tice there is no intermediate point between Daddy and Hubby. There is no "limbo land" where the girl is free to gallivant on her own, "discovering herself" as she walks in fields of gold, apart from any defining covenant head, doing whatever she sees fit.

The Botkin sisters concur with the sentiment, writing on their blog, "Dear girls—don't be afraid of losing your 'individual personhood' or the ability to think for yourself, and don't think that those are the signs of an adult. Any two-year-old girl has a mind of her own and most certainly thinks for herself…it's part of being Eve's daughters. It's not a sign of maturity to struggle for autonomy—that's toddler stuff."

In *So Much More,* the Botkin sisters likewise deride girls unwilling to place their lives in their fathers' hands as cowards, "afraid to lose a measure of childish independence." History's example, they write, is of men laying down their lives for women and children, and women also laying down their lives by dying to their selves. Though they see all women as "rebellious feminists at heart"—their understanding of feminism founded, a footnote explains, on a collection of contextless feminist quotations assembled by the antiabortion Web site Fathers for Life—repenting of rebellion can lead the way to becoming "true women."

Starting as daughters, that means giving their fathers their hearts and molding their minds in the pattern of their father's preferences. "You will love what he loves, you will hate what he hates, and you will even think his thoughts after him. This will help you know how to be his glory.… Girls, we must never underestimate the power we have over men. We can build them up or we can tear them down."

This power, of course, is always secondhand and relational. In the same way, the virtuous daughters the Botkin sisters profile in their documentary express great gratitude for the influence they have over generations of future children as they model submissive womanhood to their younger brothers in order to train them to desire a godly, fruitful wife rather than worldly, immodest women.

On a practical level, practicing being a helpmeet for a future husband with one's father can mean anything from helping fathers set up or run home businesses to bookkeeping and research to running and beautifying the home. In the Botkins' *Return of the Daughters* film, graduated homeschooling daughters forego college in order to remain at home with their fathers, and their parents are quick to argue that the women are receiving Ph.D.-level educations at home, at least in the skills they will need later on as wives and mothers. Whether or not this is true, more questionable aspects of practicing being helpmeets abound. As one of the Botkins' characters in *So Much More* suggests, it can mean fetching a father's slippers for him in order to free the father up for weightier dominion tasks in reclaiming the world for Christ.

Anna Sofia has served thus herself, as her father explains in an appendix interview included in *So Much More* so it might contain some proper male authority to address fathers. One day, while father Botkin was entertaining a "very important political leader," he called to his daughter. Anna Sofia, then five or six, came into the room to untie and remove her father's shoes, and she then asked the guest if she could untie his shoes as well. Years later, Geoffrey Botkin says, the politician brought the evening up, telling Botkin, " 'You know when I decided we should have more children? It was that night your sweet little daughter helped me with my shoes.' One simple act of hospitality had eternal consequences."

The extent to which Botkin views his daughters as his ambassadors, or extensions of himself, is perplexingly hinted at when both he and Doug Phillips slip during the conference and refer to *So Much More* as Geoffrey Botkin's book. This could seem either an indication of his daughters' total identification with their father, or else, perhaps, indication of the heavy paternal hand guiding the virtuous daughters' movement—as present in the writing of the book as it feels in every frame of the film and every still photograph taken of the two sisters.

Such lessons are repeated wide-scale at the father-daughter retreats, where daughters are given object lessons alongside the sermons through a series of ideological games, including a blindfolded obstacle course, where chains of blinded daughters were guided solely by relying on their fathers' verbal commands; contests for fathers "wooing and winning the hearts of their daughters"; and intimacy-building "unity games" that teach daughters to serve their fathers by shaving their faces, grooming their hair, and knotting their shoes and ties. As three of Phillips's young daughters, Jubilee, Liberty, and Faith, explained on a video posted on Vision Forum's Web site, "Each of the games was designed to teach us a principle about our relationship with our fathers."

Or as Doug Phillips explained to the fathers in attendance, he who "tells the story controls the culture," and storytelling—setting up the basic architecture of your children's worldview—is "one of the most significant patriarchal duties that God gives us." So, he tells fathers, it's imperative to start teaching your daughter now all "the stories she needs to know" because—in an alarming revelation about the young marriages patriarchs support—the nine-year-old before you now may, in six years' time, be not just older, but married as well.

It's a short window of opportunity for a father to guide his daughter where he wants her to go, and a short time for him to experience what Phillips calls "the greatest privilege of the ages: to have someone look at you and say, 'Father, I love you. Father, shepherd me.' Father, father. The very words we call our God and savior. God has given you fathers the opportunity to look at these girls and say, 'You are mine. You are mine.'"

"Cultivate a taste for managing domestic concerns," the Botkins write, "start to see the home as an extension of your body and love." Should this sound eerily like the "de-selving" of isolated women in patriarchal societies described by Dr. Singer, the Botkins clarify themselves to remove all doubt: thinking you belong to yourself is outlaw thinking and the biggest inhibition to father-daughter intimacy.

"Self-denial means denying that you have a 'self.' We do not belong to ourselves, but have been bought with a price. The natural 'us' deserves to spend eternity in Hell. Being true to ourselves and following our hearts condemns us to spiritual deaths. We have no selves that are worth being loyal to," write the Botkin sisters. They're loyal instead to those who and that which have made them a cosmic, eternal promise: victory through posterity. "God laughs at the militant feminists who mock the real woman for her meekness, promising that it will be the descendants of his meek servants who will inherit the earth."

This is what the Botkins unveil, at the close of their book, hoping to usher a new generation of daughters into the mold of Quiverfull mothers. Women's "final secret weapon in the battle for progressive dominion," they write, with the excitement of revealing a mystery, is "motherhood. Our posterity.... Too many women forget that the hand that rocks the cradle really does rule the world.... We should think ahead, not only to our children, but to our grandchildren and great-grandchildren, aspiring to be a mother of thousands of millions, and aspiring to see our children possess the gates of their enemies for the glory of God. This is the vision of Victory through Virtuous Womanhood."

In this, they are of course their father's daughters, and daughters of the Vision Forum curriculum as well, repeating titles from the catalogue verbatim as received wisdom. One of Geoffrey Botkin's catchiest contributions to patriarchy is his branding of the dominion vision in his "two-hundred-year plan for multigenerational faithfulness": a concept that started as an Excel spreadsheet he put together stretching from his marriage in 1980 to his projected death, in 2038, to the culmination of his vision in 2180. It has since become a cornerstone of the Vision Forum message and the focus of a new three-day ministry conference teaching Vision Forum followers to emulate Botkin's ambitious plan.

Botkin's personal plan plots major family accomplishments on his Excel sheet—both completed and those they aim for, such as books published, films made, churches planted—and priorities are set out for the family that will unfold over the course of generations: a thorough listing of life goals set down for generations of children yet unborn. The generations themselves are projected as well: Botkin's sons (still unmarried) are listed with their projected marriage dates, the projected births and number of their children, and their projected deaths. His grandsons and great-grandsons are charted as well until two hundred years' worth of Botkin heirs and accomplishments have accumulated. At the end of his two-hundred-year plan, Botkin estimates that he'll have been the patriarch of some 186,000 male descendants, all of whom, he is confident, will begin their own two-hundred-year plans modeled on Botkin's ideals. The plan, he argues, is flexible enough to not presume on the Lord and to allow his family to discuss and modify it as needed. The Botkin daughters are missing from Geoffrey's two-hundred-year plan, likely absent as property transferred to another man's legacy-machine. But the projection allows all of the Botkin family members to see themselves in the proper perspective, that "in the two-hundred-year scheme of things, I'm just a blip."

That this is the endgame of seeing family units, rather than individuals, as the basic blocks of society, its cell structure, is perhaps not a point that would resonate among the faithful, for whom self-obliteration is a virtue. But the patriarch's vision of himself at the head of this line—his sons fulfilling his destiny down the line—is an indication of what even the male patriarch becomes under this system: inconsequential to the big picture of what the patriarch decrees, a blip. Women, it follows, matter exponentially less.

But the faithful are a blip to a larger end, if that's of any consolation. Doug Phillips, seizing on the imagery on hand at the retreat, described the concept of multigenerational faithfulness to young daughters by drawing on the example of the butterfly colonies that thrive at the Calloway Gardens location. Particularly, he focused on the generational lifecycles of monarch butterflies, three successive generations of which will live short lifespans before a blessed, elect, fourth generation of monarchs is born.

This fourth generation will live for many months, rather than many weeks, and will be able to fly across entire countries. But its glorious existence depends entirely on the success of the three generations that came before, living and dying in normal, butterfly drudgery. "If the first three generations are not faithful in producing the butterfly children," Phillips explains to the roomful of daughters, "there is no fourth generation." For those too young to grasp the metaphor, he translates: "Girls, your fathers are getting a vision that has been set aside for at least one hundred years...one that is found in the Bible and transcends all cultures and time...a vision that has always been front and center at times of massive revival." You daughters, Phillips tells them, are fighting for "children you'll never look in the eyes because you will be dead before they come on this earth. But if you are faithful as a daughter now, they will come to this earth, if Jesus tarries. While the rest of the world is aborting their children and cutting off their seed, we'll be here having the children of Zion. But it won't happen if we're not faithful."

Brian Abshire, a Vision Forum associate, summed up this plan more than a decade earlier in a 1996 piece for the *Chalcedon Report*. "Time," he argued, "is something that postmillennialists have plenty of. Isn't it worth a little sacrifice now to know that your descendants will live in a Christianized world?" Lay followers have gotten the appeal of this idea as well. Mike Southerland, a father of seven and author of a blog titled "Christian Patriarchy," heard Botkin speak at Sovereign Grace Family Church in Texas and was so inspired by the two-hundred-year plan that he created his own, setting death dates for his family at a generous one hundred years. With God's help, he wrote on his blog, "I believe I can set the expectations for two centuries to come, and that my children after me will carry this same vision forward to their descendants forever."

Or as M. Manley, an attendee at Vision Forum's 2008 Two-Hundred-Year Plan conference, described the encouragement he found in such a long-term vision, in a testimony that recalls the politicization of evangelicals thirty years ago, "I was leading my family with a survivalist mindset, having lost all hope for changing the tides of God's judgment on our sinful culture. I realize now that no matter what the outcome in America, we are to advance toward victory... not plan for defeat."

Ensuring the faithfulness of one's children to the patriarch's vision means having a controlling hand in how they set up their adult lives, making sure they marry within the faith by following courtship rituals rather than dating. Courtship, Scott Brown promises, is the path for godly daughters who have "decided to see how the Lord will work through their fathers in helping them evaluate men whom they might marry." Some girls, he continues, who have truly turned their hearts to their fathers, will "even go further than this and they actually, deep within their hearts, make a commitment that they not only listen to their fathers, but they will completely submit to him in the decision about whom to marry." The actual process may vary. It may or may not involve a bride price—a suitor's literal payment to a father for his daughter—an emerging option of the courtship movement that has both Botkin's and Phillips's support. But a uniform characteristic is that the suitors court fathers first, proving themselves theologically, politically, and ideologically to a daughter's dad before the daughter herself is informed about the proposal. If a father gives his consent, a period of getting acquainted, with the express and declared purpose of marriage, begins, after which a short engagement is declared and a wedding speedily arranged.

Geoffrey Botkin summarizes, "If you have to boil courtship down to a sentence, it involves getting Dad involved and getting Cupid out of the picture." Fathers should begin priming their girls from an early age "to have the right kind of affections for the right kind of men, so that they know that they're looking for virtue and character and vision, not biceps and wavy brown hair." Furthermore, fathers should keep their daughters from novels and fictional depictions of falling in love, lest high expectations create difficulties for fathers when it comes time for the daughters to marry. "We have to guard their hearts and emotions so that they have the most clear, objective ability to evaluate the situation, so that they work with us to find out if truly this young man is the right one for us."

Part of the appeal to fathers at the conference is that the relationships they establish with other fathers—through networking amongst themselves and following up postconference by making alliances and starting family-integrated, patriarchal home churches in their own localities—will help them find suitors for their daughters down the line.

The kind of suitors the fathers have in mind are young men like the one who courted Scott Brown's daughter. If Vision Forum has a single defining talent, it's in recognizing the power of storytelling and the ability of a well-told story to convey a moral with far more weight and staying power than the sermons of Brown, Botkin, and Phillips put together. Vision Forum flourishes by setting up particular young women as bearers of its virtues, and this is no different for courtship. The fairytale marriage story for this generation of patriarchy daughters is that of the courtship and wedding of Brown's daughter, Kelly, and Peter Bradrick, a former Vision Forum intern and son of homeschooling lecturers Michael and Susan Bradrick (who were among the recipients of the smear letters written about Cheryl Lindsey Seelhoff a decade earlier).

The merging of these two families through the marriage of their young children was featured on Web sites and blogs across the patriarchy community, capturing the moment of the couple's first kiss at the altar, surrounded by scores of bridesmaids and groomsmen. Peter's courtship of Kelly had begun, breathless accounts tell, with her father, whom he approached and had to win over long before he ever displayed his interest to Kelly. Peter wrote more than a dozen "position papers" for Scott Brown on everything from politics and theology to child training and marital roles for husband and wife, all backed by biblical arguments for what Peter expected from his future wife.

Kelly, a blonde daughter of North Carolina, with a fragile, intelligent beauty in her pictures, like a young Mia Farrow, was another of Vision Forum's lofted role models for young daughters before the era of the Botkin sisters, speaking on the Vision Forum *Victory for Daughters* CD while she was a single daughter living at home after finishing homeschool. There, as a model of patient premarried womanhood, she shyly delivered the word: "These days everyone wants to be the chief and no one wants to be the Indian. But without the Indians, what would the chief be?"

Fulfilling the promise that patriarchy makes to its daughters in convincing them to be submissive and content, Kelly did attract the attention of a man in the mold of her father. Peter, a sturdy, confident redhead, is interviewed at length about his courtship process in *Return of the Daughters,* the Botkin sisters' documentary film showcasing some of the movement's prettiest daughters, moving, in slow motion, through their daily lives at home with a number of pointed indicators of the good life: sensual shots of lush meals and strawberries dipped in chocolate interspliced with footage of stay-at-home daughters helping their fathers with home businesses or sipping cups of tea in filmy, ornate hats at the Father and Daughter Retreat.

The crowning story of the film is the fable of Kelly and Peter, mythologized with still shots of the pretty bride and her noble groom. After he had successfully wooed Scott Brown, Peter received permission to correspond and talk with Kelly, where they eschewed emotion for doctrine, discussing the Bible's rules for marriage, housekeeping, and what Kelly's role would be as a helpmeet.

"I never told her 'I love you,' and I never told her she was beautiful," explains Peter, "two things that I thought would insert an emotional flutter, an emotional element, I wanted to withhold before I made a commitment.'"

Kelly, filmed just days before delivering her first child—a son she and Peter would name "Triumph"—had lost the waifish thinness of her wedding photos, but her imminent childbirth, just a year after her wedding, is of course part of this story as well. But there's a gloom to these shots, despite the best intentions of the filmmakers, who linger longer on Kelly's wedding pictures, black and white shots of the laughing, svelte, bare-faced beauty than on her married life or her filled-out and heavily rouged cheeks. The expanse of life stretching out in front of her seemed little more than an afterword, with the baton clearly passed to the next set of model daughters—young women who, for all their advocacy of the home life of wives and mothers, are still unmarried and pursuing creative projects.

"People ask me, did my dad choose my husband?" Kelly recounts, almost defiantly. "We chose together. Ultimately, God chose....I see so much the importance of a father being the one who goes out, who is in harm's way, that is looking for a young man for his daughter," she says. "It shouldn't be for a daughter to be making herself exposed searching for someone." Far from resenting her upbringing, she says, she "can't wait to apply all those things as best I can."

Her husband will be a fit co-warrior for the task as he, a young man in his twenties with the confidence of a junior senator, repeats the lessons he's been taught all his life. "There's an army of girls across the country," he says, "that are valuing their days in their father's house, staying at home and not falling for the world's cheap vision, the counterfeit vision of biblical femininity. They're new recruits. The hand that rocks the cradle rules the world. We have a new generation of girls who will rule the world."

Or rule it by proxy, through a biblical femininity that promises daughters awesome power if they remain under their father's and husband's authority for life. A covering and a protection, repeat its defenders, that guides, that saves, that ultimately frees young women from the most oppressive slavery—slavery to themselves or to sin. "Is this some sort of oppressive patriarchalism?" asks Doug Phillips. "No, this is order. This is love."

CONCLUSION

I met Donna Mauney in Jamestown, in line with a dozen other women, many in elegant colonial or Victorian homemade gowns, to use the deluxe portable johns that Vision Forum had rented for the occasion of the Jamestown Quadricentennial. One of Donna's two daughters had a nosebleed, and she held napkins to her nose to keep the blood from dripping on the dress she and her sister had made as part of a seven-person costume ensemble they'd created for the entire family. I asked them to go ahead of me, but even so the line moved slowly as women gingerly maneuvered through the temporary restrooms (fitted with two flushable toilets and a running-water sink, amenities Vision Forum provided for the ladies). While we waited, Donna introduced herself to me. An effusively friendly, ever-smiling woman in her early fifties, Donna had traveled to Jamestown from Charlotte, North Carolina, largely at the behest of her five children, all in their teens and twenties except for the youngest son, Jeremy, at nine.

In the photograph of the family I have from Jamestown, the men, three sons and father Paul, wear breeches and white stockings; the women are in open-front gowns with petticoats, blue, brown, and dusty rose. Donna wears a floppy white mob cap over shoulder-length, light brown hair and smiles with her wide, toothy grin. Paul, a gentle and soft-spoken man who used to work in construction and now runs a termite-control business, tilts his head toward Donna. Their children—sons Jason, Josh, and Jeremy and daughters Jessica and Jennifer—beam, all arranged symmetrically around their parents.

While in line for the bathroom, Donna asked me if I'd heard of the attacks on the celebration in the local papers. The Mauneys, Donna explained, "believe in patriarchy. In men leading families and women growing up to be homeworkers." She said she found it interesting that Peter Bauer's church "calls that a political agenda. If you read about it, colonial America embraced that. It's interesting that they're critical of everything colonial America stood for."

She deferred to her daughter Jessica, a seventeen-year-old recent homeschool graduate with long, light brown hair and a serious, studious disposition, for the particulars of the controversy. "It's disgraceful," Jessica said coldly when I asked what she thought of the newspaper article that inaccurately labeled Vision Forum a cult or the letter from Pastor Bauer distancing the group from local churches. Jessica and her siblings, Donna explained, are far more attuned to the news and positions of the groups organizing the celebration than she and Paul are. They've taken to the lifestyle with a fervency that pleasantly surprises Donna, but which she doesn't quite follow.

The girls are regular readers of Jennie Chancey's Ladies Against Feminism blog and other biblical womanhood sites online, while the oldest son, Jason, has led the family theologically, volunteering in a Reformed Presbyterian library and becoming an avid reader of Reconstructionist and patriarchy theology and apologetics. Jason has introduced the family to deeper expressions of the movement and has suggested new movement ideas to the family, such as courtship.

"Jason actually brought that idea up to me. I always assumed my kids would date. But at thirteen, Jason said, 'I don't want to date. I want to wait till I get married.' I had no familiarity with that. I mentioned it to a friend and she said, 'Don't you know he's talking about courtship?'"

"I've never had leaders like Vision Forum," said Donna. "My children had the vision of things before us." She laughed. "The Bible does say 'out of the mouths of babes.'" Donna adores her children, but says she doesn't always keep up with the convictions that excite them. "I get way behind. I'm not a fast reader, but they are. That's the problem when you start homeschooling: a lot of times kids will quickly excel and pass you. My kids are really independent thinkers, so I laugh to hear we're oppressing our children, spoon-feeding them this stuff."

If anything, it might be the other way around. When I asked Donna about the Reconstructionist theology being given much play in the speeches at Jamestown, she was at first concerned. She didn't know much about those arguments, and it doesn't sound quite right to her: she has her beliefs but doesn't expect others to follow them. This is surprising, because unlike the broad-draw homeschooling conferences Vision Forum and Doug Phillips use as outreach opportunities, the Jamestown event was predominantly a gathering of the already-converted. But Donna asked Jason about the theology, and he explained the basics of Reconstructionism to her and told her that critics often take it out of context.

Donna seems satisfied with this; for the most part, she's not overly interested in the motivations and deeper beliefs of the leaders of the patriarchy and biblical womanhood movement that she supports. She appreciates the atmosphere and the general message of family and submission and focuses, she says, more on perfecting her own practice. If she has questions, she often turns to her children: a wholly kind, intelligent, and respectful group who are nonetheless avid children of the movement, eclipsing their parents' devotion to the cause.

For Donna's part, she is more enthusiastic than dogmatic about her faith, which she circled back to in adulthood after years of flirtation with "new age" spirituality and what she calls her "feminist phase." The feminism Donna refers to is not feminism by the lights of the feminist movement, but it is certainly so by the definition of the leagues of "ex-feminists" among biblical womanhood advocates. In college, Donna listened to Helen Reddy and hoped to hear Betty Friedan speak. She planned for an equal marriage, prompted by her father's poor treatment of her mother: not physical abuse, says Donna, but failing to show his wife "honor or dignity as a woman" and treating her as a "second-class citizen." Paul, whom Donna met at a community college sociology class about interpersonal relationships, supported the idea of a "fifty-fifty" marriage all the way.

The Mauneys are now solidly Reformed Baptists, attending a Desiring God church plant under the leadership of John Piper's organization that Jason introduced them to. But the road there is littered with other spiritualities she and Paul dabbled in and discarded. Starting with Donna's salvation at a Billy Graham crusade at fifteen and her subsequent attendance at a charismatic church she now finds "unbiblical," she and Paul tried their hand at a lot of belief systems: Transcendental Meditation, the "Be Here Now" school of Ram Dass, the Unity School of Christ, rebirthing, Prosperity Gospel, the Bhagavad Gita, homeopathy, Silva mind control, gurus.

It didn't work. Donna became sick, then agoraphobic. She suffered crippling panic attacks. She lay in her bed and told Paul she wasn't getting back out. Paul, a sturdy, patient man slow to put down his foot, picked her up and put her on the sofa, where Donna, under the guidance of a Christian friend telling her to get back to the Bible, "cried out to God," demanding, "If you're real, help me."

"I felt like Christ appeared to me. I don't know how biblical that is, but it was my experience at the time, and I can't lie about it." The Christ of Donna's vision picked her up and Donna's overwhelming thought was, "It was Jesus. It wasn't Buddha. It was Jesus."

Donna recommitted herself to Christianity. Paul didn't immediately follow, and Donna, anxious now that she was saved, asked her new pastor how to get Paul right with God. The pastor prayed for Paul and returned with a vision of his own. "Your husband is sitting on the line. I think you ought to keep your mouth shut, go home, and pray for him. He's the leader of your home. He doesn't have to give up that territory. Go home and pray for him. It's a spiritual war. Just go home." It was the "win him without a word" lesson: praying that God would convert him and using Donna's new submissive behavior and silence as a further inducement to the lifestyle. And it worked. Two months later, Paul converted. They bounced through a series of churches—"we've probably been in every Protestant denomination there is"—and then into the homeschooling community after Paul's construction job fell through and the cost of Christian day school became untenable.

At the urging of her son Jason, Donna dedicated herself to setting aside what she sees as feminism. Donna felt that feminism—in the way that the term has come to serve as routine conservative shorthand for a jumble of accusations—wanted and even demanded that she abort her children, work full time, and, if she did have children, leave them to be raised as attention-starved misfits in a state day care center rather than be brought up as the well-behaved offspring of her stay-at-home sister-in-law. But it was her son's criticism that sparked her interest in submission, when, during a stormy season in Donna and Paul's marriage, Jason stopped speaking to his mother and wrote an e-mail to a group of pastors he corresponds with, asking them to help his parents before they divorced. Donna was ashamed, and the pastors sent the couple a CD about overcoming bitterness. "That is pretty much when we got serious about the whole love and respect/submission and headship thing," Donna says, casually blending basic relationship lessons with a comprehensive theological system that demands women's obedience.

> What the whole submission thing boils down to for me is humility and selflessness, and there is more than one way to demonstrate that. But I just believe that when these crises occurred in my marriage and family, this is exactly what God wanted me to learn. You see, I was full of pride and selfishness and in total denial about how much I was hurting and destroying my whole family because it had always been about me, me, me....Paul had condescended to me so many times just to keep the peace, but I was the type that just couldn't shut up. His weariness of dealing with my demands had turned into withdrawal and resentment toward me, and honestly, it took my kids to open my eyes to it.

I learned all this because Donna and I became friends after Jamestown. I was leaving the Fort Pocahontas celebration grounds late at night, hours after having spoken with the Mauneys, walking from the big tent across the dipping expanse of lawn to the dirt road where the cars were parked, when Donna and Jennifer, a sweet girl with a hint of enchantment behind her quietness, caught up with me, out of breath from sprinting across the field. They wanted to give me a copy of the critical articles that had been published in the local paper, which they'd gone back to the hotel to retrieve. I'd learn soon this generosity wasn't an out-of-the-ordinary gesture for Donna, who, upon learning the state of my soul, sent me not only dozens of the books that won her to Christ, or bolstered her faith once she had it, but also a number of nonproselytizing letters and birthday cards, holiday cards, and get-well cards. She is a kind friend, if a persistently self-doubting one, equally stung by silence and disagreements. Every several months she e-mailed me a variation of her concern: "What do you want?" She alternately disapproves of my criticism of conservative Christian activism and tries to convince me that my poor impression of submission and patriarchy teachings are the result of bad apples, not "real Christians." She wonders frequently if I secretly despise her. As often as not, she will apologize profusely for her doubt before I've had a chance to answer, and she'll tell me that, though she's not sure why, she thinks of me as a daughter. What follows is a week of ritual humbling on Donna's part, where she takes a spell to search herself for clues as to why she has reacted the way she has. It's both exhausting and admirably generous of spirit. I don't despise Donna, secretly or in any way, but I still don't know what to make of her.

. . .

Over the course of the year since I met them, Donna and her family also embarked on a long journey toward adoption. Donna and Paul felt it was God's desire for them to adopt, that he had called them to it, and they threw themselves repeatedly into what became a punishing process. They started a family blog devoted to the hoped-for adoption called Pure Religion, taken from James 1:27, "Pure religion and undefiled before God and the father is this, To visit the fatherless and widows in their affliction and to keep himself unspotted from the world." But Donna's drive to adopt ran into countless walls as they applied for numerous children across the country, in Florida, Texas, and Utah, and internationally, in Guatemala, Haiti, and Liberia, working with a U.S. Christian adoption agency that was later accused of coercive behaviors by a Liberian official. They had hosted a ten-year-old girl from Belarus in the past, and they were foster parents to two babies from a neglectful home, and each time they had severe difficulty returning the children to their parents. Repeatedly, paperwork got in the way of successful adoption or birthmothers chose other applicants. Donna cried and took to her bed; she would then get to work revising her "birthmother letter," a description of family life in the Mauney household written to help birthmothers choose who they will give their child to, or her testimony statement, explaining how God had led her to adopt. They solicited small donations from friends to cover the costs of the ongoing process and posted feel-good encouragement posts taken from some "Chicken Soup for the Adoptive Parent's Soul"–type source: "You know you're an adoptive parent if…" lists, or a Liberian-English Christmas story, retelling Christ's birth in a patois of some colonial imagining.

Donna's zeal to adopt was overwhelming, and she felt her friends didn't understand or support what she said was God's clear desire for her to take in a needy child. They lagged in writing recommendation letters for the family, or they asked why Donna was still pursuing so feverishly what God would either provide or not. It's hard not to entertain this criticism—that Donna's experience of God's will to help the orphans seemed to line up much more with her desires than the existence of an orphan needing help—or to speculate on what was driving her, her desire for a baby as her own children became adults and as her identity as a mother waned outstripping the readiness of birth parents to supply an adoptive child. But others of Donna's friends, particularly those who have adopted, as a sizable percentage of homeschoolers and conservative Christians have, understood, and they consoled Donna that "her baby," the one God intended for her, would surely be born very soon.

One week, the Mauneys received a rejection notice from one birthmother just days after Jason learned that he'd been rejected by the parents of a girl he'd traveled to the Midwest to court: a double blow that made Donna dizzy and tired and fearful that she'd retreat to her bed again soon.

But in June 2008, the family got a call that they were being considered, yet again, for an AA baby (African American, in the shorthand of adoption agencies) in Texas. In joy, the family packed up their minivan and drove to Dallas, and, prayer warrior friends on notice to keep them in mind, they succeeded in adopting an infant girl. One of the child's four names is mine.

After a Bible study lesson one day, Donna wrote to describe an epiphany she'd had: she's not a conservative, but a "gospel-driven person." Her definition came from a handout her Bible study teacher had distributed, explaining the difference between "liberal (hedonist)" and "conservative" approaches to other cultures. Liberals were relativistic, admitting no ultimate truth, while conservatives were judgmental and vain. Conversely, gospel-centered people approached other cultures *just right,* with both humility and certainty of the truth of their own convictions. I didn't point out that it seemed a rather self-serving definition partly because Donna, who comes to her convictions somewhat naïvely, has the virtue of innocence as well in really intending to live out her beliefs. At least most of the time.

Earlier that spring, I'd met Donna, Paul, and their three youngest children at an Atlanta soul food restaurant, where we began a day spent together before going to Martha Peace's dinner lecture at the First Baptist Church of Jonesboro. In the parking lot behind the restaurant, I saw the Mauneys' minivan long before I made my way inside to meet the family: it was covered on all five exposed surfaces with neon pink removable paint urging support of former Arkansas governor Mike Huckabee in 2008. Huckabee had withdrawn from the campaign weeks earlier, but the Mauneys were slow to let go. Inside, over okra, sweet tea, and fried chicken, Donna's daughters, in T-shirts, Crocs, and long denim skirts, chatted about their reading, which included Chancey and McDonald's *Passionate Housewives,* among other titles. Donna teased me shyly about my Yankee-ness, reveling in the cross-cultural sniping when we went to Atlanta's Cyclorama depiction of the Civil War Battle of Atlanta.

In the evening, while we waited for the dinner lecture to open, strolling on the campus of the megachurch, Donna asked me, for the fifth or sixth time that day, if I was ready to learn to submit. Her daughters giggled, and Donna swatted at them playfully, "Don't give my secrets away!" I think I know it, I told her, having watched Paul easily defer to her again and again. There's no submission here, I thought, or at least not in the sense that Donna's mentors and favorite authors mean it. During Peace's lecture, Donna nudged me like a restless classmate, coughing "liberal" and "feminist" into her hand while the table full of Women of Purpose leaders whom we sat with, in a full southern belle style that made Donna look a mischievous tomboy, politely failed to hear. After the lecture, Donna approached Peace to ask, she told me later, how she can remember to submit to her husband when they have disagreements.

Outside, as we were leaving for the night, the Mauneys got ready to head back upstate to Stone Mountain Park, north of Atlanta, where they were staying. Paul had arrived in the minivan from the movies, where he'd taken young Jeremy, a beautiful, shy-smiling boy, on a men's outing. Donna lingered outside the van, reluctant to leave, asking if I'd join the family for a vacation in Myrtle Beach the following month, or in Florida where they were going to look at possible adoptees in several weeks. Paul called to her again from the driver's seat: it was late already and an hour's drive to the hotel. Donna ignored him. He called again, and she ignored again.

"I think Paul's trying to get your attention," I told her, aware, with a weird twinge, that I was telling her to mind her husband.

"All right," she said with a teasing, exaggerated sigh. "I guess I'd better go submit": a joke because, tips from Martha Peace aside, she didn't much intend to.

When I first came across the insistence—standard throughout the literature of biblical womanhood—that love is a choice, not a feeling, I imagined the doctrine a clumsy bit of overreaching: too retrograde, too reactionary and self-denying for modern women, even these modern women with their old-fashioned aspirations. I came to see it instead as a stealth argument, containing just enough truth to resonate with women who realize that commitment frequently involves some degree of self-sacrifice and stamina through the tides of waxing and waning affection. It also resonates with women who feel that they can't be expected to "do it all," as the ubiquitous cliché has it, without suffering a breakdown on some front. But with its grain of truth comes an overabundance of ready-made solutions; it's a truism turned poisonous as a system of belief with expectations of obedience and mechanisms of enforcement.

Donna's seeker approach to patriarchy, another lifestyle slipped on like an all-covering garment, wasn't reflected in her children, who took to the convictions with a devotion and seriousness that left their parents' ambivalence far behind. Women like Donna, floating on the waves of these battles, pass the reactionary lessons on undigested, unwittingly raising a generation of revolutionaries whose learned goal is to extinguish such hesitation and doubt with cradle-taught absolutism. Donna doesn't really know the movement she is helping to build, but that doesn't matter. As the minivan left the parking lot, from the backseat, her daughters waved.

Quiverfull was written in part with the support of the Nation Institute's Investigative Fund and the MacDowell Colony. Parts of this book originally appeared as magazine articles. I am deeply grateful to the editors who worked with me to expand my research and sharpen my thoughts. Many thanks to Betsy Reed and Bob Moser of the *Nation*; Esther Kaplan, Kim Nauer, and Joe Conason of the Nation Institute; Monika Bauerlein of *Mother Jones*; Brin Stevens of the *Harvard Divinity Bulletin*; and Tom Watson of *Newsweek*. Hearty thanks to Amy Caldwell, whose direction and encouragement saw this book through from its inception, Joanna Green, and everyone at Beacon Press.

I've benefited greatly from the influence and expertise of many colleagues, writers, and scholars who spoke to me about everything from fundamentalism to feminism, global politics to local medicine. My work is much better for our conversations and their help. Thanks to this incomplete list: Frank Bardacke, Richard Bartholomew, Chip Berlet, Rev. Jennifer Butler, Pam Chamberlain and Public Research Associates, Frederick Clarkson, Evan Derkacz, Emily Douglas, Dorothy Federman, Faye Ginsburg, Michelle Goldberg, Kevin Gray, Betsy Hartmann and the Civil Liberties and Public Policy Program, Gillian Kane, Betsy Krause, Garret Keizer, Elzbieta Korolczuk, Michael McVicar, Marek Mscichowski, Jon O'Brien, David Samuels, Bruce Wilson, JoAnn Wypijewski and the Kopkind Colony, Angela Zito, and the New York University Center for Religion and Media. Thanks as well to the Swedish Association for Sexuality Education and the European Parliamentary Forum on Population and Development. And also at *Newsweek,* thanks to Cathy Fenlon, Dan Brillman, and Pierre Metivier.

I've been fortunate to have had a number of gifted teachers at both Hampshire College and New York University who helped me along the way, including Ellen Willis, Susie Linfield, Michael Lesy, Lynne Hanley, Paul Jenkins, and Susan Tracy. I'm equally lucky for the good friends who read, advised, or housed me throughout the process, including Jason Boog, Eve Burns, Marin Buschel, Jeremy Greenfield, Sarah Harrington, Kathryn Kosowicz, Kate Lynch, Andrew McKinney, Ann Neumann, Corey Noll, Molly Page, Jesse Sunenblick, Matt Williams, and Ariel Woods. Many thanks for photography and design help to Keliy Anderson-Staley, Rolf Ebeling, and Francine Dreyfus. Special thanks to Lauren Sandler, who provided critical insight, experience, and the boon of her own notes. And a world of gratitude to Jeff Sharlet, who has been an inspiring fellow traveler, an incisive and challenging editor, and a great friend.

This book would have of course been impossible without the openness, generosity, courage, and patience of the many women who agreed to speak with me in depth about their stories and convictions, even when the topics were painful or when we sharply disagreed. I'm immensely grateful to everyone I spoke with, and in particular to Donna Mauney, Jennifer Epstein, Carmon Friedrich, Cheryl Seelhoff, Dawn Irons, Jodi Jett, Traci Knoppe, and Jocelyn Andersen.

Finally, deep thanks for the stalwart support of my family, Bonnie, Michael, James, and Misa Joyce, and to Chris Kyriakos, who got me through the entire process with patience, humor, and love.